Although the author has made every effort to ensure that the information in this book was correct at the time of print, the author does not assume and hereby disclaim any liability to any party for any loss, damage, or disruption caused by errors or omissions, whether such errors or omissions result from negligence, accident, or any other cause.

978-0-473-68843-1

© 2024 Taryn Dryfhout. All Rights Reserved.
www.TarynDryfhout.com

Third edition

No part of this book may be reproduced or transmitted in any form or by any means, electronic or mechanical, including photocopying or recording, or by any information storage and retrieval system, without permission in writing from the publisher.

All photos and/or copyrighted material appearing in this book remains the work of its owners. Every effort has been made to give credit. No infringement is intended in this work. The title of this work, "You've Been Gilmored", as well as most of the chapter titles are phrases from *Gilmore Girls* and are not owned by the author. This book is not official, authorised by, or affiliated with The CW, Warner Brothers, Dorothy Parker Drank Here Productions or their representatives.

You've Been Gilmored!

A Cultural Reference Guide

Table of Contents

Preface……………………………………………………7

Introduction……………………………..………………11

How This Book Works………………………………..18

Episode Directory……...……………………………..23

Movies………………………………………………..…...32

Television…………………………………………..…..160

Books………………………………………………….....233

Music………………………………………………….....293

Stars Hollow Town Guide …………………………..363

Eating Like A Gilmore………………………………394

Love And Relationships……………..………………472

Trivia………………………………………………….....498

Documents…………………………………………....551

The Rest of the Gilmore World………………………568

Honorary Gilmores: The Fans…………………….639

How To Study Like A Gilmore……………………...655

Life's Short, Talk Fast: Quickfire Lists……………..676

Preface

It feels surreal to be sitting here, composing the foreword to yet another edition of *You've Been Gilmored*. When I first conceived of the idea of putting the first edition together, it was mainly out of my own personal desire to have a book of all the references. I suppose I could have just as easily hand-written all the information into a few notebooks, but it seemed easier to collate the lists into a word document, with the intention of getting it printed and bound for my own personal library. As I started engaging in the online fan community, people became interested in what I was doing, and encouraged me to publish, and share the research I had done, so that all *Gilmore Girls* fans could access this Gilmore 'bible'. I could not have anticipated the response that my book would get once it went to print, and I feel incredibly grateful for the support and encouragement that I have received in the past three years.

Republishing has given me a chance to add some valuable material to the book. Since the publication of *You've Been Gilmored,* several other books have been written which are germane to the lists contained in the 'Books" section. These have now been added, as well as a brand-new list, which to my knowledge, is the first of its kind. The new list, found in the chapter "You Jump, I Jump, Jack" is an inventory of every sport or game referenced in the show. This is an exciting addition to the number of unique lists that this book contains, which have never been published online, or elsewhere.

After almost three years of writing, *You've Been Gilmored,* I had hoped that my first print would be perfect. Of course, like all best laid plans, there were a small number of errors. This edition seemed like a fantastic opportunity to also fix those, and reach what I hope, is a closer level of perfection.

The last change that you will find in this edition is the absence of the fan section. Since the release of *You've Been Gilmored* I have been working on another Gilmore related book. *But I'm a Gilmore* will explore the experiences and reflections of more than 50 cast and crew, who I was lucky enough to interview over a period of six months, and more than 60 stories from fans or, 'honorary Gilmore girls'. The fan stories will outline the experiences of how fans came to the show, what it means to them, and how it has impacted their life. Because this upcoming book has the capacity to delve much deeper into the experiences of fans than the space that this book allowed for, it seemed fitting to remove that material from this one.

Readers all over the world have shared with me their reading habits in relation to this book: they take it with them to watch parties, on vacation, and throw it in their bag when they head off on a road trip. Avid fans of the show want to take the book to every place where they watch *Gilmore Girls.* In addition, readers have written notes in the margins (Jess would approve), highlighted things, and used Post It notes to divide up the reference sections. In a way, it has become a kind of living, breathing fan book, which is both unexpected, and humbling. It is my hope that this book will become an even more enriching part of your Gilmore experience.

Introduction

I came to *Gilmore Girls* late. I was in my late twenties, and the show had been finished for a year when I first picked it up. Having caught a few brief minutes on the television, years before, I picked up the first season on DVD from a department store. By the end of the first episode, I was hooked.

I like a few different television shows, but nothing has stuck with me like this one. Like many *Gilmore Girls* fans, qualities of both Rory and Lorelai resonated with me very deeply, and the world of Stars Hollow spoke to me in a way that nothing else ever has. No matter what is going on in my life, I can always put on the show and tuck myself away in a snowy, coffee-filled world of books, movies, and pop-culture references to escape for an hour.

As a part of the vibrant online fan community that keeps the spirit of *Gilmore Girls* and Stars Hollow alive, I have observed that most fans of the show have a story. Each story usually includes how they came to the show, how it fits in their lives, and what it means to them. Stepping into this tradition, I decided to open this book by sharing my *Gilmore* story, and how it led to the creation of this book.

How This Book Came to Be

When I started watching the show, I was in my second year of college. I related so much with Rory's passion for reading, and with her love for literature that I decided to take on an English paper, as an elective course, outside of my major. By the time I had finished the paper, I had also finished *Gilmore Girls* and it wasn't long before I found myself lining up at the admissions office to add another major to my study load—English.

The addition of a second major was just the beginning. The show had impacted me so profoundly that I began to see many changes. Watching Rory grow from her role as a private high school student to a Yale college graduate shaped me into a more diligent student. I found myself studying more often, and more intensely, and planning my future with more dedication than ever before. My GPA increased as a result, and eventually led to me being accepted into a post-graduate program. I acquired an interest in journalism, and joined the college newspaper—first as a reviewer, before becoming a columnist, feature writer, and eventually editor. My studying life had been transformed in the space of about a year. I was driven, focused and happy, and I owed it all to *Gilmore Girls.*

While I was still an undergraduate student, I was offered some work through a friend. The job was part-time, writing for a website that needed its content updated. When the job was done, I was taken on to write articles, and before long, I was picking up freelance writing contracts left, right and center. As my writing career progressed, I was given the opportunity to contribute to other people's blogs and books, as either a guest writer, ghost-writer, or editor. While these were amazing opportunities, there came a time where I felt that the natural next step was for me to write something of my own. I had been toying with the idea of starting a *Gilmore Girls* inspired blog for a long time, and had even written some scraggly lists of ideas for how this might look and what it might include, but it never felt right. Though I was becoming more strongly in favor of writing about *Gilmore Girls,* the blog-project wasn't thrilling me like I'd expected it would.

The idea of opening a website dedicated to my favorite show sat in the back of my mind for months, while I got on with other things. I had taken a trip to California, a 14 hour flight from my home in New Zealand. One of my main planned activities was to visit the set of Warner Bros. Studios, where I fell in love with the set of

Stars Hollow, which I knew I would. Back home I continued to work on my writing career and returned to school to take on creative writing papers, in an effort to broaden my writing skills.

When the cast of the show reunited on the ATX Television Festival, I blocked out the day to eagerly follow the events online with like-minded fans. Though no announcements were made on that day, the idea of a revival hung in the air, unspoken, and after five years of silence, there was hope that our girls would return to the screen, and that "The legend of Sherman-Palladino's unwritten ending" would finally be known.[1]

Why Now?

Apparently, Toni Morrison once said, "'If there's a book that you want to read, but it hasn't been written yet, then you must write it." During my time preparing for the blog that never was, I had spent a lot of time extracting information from the show. I published the first list available online of movies referenced in the show and had been keeping meticulous lists of everything - books, food, songs. While the internet offers many of

---

[1]Katheryn Wright, "Gilmore Girls: "Bon Voyage"."
In *Television Finales: From Howdy Doody to Girls*, ed. Howard Douglas L. and Bianculli David, (Syracuse, NY: Syracuse University Press, 2018), 148.

these lists, I have not found any that are exhaustively complete. With an increasing demand for my movie list online, I realized that this information would have to be published, in some form. What I wanted, more than anything, was to get my hands on a thoroughly comprehensive encyclopedia of all things *Gilmore Girls* so that all the information would be canonized, in something beautiful, and permanent. This book was the one I most wanted to read. It was the book that I felt the world was missing out on. This was the project I had been waiting for.

What This Book Is

While there have been some past printed contributions to the world of *Gilmore Girls,* the revival brought with it a large amount of new information to set down. After the revival, a gap existed, since no comprehensive literature had been published which included it. It was time for an all-inclusive manual that housed all of the cultural capital that this show had to offer – a Gilmore guide to life. This book is not intended to help you get to know the actors behind the series or how the set operates. This book is intended to be your handbook for living a life that is thoroughly steeped in *Gilmore Girls.*

Inside its pages, you will find how to 'live like a Gilmore' - including what music to listen to, what films and television shows to watch, what books to read, what food to eat, and how to study like a Gilmore. You will also find out everything you have ever wanted to know about the world of *Gilmore Girls* and Stars Hollow and the colorful characters and events that inhabit it. David Diffrient calls this world in which we strive to immerse ourselves the "*Gilmore*verse", and it is my hope that this book will allow you to step a little deeper into it, no matter what stage of Gilmore fandom you are at.[2]

It is impossible to articulate how much a part of my life *Gilmore Girls* has become, and I know that fans all over the world have felt the same since the show first aired on October 5th, 2000. I came alive when I found the show. I found two strong women, surrounded by a host of colorful characters, and in doing so, found myself.

Gilmore Girls has allowed me to grow into more of myself than I ever have been, and I can confidently attribute a large part of this with the

---

[2] David Scott Diffrient, "Introduction: "You're about to Be Gilmored"," In *Screwball Television: Critical Perspectives on Gilmore Girls*, ed. Diffrient David Scott and Lavery David (Syracus: NY: Syracuse University Press, 2010), xxii.

show, and the world that *Gilmore Girls* has allowed me to engage in.

This book allowed me to combine two of my great loves – writing, and *Gilmore Girls*. I hope that you will find within its pages more than just a television show – it's a lifestyle. It's a religion.

Taryn

How This Book Works

At 'Armageddon', a national comic convention in New Zealand in 2019, I was able to share this book—which was still in its infancy—with Sean Gunn who plays the recurring character of Kirk. Sean said "Oh. So, it's like Wiki, but in a book". It is my hope that this book will be so much more than Wiki, but the comparison still seems like a good place to start. It is intended to be a comprehensive compendium of everything that was included in the show.

The bulk of the book takes the form of 'lists'. These lists document all of the movies, television shows, music, food, and books that were referenced throughout *Gilmore Girls*. This book also contains lists of all of the pets that featured in the series, the businesses and events that made up the unique town of Stars Hollow and the Gilmore world, menus from the many restaurants that the Gilmore's eat at, as well as every illness, maid and geographical place ever mentioned on the show, and so much more.

The book opens with a comprehensive episode list—detailing the season, episode number, and title. After the episode list, each episode mentioned throughout the book will be marked by its season, and episode in numeral form. For example, a reference to episode five of season six, will simply be marked as (6.5). In the same way, the first episode of *A Year in the Life* will be marked as (AYITL: Winter).

The Trivia section, as well as many of the lists, are designed to accompany a re-watch of the show. Each episode is numbered with interesting information, or explanations of the many 'Gilmorism's' which feature in that episode. Lists such as the Love Interest Guide, or the Stars Hollow Town Guide are designed for reference, and of course, interest.

In the back of the book, I have included a section of 'Quickfire' lists. These lists are not as detailed as the ones found throughout the book, but do contain some of the same information. Where the more detailed lists include episode references and at times, the context of the episode, the quickfire lists are undetailed lists which can be accessed for a quick check on what books, or movies are included in the show, for example. These quickfire lists are also not repetitive. For instance, in the movie section, some films are referenced more than once throughout the series, and as such are listed with their context in the episode, for each reference. In the quickfire lists, films are mentioned only once. It is my hope that the quickfire lists will be helpful for those wanting to work their way through every book or movie mentioned on the show, and will serve as a handy reference guide.

It probably goes without saying, but this book is loaded with spoilers, and is intended for reading only after an initial watch of the show. Even reading along with the trivia section at the same time as watching, will likely reveal spoilers, as I provide connections to characters and story arcs which appear later in the show.

It is also necessary at this point to draw attention to the fact that this book has no official, or authorized connection to the show, Warner Bros., the C.W. or Dorothy Parker Drank Here. This work was fan-produced, from multiple re-watches of the show and from critical research of the show by scholars who are cited throughout. References to the show are explicit throughout, usually by the accompaniment of an episode reference (e.g. 7.2). All chapter titles are references to quotes used throughout the show, and remain the work of the copyright owner.

It is my sincere hope that reading this book, and in using it as a companion to the show that you will find this encyclopedia helpful, and that it will enrich, and enhance your enjoyment of the show. While every care has been taken to ensure that this guide is as accurate, and comprehensive as possible, I would love to hear if you think I have missed anything that could be included in any subsequent reprints of this book. (taryndryfhoutwriting@gmail.com).

In Omnia Paratus!

I Smell Snow

Episode Directory

Episode List

Season One

1. Pilot
2. The Lorelais' First Day at Chilton
3. Kill Me Now
4. The Deer Hunters
5. Cinnamon's Wake
6. Rory's Birthday Parties
7. Kiss and Tell
8. Love and War and Snow
9. Rory's Dance
10. Forgiveness and Stuff
11. Paris Is Burning
12. Double Date
13. Concert Interruptus
14. That Damn Donna Reed
15. Christopher Returns
16. Star-Crossed Lovers and Other Strangers
17. The Breakup, Part 2
18. The Third Lorelai
19. Emily in Wonderland
20. P.S. I Lo...
21. Love, Daisies and Troubadours

Season Two

1. "Sadie, Sadie"
2. "Hammers and Veils"
3. "Red Light on the Wedding Night"
4. "The Road Trip to Harvard"
5. "Nick & Nora/Sid & Nancy"
6. "Presenting Lorelai Gilmore"
7. "Like Mother, Like Daughter"
8. "The Ins and Outs of Inns"
9. "Run Away, Little Boy"
10. "The Bracebridge Dinner"
11. "Secrets and Loans"
12. "Richard in Stars Hollow"
13. "A-Tisket, A-Tasket"
14. "It Should've Been Lorelai"
15. "Lost and Found"
16. "There's the Rub"
17. "Dead Uncles and Vegetables"
18. "Back in the Saddle Again"
19. "Teach Me Tonight"
20. "Help Wanted"
21. "Lorelai's Graduation Day"
22. "I Can't Get Started"

Season Three

1. Those Lazy-Hazy-Crazy Days
2. Haunted Leg
3. Application Anxiety
4. One's Got Class and the Other One Dyes
5. Eight O'Clock at the Oasis
6. Take the Deviled Eggs...
7. They Shoot Gilmores, Don't They?
8. Let the Games Begin
9. A Deep-Fried Korean Thanksgiving
10. That'll Do, Pig
11. I Solemnly Swear
12. Lorelai Out of Water
13. Dear Emily and Richard
14. Swan Song
15. Face-Off
16. The Big One
17. A Tale of Poes and Fire
18. Happy Birthday, Baby
19. Keg! Max!
20. Say Goodnight, Gracie
21. Here Comes the Son
22. Those Are Strings, Pinocchio

Season Four

1. Ballrooms and Biscotti
2. The Lorelais' First Day at Yale
3. The Hobbit, the Sofa and Digger Stiles
4. Chicken or Beef?
5. The Fundamental Things Apply
6. An Affair to Remember
7. The Festival of Living Art
8. Die, Jerk
9. Ted Koppel's Big Night Out
10. The Nanny and the Professor
11. In the Clamor and the Clangor
12. A Family Matter
13. Nag Hammadi Is Where They Found the Gnostic Gospels
14. The Incredible Sinking Lorelais
15. Scene in a Mall
16. The Reigning Lorelai
17. Girls in Bikinis, Boys Doin' The Twist
18. Tick, Tick, Tick, Boom!
19. Afterboom
20. Luke Can See Her Face
21. Last Week Fights, This Week Tights
22. Raincoats and Recipes

Season Five

1. Say Goodbye to Daisy Miller
2. A Messenger, Nothing More
3. Written in the Stars
4. Tippecanoe and Taylor, Too
5. We Got Us a Pippi Virgin
6. Norman Mailer, I'm Pregnant!
7. You Jump, I Jump, Jack
8. The Party's Over
9. Emily Says Hello
10. But Not as Cute as Pushkin
11. Women of Questionable Morals
12. Come Home
13. Wedding Bell Blues
14. Say Something
15. Jews and Chinese Food
16. So...Good Talk
17. Pulp Friction
18. To Live and Let Diorama
19. But I'm a Gilmore!
20. How Many Kropogs to Cape Cod?
21. Blame Booze and Melville
22. A House Is Not a Home

Season Six

1. New and Improved Lorelai
2. Fight Face
3. The UnGraduate
4. Always a Godmother, Never a God
5. We've Got Magic to Do
6. Welcome to the Doll House
7. Twenty-One is the Loneliest Number
8. Let Me Hear Your Balalaikas Ringing Out
9. The Prodigal Daughter Returns
10. He's Slippin' 'Em Bread...Dig?
11. The Perfect Dress
12. Just Like Gwen and Gavin
13. Friday Night's Alright for Fighting
14. You've Been Gilmored
15. A Vineyard Valentine
16. Bridesmaids Revisited
17. I'm OK, You're OK
18. The Real Paul Anka
19. I Get a Sidekick Out of You
20. Super Cool Party People
21. Driving Miss Gilmore
22. Partings

Season Seven

1. The Long Morrow
2. That's What You Get, Folks, for Makin' Whoopee
3. Lorelai's First Cotillion
4. 'S Wonderful, 'S Marvelous
5. The Great Stink
6. Go, Bulldogs!
7. French Twist
8. Introducing Lorelai Planetarium
9. Knit, People, Knit!
10. Merry Fisticuffs
11. Santa's Secret Stuff
12. To Whom It May Concern
13. I'd Rather Be in Philadelphia
14. Farewell, My Pet
15. I Am Kayak, Hear Me Roar
16. Will You Be My Lorelai Gilmore?
17. Gilmore Girls Only
18. Hay Bale Maze
19. It's Just Like Riding a Bike
20. Lorelai? Lorelai?
21. Unto the Breach
22. Bon Voyage

A Year in the Life

1. Winter
2. Spring
3. Summer
4. Fall

I Enjoy Watching people watch certain parts of certain movies

Movies

Movies in Gilmore Girls

Movies are such an enormous part of *Gilmore Girls* that it is impossible to even get through the pilot without realizing the impact that movies have on the girls.

This book was born out of my desire to put together a complete movie list for each season, and out of that small project arose this encyclopedia. I chose to compile the movie lists first, before anything else, because I felt that in a way, Rory and Lorelai were a product of all of the films they had watched, as many of us are. Theodore Roosevelt said, "I am a part of everything I have read" and in the same way, Lorelai and Rory are a part of everything they have watched, and those films have become a part of them. So, in a way, this section represents the heart of *Gilmore Girls*.

Just as *Gilmore Girls* has become a part of my life canon, and the life canons of all the fans who feel the same way about the show, the following movies are a part of the Gilmore canon. I can think of no better way to immerse oneself in the Gilmore world than to work through this list of films that saturated the atmosphere of the show, and which became material for Lorelai's jokes, conversation starters for Rory, and company for Emily when she was lonely.

This section opens with Lorelai's movie rules, which are especially important for 'true classics', but which I am sure she would enforce for the viewing of any of the films, in the lists that follow.

Lorelai's Movie Rules

(especially for a true classic like *Casablanca*)

(4.5)

- Get situated
- Squish around a little
- You can't squish around during the movie
- No talking during the movie
- Minimise distraction
- No shifting around a lot
- No phone calls
- No going to the bathroom
- We're not pausing the movie
- No talking during the movie

Warning:

When they showed the first motion picture over a hundred years ago, it featured a train rushing toward the camera, and people were so sure the train was going to burst off the screen and crush them that they ran away in terror. Now, the train is not going to leave the screen.

Season One

1.

West Side Story (1961)
Lorelai: "Look, Officer Krupke. She's right at that table, right over there."

Rosemary's Baby (1968)
Rory: "You're like Ruth Gordon just standing there with the tannis root. Make a noise!"

Mommie Dearest (1981)
Lorelai: "You're not going to give me the 'Mommie Dearest' treatment forever, are you?"

2.

Alice in Wonderland (1951)
Lorelai: "I remember it being smaller. And less..."
Rory: "Off with their heads?"

The Shining (1980)
Lorela: "Well, we like our Internet slow, okay? We can turn it on, walk around, do a little dance, make a sandwich. With DSL, there's no dancing, no walking, and we'd starve. It'd be all work and no play. Have you not seen The Shining, Mom?"

The Goonies (1985)
Madeline: "I hate nature!"

Schindler's List (1993)
Rory: "I work at my mother's inn after school sometimes. And I was in the German Club for a while, but there were only three of us, and then two left for the French Club after seeing Schindler's List, so…"

The Hunchback of Notre Dame (1996)
Lorelai: "I'm just trying to see if there's a hunchback up in that bell tower"

3.

Peyton Place (1957)
Richard: "It's Peyton Place"

Looney, Looney, Looney Bugs Bunny Movie (1981)
Drella: "Hey, Pepe le Pew, you wanna give me a hand with this?"

4.

The Deer Hunter (1978)
Title reference

Flashdance (1983)
Lorelai: "Oh no that's true. I added that. Wouldn't want you to get in trouble with 'Il duce' here. I thought this place was going to be so great! And now I guess this goes on the 'Boy was I wrong'

list, right above gauchos but just below the 'Flashdance' phase."

5.

Valley of the Dolls (1967)
Lorelai: "It's like a scene from a kitty version of 'Valley of the Dolls.'"

The Sixth Sense (1999)
Lane: "M. Night Shyamalan lives there"
Rory: "Who?"
Lane: "The guy who directed 'The Sixth Sense'."

6.

Bright Eyes (1934)
Lorelai: "I got your Good Ship Lollipop right here, mister."

The Fly (1958)
Lorelai: "You didn't build one of those machines like in 'The Fly,' did you?"

Freaky Friday (1976)
Lorelai: "Yeah, huh? That was a pretty 'Freaky Friday' moment we had back there."

7.

Invasion of the Body Snatchers (1956)
Luke: "Guess my pod is defective."

Sleeping Beauty (1959)
Cinderella (1950)
Lorelai: "Don't even get me started on your Prince Charming crush, OK? At least my obsessions are alive. You have a thing for a cartoon."
Dean: "Ooh, Prince Charming, huh?"
Rory: "It was a long time ago. And not the Cinderella one, the Sleeping Beauty one."

Shaft (1971)
Lorelai: "I'm going to be so cool in there you will mistake me for Shaft."

The Way We Were (1973)
Lorelai: "Oh I've got one. At the end of The Way We Were, you wanted Robert Redford to dump his wife and kid for Barbra Streisand."
Dean: "I've never seen The Way We Were."

Ice Castles (1978)
Rory: "The theme from Ice Castles makes you cry."

9½ Weeks (1986)
Lorelai: "Yeah, well by the time that gets to Miss Patty's it's a scene from 9 1/2 Weeks."

The Crucible (1996)
Lorelai: "Not going to talk about how good you'd

look dressed like one of the guys from The Crucible."

Boogie Nights (1997)
Dean: "I don't know...Boogie Nights, maybe."

Magnolia (1999)
Rory: "She had a bad reaction to Magnolia. She sat there screaming for three hours 'I want my life back!' and then we got kicked out of the theater. It was actually a pretty entertaining day."

Willy Wonka & the Chocolate Factory (1971)
Lorelai: "Oooh -- Oompa Loompas!"
Rory: "My mom has a thing for the Oompa Loompas."

8.

Shall We Dance (1937)
Richard: "Potato, po-tah-to."

Rosemary's Baby (1968)
Lorelai: "Hey, sweets. I have a locksmith coming to the house today like five-ish, and I don't know how long it'll take, so will you tell Grandma and Grandpa that I'm gonna be late, and that I'm having Satan's baby. You pick the order."

Yellow Submarine (1968)
Lorelai: "Hey babe. Sergeant pepper."

House on Haunted Hill (1959)
Lorelai and Max watch the film at the Black, White and Read Movie Theater

9.

Gone with the Wind (1939)
Lorelai tells Emily that she is making Rory's dress for the dance. Emily responds, "You're not using the curtains are you?"

The Glass Menagerie (1950)
Rory: "He's my...gentleman caller."

A Streetcar Named Desire (1951)
Lane: "Okay, Blanche."

Midnight Express (1978)
Lorelai: Absolutely. And then we can go to Turkey and stay in that place from Midnight Express."

The Outsiders (1983)

Rory: "And these kids at my school -- awful. Have you seen The Outsiders?"
Dean: "Yeah, I have."
Rory: "Just call me Ponyboy. I heard this place is beautiful though -- old and historic."

Sixteen Candles (1984)
Lorelai: "That's true. However, not really, since you've never actually been to one you're basing

all your dance opinions on one midnight viewing of Sixteen Candles."

Fried Green Tomatoes (1991)
Lorelai: "Well I was all out of Saran Wrap."

Pleasantville (1998)
Lorelai: "This is a life. It has a little color, which you might not recognize."

Double Indemnity (1944)
Lorelai and Emily watch this film

10.

The Wizard of Oz (1939)
Lorelai: "Where's the scarecrow when you need him?"

The Miracle Worker (1962)
Rory: "Nope. Things are still Miracle Worker at my house. God, how did everything get so screwed up?"

The Deer Hunter (1978)
Emily: "What? You'll do what? I'd like to hear in your most condescending tone what my punishment will be for not filling out these forms in a timely manner. Are there bamboo shoots involved? Some sort of dark deep hole in the ground? Rats nibbling at my toes?"

11.

Psycho (1960)
Max: "I look like a Norman to you?"
Rory: "I'm sorry, 'Psycho' was on earlier and it was just the first name that came to mind. I'll think of something else. How about Alfred?"

The Odd Couple (1968)
Rory: "Oscar!"

Lorelai: "Felix!"

The Omen (1976)
Lorelai: "Look, I know it was bad, but this was a vicious hamster. This was like a Damien hamster with little beady eyes and a big forked tail and...a cape with a...hood...and bye bye Buttercup. Bye Luke."

The Shining (1980)
Lorelai: "Here's Johnny!"

Heathers (1988)

Lorelai: "Wow, you're the new 'Heather'"

Paris Is Burning (1990)
Title reference

12.

The Great Santini (1979)
Lorelai: "Look, I know that Mrs. Kim and Robert

Duvall in 'The Great Santini' share a striking resemblance, but she is Lane's mom."

Mask (1985)
Lorelai: "You're nervous? You don't have some guy staring at you like he's Cher and you're the kid from 'Mask'."

Beethoven (1992)
Todd: "Beethoven."
Lane: "Beethoven? The one with the dog?"

Donnie Darko (2001)
The opening scene of this episode mimics the scene from this film, when Donnie first arrives at school.

Attack of the 50 Foot Woman (1958)
The poster for this movie is visible when Rory, Dean and Lane go to the Black, White and Read theater, and brief clips of it are shown in the episode

13.

The Wizard of Oz (1939)
Lorelai: "I'm the good witch of the . . ."

How the Grinch Stole Christmas! (1966)
Lorelai: "Here Grinch."

Carrie (1976)
Rory: "Let's not get ahead of ourselves. They've

basically just moved off the plan to dump the pig's blood on me at the prom, that's all."

Everest (1998)
Sookie: "Did you ever see Everest?"

14.

A Streetcar Named Desire (1951)
Lorelai: "Stellaaaaaaaaa!"

The Music Man (1962)
Taylor: "You got trouble, my friends"

Lorelai: "Right here in River City"

15.

Citizen Kane (1941)
Lorelai: "No, they were directing them at me because I screwed up their big 'Citizen Kane' plans. That's all."

How the Grinch Stole Christmas! (1966)
Christopher: "All is not right in Who-ville."

2001: A Space Odyssey (1968)
Christopher: "Holy mother. This is the monolith from 2001."

Fiddler on the Roof (1971)
Lorelai: "That's very 'Fiddler on the Roof' of you"

You're a Good Man, Charlie Brown (1985)
Emily remembers Lorelai and Christopher's performance of "Suppertime" from this film

16.

Gone with the Wind (1939)
Paris: "Yup. Right behind Belle Watling."

Bambi (1942)
Rory: "Nobody eats cute…Bambi maybe, but he's a cartoon."

Lady and the Tramp (1955)
Lorelai: "Wow, it's gonna be just like Lady and the Tramp. You'll share a plate of spaghetti, but it'll just be one long strand, but you won't realize it until you accidentally meet in the middle. And then, he'll push a meatball towards you with his nose, and you'll push it back with your nose, and then you'll bring the meatball home and you'll save it in the refrigerator for years and…"

Lovers and Other Strangers (1970)
Title reference

The Boy in the Plastic Bubble (1976)
Rory: "Well, that special occasion better include my being relocated to a plastic bubble if my grandmother's gonna let me out of dinner."

Christine (1983)
Dean: "Okay. Uh, did you ever see Christine?"

Misery (1990)
Lorelai: "Oh God. Mom has gone a little crazy with the figurines here, huh? A little Kathy Bates. Although you probably haven't seen Misery, which is a good thing because Rory couldn't sleep alone for a week after we watched it."

Tuesdays with Morrie (1999)
Lorelai: "Yeah, we're having a great conversation, me and Morrie."

17.

Lady and the Tramp (1955)
Rory: "I forgot your meatball in the car."

An Affair to Remember (1957)
Love Story (1970)
Ishtar (1987)
The Champ (1979)
Lorelai: "One day, one day of pizza and pajamas. I'll rent 'Love Story' and 'The Champ', 'An Affair to Remember', 'Ishtar'."

Old Yeller (1957)

Lorelai: "So should we rent 'Old Yeller' too or is that just a guy's crying movie."

Who's Afraid of Virginia Woolf? (1966)
Rory: "And to make it interesting, we should come up with like a reward system so once we're done with everything on the list we could go get

manicures or we could go to the Swiss place for fondue for dinner or we could stuff our purses full of sour patch kids and milk duds and go see the Stars Hollow elementary school production of 'Who's afraid of Virginia Woolf.'"

The Godfather (1972)
Lorelai: "Hey, it sleeps with the fishes."

Footloose (1984)
Lorelai: "Ha! Jumpback!"

G.I. Jane (1997)
Lorelai: "No, this is good. This is like 'G.I. Jane' but we get to keep our hair."

18.

Casablanca (1942)
Rory: "Louis, I think this is the beginning of a wonderful friendship."

Gaslight (1944)
Lorelai: "I have to change and go to tea with Gran and the cast of 'Gaslight'."

Cabaret (1972)
Sookie: "Call her now. Ooh, page her, or page her and have her call my cell phone and we can sing the money song from 'Cabaret'. You be Liza, I'll be Joel."

Grease (1978)
Madeline: "Looks like we're going to have to do the Pink Ladies makeover on you."

The Silence of the Lambs (1991)
Rory: "No I think you can, I just think it would be hard for you. It'd probably involve some kind of lock up facility, one of those Hannibal Lector masks."

Elizabeth (1998)
Louise: "I'll be the lady-in-waiting. The one with the low-cut blue velvet renaissance dress."

19.

The Grapes of Wrath (1940)
Emily: "It's the Grapes of Wrath."

The Lost Weekend (1945)
Sookie: "Yes, the lost weekend."

To Kill a Mockingbird (1962)
Lorelai: "The old potting shed? That's where Rory and I lived when she was a baby. It has memories and little rosebud wallpaper. I don't want Boo Radley touching my rosebud wallpaper."

Working Girl (1988)
Lorelai: "What's up, working girl?"

Saving Private Ryan (1998)
Lorelai: "It would be like the first 15 minutes of

Saving Private Ryan but at least those guys got to be in France."

Queen of Outer Space (1958)
The Black, White and Read Movie Theater plays this film

20.

Seven Brides for Seven Brothers (1954)
Lorelai: "Hey, it's not like the lumberjack look will ever go out; it won't. But just once wouldn't it be nice not to be dressed like an extra from "Seven Brides for Seven Brothers"?"

Patton (1970)
Dean: "Has she seen Patton?"

The Amityville Horror (1979)
Lorelai: "No, that house is not safe. It's like The Amityville Horror, without all the good times."

Out of Africa (1985)
Lorelai: "Good. Okay, last week we were talking about Meryl Streep and the whole accent thing and Rachel said that she loved "Out of Africa" but she'd never read the book, remember?"

21.

Snow White and the Seven Dwarfs (1937)
Lane: "I so encourage this. I love you, but you've

been mopey, dopey, and about 12 other melancholy dwarves for the past 5 weeks and I miss the old Rory."

The Matrix (1999)
Lane: "I almost went full matrix on her. Have you heard a word I've said?"

Anywhere But Here (1999)
Luke: "It's just like all the other times Rachel. You're the anywhere but here girl, you're restless, you're bored, it is what it is."

Life with Judy Garland: Me and My Shadows (2001)
Madeline: "So I've decided I'm now completely into Judy Garland. Did you see the TV movie? Pretty intense."

Season Two

1.

Funny Girl (1968)
Sookie: [Sings] "Sadie, Sadie, Married Lady"

The Great White Hope (1970)
Lorelai: "You are the great white hope of the Gilmore clan. You are their angel sent from up above. You are the daughter they didn't have."

Fame (1980)
Lorelai: "Like, on 'Fame'?"

Cujo (1983)
Max: "Mm hmm. Put Cujo on the phone please."

Not Without My Daughter (1991)
Lane: "It's gonna be just like that Sally Field movie when her husband took them to Iran and wouldn't let them come back, except that I won't have to keep my head covered."

Tears and Laughter: The Joan and Melissa Rivers Story (1994)
Rory: "The Joan and Melissa Rivers Story, starring…"
Lorelai: "Joan and Melissa Rivers. A mother and daughter torn apart by tragedy."

2.

The Naughty Nineties (1945)
Rory: "It's for charity and I'm late, and why don't you go on inside and you and my mother can continue the 'Rory's building a house' routine and when that gets boring you can move on over to 'Who's on First?'"

Lassie (1954)
Lorelai: "I mean it, Timmy. No falling down the well."

Barbarella (1968)
Dean: "The day is over. Let's talk about the night. Uh, there's a 7:30 showing of Barbarella, and I thought you can bring your mom's purse, you know the one with that monkey face and we'll sneak in some burgers and... what?"

Fatal Attraction (1987)
Lorelai: "Rory, I love you Rory. Rory, I will not be ignored Rory…"

Thelma & Louise (1991)
Paris: "I'm sorry if you thought we had some kind of deep Thelma and Louise thing going here, but we didn't."

3.

Them! (1954)
Rory: "Like the giant ants in 'Them'?"

Monty Python and the Holy Grail (1975)
Rory: "We can watch "Holy Grail" on tape again"

Saturday Night Fever (1977)
Sookie: "You need to strut Tony Minero?"

Life of Brian (1979)
Dean: "Life of Brian?"

Misery (1990)
Luke: "No. I mean, I guess, for some people marriage, you know, isn't the worst thing in the world. I mean, it's probably better than being hobbled or something like that."

Pulp Fiction (1994)
At Lorelai's Hen's party, Michel dances with a drag queen dressed up as Mia Wallace

A.I. Artificial Intelligence (2001)
Lorelai: "Oh, Max, Rory is very low maintenance. Kind of like that robot kid in A.I., only way less mother-obsessed. Oh my God, that kid was so annoying. I would've pushed him out of the car while it was still moving."

The Born Losers (1967)
Rory, Lorelai, and Max watch a VHS copy of this for movie night

4.

Summertime (1955)
Lorelai: "Come on! Mom, I may never get married. I may be a free spirit my whole life or

fall in love with a separated catholic guy like Katherine Hepburn did and then, and then not get to go to his funeral when he dies."

Chinatown (1974)
Rory: "Forget it Jake, It's Chinatown"

Midnight Express (1978)
Lane: "Well, I strapped them to my body like in Midnight Express."

Grease (1978)
Rory: "Okay, Rizzo. I'd like to listen a little bit more."

Captain Corelli's Mandolin (2001)
Rory: "Captain Corelli's Mandolin."
Lorelai: "I'm serious."
Rory: "Bella bambina at 2 o'clock."

5.

The Thin Man (1934)
Title Reference
Lorelai: "Rory, this was a bad one, okay? This was not Nick and Nora, this was Sid and Nancy, and I'm not going in there."

West Side Story (1961)
Rory: Yeah, Riff, everything's fine."

The Godfather: Part II (1974)
Lorelai: "Yes, I respect that, but what if he turns out to be Fredo?"

The Breakfast Club (1985)
Lorelai: "Outside working on his 'Breakfast Club' audition. He's getting good."

Sid and Nancy (1986)
Title reference

The Shawshank Redemption (1994)
Lorelai: "Well, you might want to find out. Ask a couple of subtle questions, you know, has he seen The Shawshank Redemption, did the setting seem homey to him? Stuff like that."

6.

Cinderella (1950)
Lorelai says that Rory will need "some mice, a dog, a pumpkin" for her upcoming debutante ball

The Sound of Music (1965)
Lorelai: "Okay, Liesl. I'm Brigitta, this is Gretl. And, uh, Emily and Richard are expecting us."

Who's Afraid of Virginia Woolf? (1966)
Lorelai: "I don't know. I think George and Martha are joining us for dinner."

Moment by Moment (1978)
Lorelai: "I am still convinced she had something to do with Lily Tomlin doing that movie with John Travolta."

This is Spinal Tap (1984)

Lorelai: "Ugh. Rory, that's like accepting the position as the drummer in Spinal Tap."

Endless Love (1981)
Lorelai: "Now, I know you would rather sit through "Endless Love" than ever be apart of this scene again."

Dirty Dancing (1987)
Lorelai: "Nobody puts Baby in a corner"

The Lion King (1994)
Lorelai: "We didn't know we were walking in on The Lion King without the puppet heads"

7.

The Wizard of Oz (1939)
Rory: "Toto, we're not in Kansas anymore"

Coming Home (1978)
Francie: "We were just discussing homecoming. Thoughts?"
Rory: "Great movie. Oh wait, that was Come Home. Sorry."

The Outsiders (1983)
Lorelai: "Hey, I told you not to become a soc, but you didn't listen."

Like Father Like Son (1987)
Title reference

Rain Man (1988)
Francie: "So I drop a box of matches on the floor, she can tell me how many there are?"

The Matrix (1999)
Lorelai: "You don't own a long black leather Matrix coat"

8.

To Kill a Mockingbird (1962)
Jess: "You actually went to that bizarro town meeting? Those things are so 'To Kill a Mockingbird.'"

The Money Pit (1986)
When Lorelai and Sookie are trying to come up with a name for their inn, Michel suggests, 'The Money Pit'.

Glitter (2001)
Lorelai: "I heard he controls the weather and wrote the screenplay to Glitter."

9.

The Shining (1980)
Bringing Up Baby (1938)
Lorelai: "Mmkay, I couldn't make up my mind so I got The Shining and Bringing Up Baby"

On the Town (1949)
Madeline: It's very On the Town"

My Fair Lady (1964)
Rory: "By George, I think he's got it"

Butch Cassidy and the Sundance Kid (1969)
Paris: "Hey, anyone stupid enough to hand out with Butch Cassidy and the Sun-dunce kid deserves whatever they get"

Cocoon (1985)
Louise: "What's up with the cast of Cocoon?"

Mystic Pizza (1988)
Paris: "Look, I understand the whole Mystic Pizza, small town, 'we don't let a clock run our lives' thing, but I come from the big city where money talks and I'm paying good money for this place and I have a schedule to keep."

The River Wild (1994)
Lorelai: "Plus, he's outdoorsy. Remember that Meryl Streep movie where she and her family take a rafting trip and then psycho Kevin Bacon forces them to take them down the river?"

Romeo + Juliet (1996)
Lane shows this film to Mrs. Kim so that she can attend Rory's Shakespeare production at Chilton

10.

Invasion of the Body Snatchers (1956)
Lorelai: "Your pod Grandpa is still happy as a clam."

Ben-Hur (1959)
Lorelai: "Come on. We can pull a Ben Hur and take down Taylor's sleigh"

Doctor Dolittle (1967)
Lorelai says: "I speak horse language. I'm Doctor Dolittle"

The Thomas Crown Affair (1968)
Rune: "I thought an alarm would go off, like in The Thomas Crown Affair"

The Rocky Horror Picture Show (1975)
Lorelai: "I offered to fund the instant invention of a molecular transport device but they just didn't go for it"

The Shining (1980)
Lorelai: "It would be like The Shining, except instead of Jack Nicholson, we have Rune"

Knowhutimean? Hey Vern, It's My Family Album (1983)
Lorelai: "We're Ernest Builds a Snowman."

The Godfather: Part III (1990)
Rory: "Oh, we have to rent Godfather 3 on DVD"

The Joy Luck Club (1993)
Lorelai: "The Joyless Luck Club."

11.

Gone with the Wind (1939)
Lorelai: "It's okay. I won't think about it tonight. I'll think about it tomorrow - at Tara. You ready?"

Fiddler on the Roof (1971)
Rory: "And you played Tevye in the, uh, Stars Hollow Community Theater production of Fiddler on the Roof"

The Rocky Horror Picture Show (1975)
Lorelai: "Okay. So, we should celebrate. Hey, how about we get all dressed up tonight and hit the Rocky Horror Picture Show?"

Silkwood (1983)
Rory: "And then she chased me halfway down the street with the hose. It was like a scene from Silkwood"

Purple Rain (1984)
Sookie: "Absolutely. We can raid the fridge. We can make a nice avocado- mango face mask. Get out the tarot cards, tell fortunes, play Twister, make a Häagen-Dazs chocolate chocolate chip ice cream milkshake, and we'll watch Purple Rain"

Secrets & Lies (1996)
Title reference

Coyote Ugly (2000)
Lorelai: "I was thinking about opening a Coyote Ugly lemonade stand"

12.

Bambi (1942)

Dumbo (1941)
Rory: "The only videos not behind that curtain are 'Bambi' and 'Dumbo.'"

It's a Wonderful Life (1946)
Paris: "Nothing, not even a cigarette butt on the ground, I can't believe it. This town would make Frank Capra wanna throw up"

Rosemary's Baby (1968)
Harold and Maude (1971)
Rory: "Ooh, we could do a Ruth Gordon film festival. Harold and Maude, Rosemary's Baby, and that really great episode of Taxi"

Three Days of the Condor (1975)
Shoah (1985)
The Jerk (1979)
Lorelai: "How about a triple feature? Three Days of the Condor, Shoah and The Jerk?"

Grease (1978)
Lorelai: "Don't you feel like one of us should've been standing between them waving a flag or something?"

Breakin' 2: Electric Boogaloo (1984)
Cool as Ice (1991)
Hudson Hawk (1991)
Lorelai: "Got it. The worst film festival ever. Cool as Ice, Hudson Hawk, and Electric Bugaloo"

Bull Durham (1988)
Dances with Wolves (1990)

The Postman (1997)
Lorelai: "The three faces of Costner – Bull Durham, Dances with Wolves, The Postman. Tom Petty playing Tom Petty, that great big speech about 'Once upon a time there was a thing called mail.' It'll make you laugh, it'll make you cry, it'll make you wanna mail something"

Goodfellas (1990)
King Kong (1976)
Rush Hour (1998)
Jack Frost (1998)
Sweet November (2001)
Cats & Dogs (2001)
These films can be seen in the background of the video store

Babe (1995)
Rory: "No, being the poster girl for censorship is not a little funny. The only videos not behind that curtain are Bambi and Dumbo. I mean, they actually had a meeting earlier about whether or not Babe should be behind the curtain so as not to offend people who keep kosher"

Showgirls (1995)
Two boys giggle over the cover of this film in the video store

Valentine (2001)
Blow (2001)
The poster for these movies can be seen at the video store

Legally Blonde (2001)
Richard: "But that's ridiculous. Who's going to help her get into Harvard?"
Lorelai: "Reese Witherspoon."

13.

Sunset Boulevard (1950)
Stalag 17 (1953)
Sabrina (1954)
Lorelai: "Hey, I'm sorry. Sunset Boulevard was on last night, and I don't know…I've known him for years – Sabrina, Stalag 17 – and yet last night something snapped"

From Here to Eternity (1953)
Jess: "Well, you're having your vertical From Here to Eternity moment right in front of the super glue"

Oklahoma! (1955)
The bid-on-a-basket auction is based on a scene from this musical

The Boy in the Plastic Bubble (1976)
Lorelai: "Boy in the plastic bubble' kind of careful"

Julia (1977)
Rory: "The other night when we were watching Julia, and Jane Fonda was playing Lillian Hellman"

Ghostbusters (1984)
Lorelai: "Okay, uh, you guys talk, I have to go call Patty and stop the forced mating process. I feel like Ling-Ling the panda bear. Oh, hey, one of them's seen Ghostbusters 124 times. Can you say score?"

14.

Harvey (1950)
Lorelai: "Yeah, duck Harvey"

The Godfather (1972)
Lorelai: "Hm. Or we could sit in the corner - you know, the Mafia table so that no one can come up behind you and whack you with a cannoli"
Rory: "Whack you with a cannoli? Oh, because he left the gun and took the cannoli"

Ferris Bueller's Day Off (1986)
Rory: "Yeah. Oh, and later I pictured you marrying Matthew Broderick, and we lived in New York in this great apartment in the village and we would talk about his Ferris Bueller days"

Fatal Attraction (1987)
Rory: "Well, what did she think, that you were gonna come home and find a rabbit boiling on the stove?"

15.

Bye Bye Birdie (1963)
Jess: "I mean, I know it's got an 'I've been pinned' Bye, Bye, Birdie kind of implication to it, but it was just a bracelet"

Mary Poppins (1964)
Taylor: "Isn't that a great idea? Elvis, The Beatles, Mary Poppins, all the greats. You can hang 'em on the wall or you buy a little stand and set 'em up on the coffee table"

Young Frankenstein (1974)
The 2000 Year Old Man (1975)
Silent Movie (1976)
Lorelai: "What do you mean, why? The Two Thousand Year Old Man, Young Frankenstein, Silent Movie – you don't think Mel has earned the right to have his face on my butt?"

Autumn in New York (2000)
The Lord of the Rings: The Fellowship of the Ring (2001)
Dean: "You go look at the astronomy section, we'll go see Lord of the Rings, and on the way home we'll rent Autumn in New York and mock it for the rest of the afternoon"

16.

West Side Story (1961)
Jess: "Okay, I'm going. Look, man, I really was

just dropping off some food, so don't get all West Side Story on me, okay?"

The Godfather (1972)
Lorelai: "Yes, it's in the Luca Brasi mobile out front"

Risky Business (1983)
Lorelai: "Rory, you have to do something bad when Mommy's out of town. It's the law. You're seen Risky Business, right? Now I'm not asking for a prostitution ring, but how about a floating craps game or something?"

Driving Miss Daisy (1989)
Lorelai: "I guess so, Miss Daisy. Bye sweets"

17.

The Wizard of Oz (1939)
Kirk: "Toto was always different after that"

The Goofy Gophers (1947)
Lorelai: "We certainly are entertaining, Mac"
Rory: "Indubitably, Tosh"

David and Lisa (1962)
The Second Troubadour: "Don't like to be touched, that's cool. Got a little David and Lisa thing happening? Made a mental note, no problem. Can I help you find something?"

The Money Pit (1986)
Lorelai: "How's the money pit coming?"

18.

Mens vi venter på Godot (1965)
Lorelai: "Godot was just here. He said, 'I ain't waiting for Richard,' grabbed a roll, and left"

Doctor Dolittle (1967)
Michel: "Yes, a regular Dr. Dolittle"

The Odd Couple (1968)
Paris: "I'm sorry, group leader, could you ask the Pigeon sisters if there is a point to this opus?"

19.

The Wizard of Oz (1939)
Where Are Your Children? (1943)
Suspense (1946)
Killer Shark (1950)
Arctic Flight (1952)
Sudden Danger (1955)
The Sting (1973)
Rocky (1976)
Urban Cowboy (1980)
Arthur (1981)
Sophie's Choice (1982)
Desperately Seeking Susan (1985)
Fletch (1985)
The Singing Detective (1986)
Crimes and Misdemeanors (1989)

Cabin Boy (1994)
These films are considered as possible choices for 'Movie in the Square' night

The Yearling (1946)
Lorelai: "You chose The Yearling again?"

Cinderella (1950)
Lorelai: "And over here you have a tiny but annoying bell in case there's something here that you need but you don't have and you want to summon the common but lovely house wench who will promptly leave her talking mice and come to fetch the Contessa whatever she may require"

All About Eve (1950)
Lorelai: "Just as Marty, aka Eve Harrington, shows up trying to take Dean's job, Taylor's ladder mysteriously disappears, suddenly making Dean invaluable no matter what fancy tricks Lon Chaney Junior over there pulls. Good thinking, Dean – smart thinking, my friend"

Seven Samurai (1954)
Lorelai: "Akira Kurosawa directed Seven Samurai. It's a great Japanese movie"

What Ever Happened to Baby Jane? (1962)
Lorelai: "Hello, I get calls there, too. I'm not 'whatever happened to Baby Jane?' yet, thank you very much"

Terms of Endearment (1983)
Lorelai: "Hey, do you remember in Terms of

Endearment, that scene where Shirley MacLaine is in the hospital and freaks out because they won't give her daughter a shot?"

Cocktail (1988)
Lorelai: "Wow, Marty does the jar twirl before putting the salsa in the bag. Impressive, very Cocktail"

Babe (1995)
Babe: Pig in the City (1998)
Kirk: "It's not exactly Babe, it's more like Babe 2"

Snow Dogs (2002)
Lorelai: "Suspense – ice skater falls in love with hired help. Well, at least now I know how Snow Dogs got made."

20.

Nanook of the North (1922)
Lorelai: "So you've been just Nanooking it this whole time, just sending out for whale blubber and mukluks?"

The Man in the Gray Flannel Suit (1956)
Lorelai: "Just now, the handshake with the man in the gray flannel suit – did you score a deal?"

21.

The Graduate (1967)
Christopher includes a copy of this film on DVD, in Lorelai's graduation gift basket

The Lottery (1969)
Rory: "Oh yeah, right after they stoned the woman who won the lottery"

Annie Hall (1977)
Lorelai: "Great, I'm Woody Allen in Annie Hall"

High Fidelity (2000)
Jess: "There's a record store you should check out. It's run by this insane freak who's like a walking encyclopedia for every punk and garage-band record ever made. Catalog numbers. . .it's crazy. The place is right out of High Fidelity"

A Beautiful Mind (2001)
Lorelai: "I guess, unless I turn into John Nash and start drooling on people"

22.

Rebecca of Sunnybrook Farm (1938)
Paris: "See, that is exactly what I need from you, Rebecca of Sunnybrook Farm for the new millennium. Hey, wear some braids tomorrow with bows. I mean, hell, let's sell it, sister!"

Bambi (1942)
Lorelai: "Dad, glad you're here. We're just talking about how pretty Rory is. Big eyes, baby. Give him the Bambi face"

Cinderella (1950)
Paris: "Because people think you're nice. You're quiet, you say excuse me, you look like little birds help you get dressed in the morning. People don't fear you"

Brigadoon (1954)
Christopher: "It was counting up how many Brigadoon references you could come up with to torture him with at a later date"

The Miracle Worker (1962)
Lorelai: "Anybody not hanging out with Annie Sullivan by the water pump"

Basic Instinct (1992)
Paris: "Just make sure you mention that Schatzi pulling the Sharon Stone/Basic Instinct bit was a cheap attempt to distract the whole student body from my mandatory recycling program"

Sleepless in Seattle (1993)
Luke: "Now I didn't expect you to call me back so we could sit on the phone in bed and watch Sleepless in Seattle together."

There's Something About Mary (1998)
Madeline: "The hairstyles alone proved the Farrelly brothers are not making this stuff up"

Girl, interrupted (1999)
Rory: "I'll tell you what, Sookie. How about Lane and I come up with a few more suggestions for you? Still melodic, but not quite as Girl, Interrupted."

Season Three

1.

Wonder Woman: Who's Afraid of Diana Prince? (1967)
Lorelai: "No, it's not so bad. I'm lucky, I know. I just...I feel like I'm never gonna have it...the whole package, you know? That person, that couple life, and I swear, I hate admitting it because I fancy myself Wonder Woman, but...I really want it – the whole package"

Sid and Nancy (1986)
Luke: "Goodbye crazy lady. [to Lorelai's stomach] Goodbye Sid and Nancy".

Reversal of Fortune (1990)
Paris: "They give up careers and become alcoholics, and if you're Sunny von Bülow, wind up in a coma, completely incapable of stopping Glenn Close from playing you in a movie."

Nell (1994)
Lorelai: "I thought I'd do it like Nell. You know, chicka chicka chickabee"

Austin Powers: The Spy Who Shagged Me (1999)
Taylor: "Yes-sir-ee, mini-me, I did not put the word madness in the title for nothing. This place

is gonna be crazy, wild – food, games, we've even got a band coming all the way from New York!"

Divine Secrets of the Ya-Ya Sisterhood (2002)
Rory: "Eventually, maybe, but for now – solidarity sister."
Lorelai: "Ya ya!"

2.

Shane (1953)
Jess: "Her name's Shane."
Rory: "As in 'come back'?"

The Godfather (1972)
Lorelai: "Saying yes to this lunch with my mother is like saying "Sounds fun!" to a ride with Clemenza."

Freaky Friday (1976)
Lorelai: "My life stinks. Hey, let's look into each other's eyes and say "I wish I were you" at exactly the same time – maybe we'll pull a Freaky Friday!"

Bugsy (1991)
Francie: "Because talking to Paris is like shopping for a bathing suit in December – frustrating, fruitless, and a complete waste of time. Now, you, you might be the wallflower, but

you're obviously the Meyer Lansky behind this organization."

The Legend of Bagger Vance (2000)
Lorelai: "Well, I was trying to watch The Legend of Bagger Vance again."

3.

Fiddler on the Roof (1971)
Lorelai: "So what do we call this guy, alumnus Darren, you know, like you'd say farmer John or the butcher Lazar Wolf?"

The Karate Kid (1984)
Rory: "Wax on, wax off."

Sid and Nancy (1986)
Carol: "Like I was holed up in the Chelsea with a needle sticking out of my arm screaming Sid at the top of my lungs?"

Dogtown and Z-Boys (2001)
Taylor: "Slaloming around pop bottles right down the middle of the street. I'm telling you, Luke, if we don't quick furnish these skateboarding z-boys with a moral distraction, they're gonna turn Stars Hollow into Dogtown."

4.

The Wizard of Oz (1939)
Lane: "I feel like I should be singing 'If I Only Had a Brain.'"

Song of the South (1946)
Luke: "Yep, Zip-a-dee-doo-dah."

High Noon (1952)
Luke: "Looks like High Noon in Stars Hollow."

Hello, Dolly! (1969)
Lorelai: (in Louis Armstrong voice) "This is Louis, Dolly!"

Ace Ventura: Pet Detective (1994)
Rory: "Got a package!"
Lane: "What's that?"
Rory: "Oh, Jim Carrey says that in Ace Ventura."

5.

The Wizard of Oz (1939)
Lorelai: "Apparently, Dwight's last home was Oz, and not as in 'The Wizard Of.'"

Psycho (1960)
Lorelai says: "Absolutely not. Key, please. Let me just say, if we walk in there and his dead mother is sitting in a rocking chair, not a bit surprised."

Marathon Man (1976)
Lorelai: "We were both in pain – deep pain, Marathon Man kind of pain."

Erin Brockovich (2000)
Doris: "Dwight, hi… it's Doris. Doris - your wife. Remember me? The woman who was asleep in bed when you snuck out the window like a spineless little worm! How dare you sneak out like that, you sniveling little pond scum sample! I should call Erin Brockovich to bring a lawsuit against your parents, you steaming lump of toxic waste!"

Blue Crush (2002)
Jess: "I like the new look. It's very Blue Crush."

6.

To Kill a Mockingbird (1962)
Rory: "Every town needs as many Boo Radley's as they can get."

Annie Hall (1977)
Rory: "No, do not do Duane from 'Annie Hall!'"

For Keeps? (1988)
Lorelai: "No, "For Keeps." Uh, Molly Ringwald, Randall Bantikoff, really underrated little post-John Hughes flick. She went to the prom fat. I found it really inspirational."

7.

They Shoot Horses, Don't They? (1969)
Title Reference

Rocky (1976)
Rory: "And ooh, I told him about how when Kirk wins, he likes to take his victory lap around the floor to the theme from Rocky. I was gonna show him all those things, and I was gonna show them to him sitting down."

Saturday Night Fever (1977)
Lane: "Go away, Jess. No one asked for a Tony Manero wannabe to drop by."

Fast Times at Ridgemont High (1982)
Paris: "Madeline -- or may I call you Spicoli?"

Blue Velvet (1986)
Dave: "Uh, well, you mentioned this thing last time we talked and it sounded very Blue Velvet so I figured I would come by and check it out."

Boxing Helena (1993)
Paris: Look, you don't have to be nice, you don't have to tie up loose ends. I get it, I'm a distraction. Now either pull a Boxing Helena, or give me back my hand.

8.

The Wizard of Oz (1939)

Lorelai: "Lions and tigers and bears. . ."

Love Story (1970)
Lorelai: "Says the man who yelled "Finally!" at the end of Love Story."

9.

West Side Story (1961)
Jess: "It's getting a little West Side Story here, Dean, and I gotta warn you, my dancing skills are not up to snuff."

Mad Max Beyond Thunderdome (1985)
Lorelai: "Wow, it's like Thunderdome in here."

The Banger Sisters (2002)
Paris: "My life with the Banger sisters."

Grey Gardens (1975)
Lorelai: "Ah, we're mad, Edie."

How the Grinch Stole Christmas! (1966)

Lorelai: "Hmm…he's the Grinch and we're Cindy Lou Who."

10.

Gidget (1959)
Francie: "Hey, no one is denying Gidget a chance to snag Moondoggie for the clambake, but the

rest of us have things to accomplish."

Annie Hall (1977)
Lorelai: "I have a spider whose previous credits include the bathtub scene from Annie Hall trapped under that cup."

Shoah (1985)
Paris: "But disgusting in a really great way. And they had tiny wreaths hanging from every doorknob, and mistletoe and candles everywhere. I couldn't believe it. I mean, I've never had a Christmas before. One year, I asked my mother if we could get a Chanukah bush. She made me watch Shoah the rest of the week."

Rain Man (1988)
Rory: "Well, if you need any help with anything, I've become the Rain Man of college application requirements."

Babe (1995)
Title Reference.

Stuart Little (1999)
Jess: "I can't concentrate with your annoying midget voice yammering on and on. It's like having Stuart Little shoved in my ear."

11.

Ben-Hur (1959)
Lorelai: "Okay. Well, do you remember the rowing scene in Ben Hur?"

All the President's Men (1976)
Francie: "These were shoved in my locker this morning, and I didn't know what to do, so I thought to myself, 'I'll just show them to Paris and I'll explain and she'll understand.'"

Shields and Yarnell (1977)
Lorelai: "Uh, well, if you like, I could recommend a few places in town. Uh, okay, uh huh, sure. Why don't you talk to your wife and call me back. Okay, bye. [hangs up] Hey, Shields and Yarnell, what's going on?"

Xanadu (1980)
Francie: "This is Xanadu-level of insane."

12.

Doctor Dolittle (1967)
Lorelai: "Yes, it scared me while you stood by calmly like Dr. Dolittle chatting with the bat."

Thelma & Louise (1991)
Luke: "Okay, Thelma, Louise, possibly there's another way to learn to fish."

13.

Easter Parade (1948)
An American in Paris (1951)
Singin' in the Rain (1952)
Funny Girl (1968)
Saturday Night Fever (1977)
Grease (1978)
Urban Cowboy (1980)
Flashdance (1983)
Footloose (1984)
Lorelai: "Plus, I picked up Singin' in the Rain, Funny Girl, Easter Parade, An American in Paris, and as an added bonus, the new classic dance series – Urban Cowboy, Saturday Night Fever, Grease, Footloose, and Flashdance. Trust me, you're gonna be cutting up your sweatshirts all weekend."

My Fair Lady (1964)
Lorelai: "Oh no, it's raining in Spain. But since the rain in Spain stays mainly in the plain…"

14.

Gone with the Wind (1939)
Lorelai: "Hmm? Is that you, Rhett?"

Bambi (1942)
Luke: "Does it act all peaceful and Bambi-like

and then suddenly attack like the rabbit in Monty Python?"

Sunset Boulevard (1950)
Lorelai: "Yeah. They've got those fancy beds that don't sag, and you're guaranteed a great Norma Desmond style breakfast the next morning. You don't have school, it works out perfectly."

Guys and Dolls (1955)
Miss Patty: "Okay, here we go. Hey, did you know that I once met the great Bette Davis? I was a chorus girl in a bus-and-truck tour of 'Guys and Dolls.'"

Lord Jim (1965)
Emily: "Oh, and that attitude – I wanted to slap that monosyllabic mouth of his. And God forbid they're in another accident together or his heap of a car breaks down and Lord Jim has decided cell phones are beneath him and they're stranded in the middle of nowhere. How can you let this happen? He had a black eye. He belongs in jail!"

Chitty Chitty Bang Bang (1968)
Lorelai: "Toute de suite, and I don't mean the candy."

Monty Python and the Holy Grail (1975)
Luke: "Does it act all peaceful and Bambi-like and then suddenly attack like the rabbit in Monty Python?"

Footloose (1984)
Rory: "Well, let's watch Footloose again."

The Lord of the Rings: The Fellowship of the Ring (2001)
Rory: "Good. Hey, it's still early. Do you wanna watch more of the extra supplementary stuff on the Lord of the Rings DVD?"

15.

Love in the Afternoon (1957)
Emily: [sings] "Love in the afternoon…"

Hoosiers (1986)
Taylor: "Well, I admit it's not exactly the plot of Hoosiers, but still it's very, very exciting."

Full Metal Jacket (1987)
Zack: "Dude, remember the drill instructor in Full Metal Jacket?"

Face/Off (1997)
Title reference

16.

Frankenstein (1931)
Rory: "It's amazing how you manage to hide those bolts on the side of your neck. What is that, just really good cover up?"

Accepted (2006)
Paris: "What if he doesn't love me anymore? What if he doesn't think I'm special anymore? How am I going to tell him I didn't get into Harvard? What am I gonna do?"

17.

The Wizard of Oz (1939)
Michel: "Every place that sounds like Glinda the Good Witch threw up, yes – all booked."

A Streetcar Named Desire (1951)
Lorelai: "Luke! Luke! Stella!"

Ed Wood (1994)
Lorelai: "It's from Ed Wood, the movie."

18.

Mary Poppins (1964)
Rory: "Because you need to be a chimney sweep to sweep a chimney."
Lorelai: "Please. If Dick van Dyke can do it, so can Luke."

Willy Wonka & the Chocolate Factory (1971)
Luke: "Yeah, you can send over a couple of Oompa Loompas to kick the crap out of Aunt Tilly."

Saturday Night Fever (1977)
Jess: "Okay, fine – tonight, Indian food, but tomorrow, Saturday Night Fever and Thai food."

Brazil (1985)
Paris: "She has to sleep on her back for a month, otherwise her face will flatten like a crepe."

Rory: "Oh my God, it's Brazil."

Ed Wood (1994)
Rory: "Hey, last night when we watched Ed Wood we got burgers like you wanted to."

Almost Famous (2000)
Rory: "What'd you get?"
Jess: "Almost Famous."

Blow (2001)
Murder by Numbers (2002)
Movie poster at the Stars Hollow video store

Gangs of New York (2002)
Rory: "This is not Gangs of New York now with Cameron Diaz. This is Gangs of New York twenty years ago with Meryl Streep as Scorsese originally imagined it."

19.

Fame (1980)
Lorelai: "No, no, but this is where you start paying - in sweat."
Luke: "What?"

Nicole: "Fame, right?"
Lorelai: "Yeah, Debbie Allen. In sweat. I just loved how she said that. Let's see. . .uh, you need towels."

The Lord of the Rings: The Two Towers (2002)
Kyle: "Oh, oh, and the part where Gimli the Dwarf is riding his horse, then Legolas grabs the front straps and swings himself up on top of it."

20.

The Man Who Knew Too Much (1956)
Sookie: "Right. Like Doris Day."
Lorelai: "Que sera."
Sookie: "Sera."

The Stepford Wives (1975)
Lane: "No, it was more Stepford than cold. You know, very calm, very serene."

Animal House (1978)
Luke: "Seems a little party you went to last night got a little Animal House, huh?"

Footloose (1984)
Rory: "Oh, no, but Stars Hollow is a much more casual kind of a prom. Less Cinderella, more Footloose."

Beaches (1988)
Lorelai: "[sings] Did you ever know that you're

my hero? You're everything I would like to be. And I could fly higher than an eagle, 'cause you are the wind beneath my wings."

Robert Benchley and the Knights of the Algonquin (1998)
Lorelai: "How was Benchley?"

21.

The Wizard of Oz (1939)
Sasha: "Hey, did you ever see The Wizard of Oz?"

Sabrina (1954)
Miss Celine: "You're Audrey Hepburn in Sabrina. Just a waif with eyes."

South Pacific (1958)
Lorelai: "'I loved you in South Pacific.' When did you do South Pacific?

Broadcast News (1987)
Lorelai: "Hey, listen, my little Holly Hunter in Broadcast News, I'm gonna let you freak out and study like a mad woman and stress yourself out until finals, but once they're over, we are gonna celebrate big time. . .'cause this is amazing."

Armageddon (1998)
Lorelai: "Does that sexy guy in the Peugeot ad who had a bit part in Armageddon live near here?"

22.

Bambi (1942)
Gypsy: "You wanna kill the little romping Bambi's?"

Rocky III (1982)
Richard: "We have a deal. Listen, if journalism doesn't work out, you might consider working for me after you graduate. You've got good deal-making skills. Eye of the tiger."

The Money Pit (1986)
Lorelai: "So, what's the final prognosis, Luke? We're not buying a money pit, are we?"

Season Four

1.

The Wizard of Oz (1939)
Rory: [to her clothes] "I had a dream about you in Copenhagen. You were there, and you, and you, and you!"

Mary Poppins (1964)
Luke: "Look at this place! Look at you. All you need is six dancing penguins and Mary Poppins floating in the corner to bring back two of the worst hours of my childhood."

The Godfather (1972)
The Godfather: Part II (1974)
The Godfather: Part III (1990)
Rory: "Well, I'm not ready. I haven't packed. I have things I need to get. We were supposed to watch the three Godfather's and Sofia dying over and over and eat our biscotti and – "

Midnight Express (1978)
Rory: "If we were caught smuggling hash over the border and we were thrown in some Turkish prison, wouldn't you want someone to know that we were in Turkey?"

The Mambo Kings (1992)
Lorelai: "Um…you know, you've got Rory locked

in here with the Mambo Kings, and, um...and Dad went to bed."

2.

Casablanca (1942)
Rory: "Of all the gin joints."

The Matrix (1999)
Luke: "They're gonna multiply like the matrix."

Monty Python and the Holy Grail (1975)
Lorelai: "That'll get the girls talking. We'll be those dirty, filthy, almost-French Stars Hollow girls. [in French accent] Oh, we spit on you, you repressed puritanical ninnies."

3.

Mommie Dearest (1981)
Sookie: "I make them eat jalapeno-chipotle cream sauce. I'm Mommie Dearest!"

The Lord of the Rings: The Fellowship of the Ring (2001)
Lorelai and Sookie cater a Lord of the Rings themed children's party. A poster for the film can be seen.

The Lord of the Rings: The Two Towers (2002)

The film is shown at the Lord of the Rings themed party.

A Beautiful Mind (2001)
Paris: "Janet's a runner, so she'll automatically be in the jock group. Tanna's a freak, so she'll be in the John Nash group. You've got your grandmother's obligation friends, and I'm stuck over there listening to a bad talk-radio session. This sucks."

4.

The Wizard of Oz (1939)
Rory: "So I should follow the yellow stick road?"

The Glenn Miller Story (1954)
Zach: "Did you ever see that Glenn Miller movie?"

Willy Wonka & the Chocolate Factory (1971)
Lorelai: "Thank you. Let's go, Sook, Augustus Gloop."

The Godfather (1972)
Lorelai: "Remember in The Godfather, Michael telling Sonny how he was gonna kill Tattaglia and Captain McCluskey in that Italian restaurant?"

Star Trek: The Motion Picture (1979)
Lorelai: "Yes, Meg sends her love. Don't worry - I'll stop by on my way to the inn. And what are your plans today, Persis Khambata?"

Wall Street (1987)
Lorelai: "I've had a business epiphany. It's like I'm Bud Fox, saying, "Thanks for the lesson, Mr. Gekko."

G.I. Jane (1997)
Lorelai: "A spur-of-the-moment, 'let's not tell my mother I'm pulling a G.I. Jane'?"

5.

The Arrival of a Train (1896)
Lorelai: "Okay, just one more warning - when they showed the first motion picture over a hundred years ago, it featured a train rushing toward the camera, and, um, people were so sure the train was going to burst off the screen and crush them that they ran away in terror. Now, Luke, the train is not going to leave the screen."

It Happened One Night (1934)
His Girl Friday (1940)
The Treasure of the Sierra Madre (1948)
Diner (1982)
Lorelai: "It Happened One Night? His Girl Friday? Treasure of the Sierra Madre? Diner?

Casablanca (1942)
Hardbodies (1984)
Lorelai:" Oh, yeah, especially for a true classic like Casablanca. It's not like we're watching a there's-nothing-else-on movie or a guilty pleasure

like Hardbodies. Oh, my God! Have you seen Hardbodies?"

National Velvet (1944)
Luke: "Great. Listen, National Velvet, you have to move this stuff out of here."

Bonnie and Clyde (1967)
Lorelai: "Bonnie and Clyde?"

The Poseidon Adventure (1972)
Lorelai: "Oh, hey. Uh, oh, oh, hold on, whoa. Wow, that could have been very ugly, huh? The great cappuccino disaster of 2003. Very sad -- Shelley Winters drowns. Think the coffee was stronger than I thought."

Chinatown (1974)
Lorelai: "Chinatown?"

Benji (1974)
Lorelai: "No, Benji, you don't."

Grey Gardens (1975)
Lorelai: "You've seen Grey Gardens - It could go on forever."

Friday the 13th (1980)
A Nightmare on Elm Street (1984)
Luke: "What a threat! Boy, you're a real master of fear, there, Ed. Look out, Jason and Freddy. Ed may never mooch off of either one of you ever again!"

Cujo (1983)
Lorelai: "Yes, Cujo, you have."

The Breakfast Club (1985)
Marty: "Well, we all just started eating breakfast together every morning, so someone came up with the name The Breakfast Crew."

Mr. & Mrs. Bridge (1990)
Luke: "I saw Mr. and Mrs. Bridge."

Casablanca (1942)
Lorelai: "Okay. You are one click away from Casablanca."

6.

Citizen Kane (1941)
Sookie: "This is Citizen Kane's house."
An Affair to Remember (1957)
Title reference

The Godfather: Part II (1974)
Lorelai: "Well, every family has a Fredo."
Jason: "Yeah, and Fredo's family put two in the back of his head."

Pretty in Pink (1986)
Kirk: "I was doing my Jon Cryer from Pretty in Pink impression."

7.

Sunset Boulevard (1950)
Rory: "You ready for your close-up, Miss Desmond?"

The Godfather (1972)
Rory: "Bada-bing all over his nice ivy-league suit."

Tommy (1975)
Lorelai: "Well, they must be down to the deaf, dumb, and blind ones. Ahhh, he found it."

The Meaning of Life (1983)
Sookie: "I'll get so huge, I'll be the fat guy in Monty Python's Meaning of Life. I'll explode and slime the whole room. People could die."

The Matrix (1999)
The Matrix Reloaded (2003)
Troubadour: "You guys watched the first two Matrix's on DVD together, too. I heard all about it."

Ocean's Eleven (2001)
Rory: "Was that Manet or Monet?"

8.

The Wizard of Oz (1939)
Paris: "Oh, please! That would be like Dorothy pissing off the Tin Man. It's impossible."

Fame (1980)
8 Mile (2002)
Rory: "Well, no, but these are simply background facts of a fascinating personal journey. A personal journey of an artist struggling against the indifference of an indifferent society, just dancing as fast as she can. Well, it's 8 Mile meets Fame."

The Brown Bunny (2003)
Lorelai: "Man oh man. If Vincent Gallo could just see this, he'd feel a whole lot better about Brown Bunny."

9.

The Breakfast Club (1985)
Rory: "He's like the lost Farrelly brother. He's so stupid. He watched The Breakfast Club and decided to tape his own butt cheeks together."

Kill Bill: Vol. 1 (2003)
Lorelai: "Do you have a samurai sword under those pom-poms, Mom? Because you're gonna have to Kill Bill me to get me into that"

11.

Superman (1941)
Lorelai: "Who, Lane? She's super waitress, able to leap tall pancakes in a single bound. Or is that pans-cake?"

Casablanca (1942)
Lorelai: "Yes, well…he'll always have Paris."

The Sound of Music (1965)
Emily: "We toured their cloister; it was right out of The Sound of Music."

Fast Times at Ridgemont High (1982)
Lorelai: "I watched The Daily Show, fell into the best sleep I ever had, woke up, watched Fast Times at Ridgemont High, and had a vanilla-scented jacuzzi bath."

Babe (1995)
Jason: "She thinks that Babe can really talk."

The Witches of Eastwick (1987)
Lorelai: "We are the Witches of Eastwick."

12.

The Court Jester (1955)
Lorelai: "The vessel with the pestle holds the brew that is true…"

The Graduate (1967)
Lorelai: "Are you doing like a Mrs. Robinson thing with my mother?"

Easy Rider (1969)
Rory: "Paris. She likes to do this thing in the morning with the triple espresso. It's like Jack Nicholson in Easy Rider."

Good Morning, Vietnam (1987)
Paris: "Oooh! Good morning, Vietnam!"

13.

Rocky (1976)
Lorelai: "Nothing wouldn't happen to wear a leather jacket and be able to pull off an extremely convincing 'Adrian!' would it?"

Alive (1993)
Rory: "Before or after our re-enactment of Alive?"

14.

The Incredible Shrinking Man (1957)
Title Reference

Mary Poppins (1964)
Emily: "Just be here and be on time, and get your hair cut. You looked like the bird lady from Mary Poppins the last time I saw you."

Taxi Driver (1976)
Rory: "You really gotta stop watching Taxi Driver Glenn."

Sophie's Choice (1982)
Sookie: "And who's making that choice, Sophie?"

The Lord of the Rings: The Fellowship of the Ring (2001)
Paris: "Kids were skateboarding up and down it,

Gandalf the Grey is still falling down it - It was a big hole."

Monster (2003)
Rory: "Seriously, if I had this analyzed, Charlize Theron would be playing me in a movie... 'Cause I'd be a serial killer, and pretty girls like to get fat and play serial killers 'cause they win an Oscar and - I'm sorry, should I go on?"

15.

Mary Poppins (1964)
Lorelai: "Tuppence a bag."

Star Wars: Episode V - The Empire Strikes Back (1980)
Lane: "Hey Kid, do I look green and wrinkly to you? No? That's right. I'm not Yoda"

Galaga (1981)
Seen at the video arcade

Scenes from a Mall (1991)
Title reference

The Lord of the Rings: The Two Towers (2002)
Lorelai: "Oh, me wants them, my precious."

16.

Welcome to the Dollhouse (1995)
Glenn: "Welcome to the dollhouse."

Charlie's Angels: Full Throttle (2003)
Michel: "Ugh. I could just kill my cable provider. No Westminster dog show, but please enjoy Charlie's Angels: Full Throttle 24 hours a day. Aaah, there, it's recording."

17.

Gidget (1959)
Paris:" Ever since I broke up with Moondoggie, soakin' up the rays hasn't been the same."

Top Gun (1986)
Paris: "You do when there's a band of Huns re-enacting Top Gun in back of you."

18.

Grease (1978)
Lorelai: "No, my song - Summer Lovin. I had to sit on his lap. It was very uncomfortable.

Dorf on Golf (1987)
Jason: "Whatever is gonna make me look less like Dorf."

Pulp Fiction (1994)
Kirk: "Let me go door to door and make sure every townsman looks under his house, Taylor. I'll even knock some heads together - get medieval on their ass."

19.

The Wizard of Oz (1939)
Lorelai: "Inn stuff. I had to pick up hinges and doorknobs and faucets."
Rory: "Oh, my."

20.

The Wizard of Oz (1939)
Lorelai: "I do recall Toto running through fields of it. Coffee to go, please."

The Miracle Worker (1962)
Rory: "Well, Annie Sullivan, look at you go. So, how's everything at the inn coming along?"

Camelot (1967)
Liz: "Oh, stop it. It's about a zillion years old with flowing sleeves. I'm like Vanessa Redgrave in Camelot. Seriously, I love myself in this dress."

The Lords of Flatbush (1974)
Luke: "You left me hanging with the Lords of Flatbush here."

Encino Man (1992)
T.J.: "Check out the fresh nooks."

American Splendor (2003)
Paris: "You were gonna ask him after class, but Toby from American Splendor wouldn't stop yapping and you couldn't."

Fatso (1980)
Rory and Lorelai watch the film

21.

The Shining (1980)
Chester: "All work and no play makes Jack..."

The Passion of the Christ (2004)
Lorelai: "It involves the J word."
Rory: "Oh, not more about Jesus. I'm sick of him and Mel Gibson."

22.

The Bad Seed (1956)
Rory: "Bye. You are the bad seed."

The Parent Trap (1961)
Lorelai: "I'm going to lock those two in a room, and they are either coming out reconciled or in a body bag. Believe you me, I'm fine either way."
Rory: "Well, look who died and made you Hayley Mills."

Better Off Dead... (1985)
Rory wakes up from a nap with a post-it note stuck to her forehead, like a character from this film.

Pretty in Pink (1986)
Rory: "James Spader in Pretty in Pink.

Heathers (1988)
Rory: "What's your damage, Heather?"

Season Five

1.

Gigi (1958)
Emily: "That is just wonderful! I'll call Ralphie right away and tell him to bump another Baptist. We'll have a wonderful time, you and I. It'll be just like "Gigi."

Bull Durham (1988)
Sookie: "You know. Was it on top of a table? 'Cause I always thought it would be on top of a table -- oh, like in "Bull Durham"!"

Fahrenheit 9/11 (2004)
Features on a poster that is visible in Lane's bedroom

2.

Apocalypse Now (1979)
Sookie: "It's Apocalypse Now, baby! I yelled at the staff, but now I know. It was you."

Raging Bull (1980)
Sookie: "We walked past Dean's place, and Lindsay was throwing his stuff out on the street. They were really going at it. It was like Raging Bull. There's yelling and screaming."

Showgirls (1995)
Lorelai: "Will you be mad if it's Showgirls again?

I got the deluxe edition with shot glasses and a drinking game."

A Room with a View (1985)
Watching TV - Rory plays this for Lorelai, calling it 'home movies' from her trip with her grandmother.

3.

Some Kind of Wonderful (1987)
Lorelai: "Alright, but no taking me to an art museum after hours and then to an empty Hollywood bowl where you give me a pair of diamond earrings that you bought with your college money when all the time you're really in love with your best friend, the drummer, who's posing as our driver for the evening."

The Lord of the Rings: The Fellowship of the Ring (2001)
Lorelai: "Oh. Oh, wow. Very 'Prancing Pony'."

Master and Commander: The Far Side of the World (2003)
Logan: "Tell Marty I said hi, and I promise to remember you instantly next time. Now, tell me that wasn't fun? Master and Commander."

4.

The Wizard of Oz (1939)
Lorelai: "This is a nice man who is growing some

very nice tomatoes, and you just need to oil your knees and go see the wizard and get a heart and drop this!"

The Manchurian Candidate (1962)
Lorelai: "Hmm. Very Manchurian Candidate of you."

Shoah (1985)
Paris: "Please. You're 19. Unless it's Shoah, you two are getting carnal."

Say Anything... (1989)
Lorelai: "Oh, no, no, no. Sorry, don't, no. Rory, Luke is fully dressed. He never came in the house. He just stood outside all night playing "In Your Eyes" on a boom box."

A Beautiful Mind (2001)
Zach: "Yo, John Nash, enough with the numbers."

Swept Away (2002)
Lorelai: "I know, but no votes? None? That's humiliating. That's Swept Away kind of humiliating."

5.

My Fair Lady (1964)
Lorelai: "By George, I think she's got it."

Cool Hand Luke (1967)
Lorelai: "They're playing a great movie tonight. Cool Hand Luke.

Last Tango in Paris (1972)
Lorelai: "But having Kirk reenact things can be pretty disturbing. He totally ruined Last Tango in Paris for me."

An Officer and a Gentleman (1982)
Zach: "I hope you weren't expecting an Officer and a Gentleman kind of thing when I came in just now."

Dances with Wolves (1990)
Zach: "You probably know me better than most people, including my parents. Neither of them have seen me cry during Dances with Wolves, and you have."

Panic Room (2002)
Emily: "I bought a panic room."

Auto Focus (2002)
Lorelai: "Yeah. Dad mentioned he had the Barbi twins up here a couple nights ago. He and his butler have a little "auto focus" thing going on."

Pippi Långstrump (1969)
Lorelai, Luke, Rory and Dean watch the movie in the local cinema.

6.

Bambi (1942)
Lorelai: "You've got Bambi voice."

Being There (1979)
Doyle: "It's like Being There. And he's Chauncey Gardiner."

Field of Dreams (1989)
Lorelai: "If you build it, they will come."

The Mothman Prophecies (2002)
Lorelai: "Oh, no? Did you see Mothman Prophecies?"

7.

Gone with the Wind (1939)
Lorelai: "Rhett is my gentleman friend, yes."

All the President's Men (1976)
Doyle: "I love this. We just had a very All the President's Men moment."

Happy Gilmore (1996)
Lorelai: "Luke's! I have to un-stress him after his unhappy Gilmore outing. Dad tried to take over his whole life. He wants to franchise Luke's."

Titanic (1997)
Rory: "You jump, I jump, Jack."

The Sixth Sense (1999)
Lorelai: "I see dead people."

Stop Making Sense (1984)
Lane and Zach watch the film on their date

8.

The Passion of the Christ (2004)
Finn: "I'll reenact the Passion of the Christ."

9.

Roman Holiday (1953)
Marty: " Rome. Rome. Romans lived there. Aah...Audrey Hepburn took a holiday there."

Butterfield 8 (1960)
Lorelai: "Just tell him you're obsessed with "Butterfield 8" and go like that."

The Godfather (1972)
Jackson: "This is the fish on the doorstep. It's the horse head in the bed. It's the "either your signature or your brains are going to be on the contract."

The Way We Were (1973)
Lorelai: "She was so serious. You know how she gets really serious, like when she saw The Way We Were, and she couldn't believe that Hubbell was going to leave Katie after she had the baby?"

St. Elmo's Fire (1985)
Lorelai: "If you try hard enough, you can eventually find a showing of St. Elmo's Fire on the big screen."

Less Than Zero (1987)
Lorelai: "And also, Andrew McCarthy at his best.

Though Less Than Zero runs a very close second."

The Bourne Supremacy (2004)
Lorelai: "I don't think so. Good thing we ditched that Audi in Marseilles. Now we just have to find that tracking device. Sookie, honey, what's wrong?"

10.

All About Eve (1950)
Paris: "Eve Harrington has arrived."

Sabrina (1954)
Rory: "Like Sabrina!"

Willy Wonka & the Chocolate Factory (1971)
Lorelai: "Ah! Its heaven! One quick trip downstairs and I have all the treats I want. You're like Willy Wonka, but hotter. Slap on a purple top hat and you're close. This is nice."

Alice Doesn't Live Here Anymore (1974)
Lorelai: "And over here we have the world famous Luke's diner, home of the best coffee on the east coast and the most delightful and chatty proprietor since Mel kissed Flo's grits."

Austin Powers: The Spy Who Shagged Me (1999)
Lorelai: "Hey! Did your mini-me show up?"

Fahrenheit 9/11 (2004)
A poster of this film is visible in Paris and Rory's dorm room.

11.

Gone with the Wind (1939)
Lorelai: "Tomorrow is another day."

The Sound of Music (1965)
Reverend: "Well, do you picture me watching Sound of Music every night, Taylor? Gag me."

Monty Python and the Holy Grail (1975)
Lorelai: "Or at least some coconuts to bang together for a nice sound effect."

Xanadu (1980)
Lorelai: "A snowy xanadu of goodness."

Oxford Blues (1984)
Chris: "Right. College. Classes. I've seen Oxford Blues, I should have put that together."

Beverly Hills Cop (1984)
Lorelai: "It was in Beverly Hills Cop, remember?"

Farewell My Concubine (1993)
Reverend: "Anyone seen Farewell My Concubine? Beautiful film. Gorgeous cinematography."

From Justin to Kelly (2003)
Lorelai: "Seriously. This dialogue is worse than From Justin To Kelly."

12.

Ghost (1990)
Lorelai: "Or Patrick Swayze."

13.

I Am a Camera (1955)
Lorelai: "I am a camera."

Breakfast at Tiffany's (1961)
"Moon River" is played at the reception.

Bugsy Malone (1976)
Chris: "I do. It's very Bugsy Malone."

Pulp Fiction (1994)
Lorelai: "Yeah. We're doing the one from Pulp Fiction. Do you want to be Uma, or should I?"

14.

The Way We Were (1973)
Lorelai: "Hey, Luke, it's me. I know I'm not supposed to be calling, but I am not doing really great right now, and - [Pause] I was just wondering, if, do you remember in The Way we Were, how Katie and Hubbell broke up because his friends were joking and laughing, and the president had just died, and she yelled at them

and he was mad and he was going out to Hollywood, and, I mean, which she hated, and he broke up with her and she was really upset."

Annie (1982)
Rory: "The party for the little girls and their dolls? Michel apparently really came through and it was a big hit. He sang a medley from Annie."

Bride of Chucky (1998)
Michel: "Teeth? Throat? Colons? They don't have these things either? Unless they are Brides of Chucky."

Crouching Tiger, Hidden Dragon (2000)
Rory: "Then they'll feel the wrath of the Green Destiny."

My Man Godfrey (1936)
This film is shown in the theater where Lorelai finds Luke

15.

Snow White and the Seven Dwarfs (1937)
Lorelai: "No, honey, honestly, the whole thing reeks of Emily. I mean, not that I think he would have discouraged it, but I'm pretty sure she's the one who poisoned the apple and gave it to Dopey to bring to the party."

Fiddler on the Roof (1971)
Kirk plays Tevye in the Stars Hollow Elementary production of Fiddler on the Roof.

Jesus Christ Superstar (1973)
Lulu: " And you know, we had a terrible experience last year when we did Jesus Christ Superstar."

Moulin Rouge! (2001)
Lorelai: "Hmm. Hey, Moulin Rouge, what do you think? Jeweled elephant in one corner, Ewan McGregor in the other."

Duck Soup (1933)
Rory and Marty watch the film.

16.

A Star Is Born (1937)
A Star Is Born (1954)
A Star Is Born (1976)
Lorelai: "I Netflix'd all three 'A Star is Born's."

A Woman Under the Influence (1974)
Rory: "Woman Under the Influence?"
Lorelai: A.k.a. the story of me."

17.

The Godfather (1972)
Lorelai: "At least I didn't ask you for a favor on this, the day of our daughter's wedding."

Jackie Brown (1997)
Reservoir Dogs (1992)
Kill Bill: Vol. 1 (2003)
Several students at the Quentin Tarantino party dress as characters from these films

Pulp Fiction (1994)
Title Reference
Several students at the Quentin Tarantino party also dress as characters from this film

Bridget Jones's Diary (2001)
Rory: "Yeah, I heard Renee Zellweger is gaining a ton of weight to play the peasant."

18.

Live and Let Die (1973)
Title Reference

19.

Bambi (1942)
Lorelai: "That's impossible. It's like hating Thumper. No one hates Thumper."

The Exorcist (1973)
Lorelai: "Oh, here, before I forget. Um, this fell out of your pocket last night while you were pulling an Exorcist."

Star Wars: Episode V - The Empire Strikes Back (1980)
Doyle: "Oh, God. Do you remember when Han

Solo finds Luke Skywalker in the snowstorm and he cuts open their dead Taun-taun to hide inside? That's what I smell like at this moment."

The Meaning of Life (1983)
Paris: "Stop saying the word 'vomiting'. Unless you want a Mr. Creosote situation on your hands here."

Good Morning, Vietnam (1987)
Lorelai: "Good morning Vietnam! How's everyone feeling today?"

Jerry Maguire (1996)
Lorelai: "Ah, baby, you lost me at carrots. Which, ah, by the way, was the first draft of 'you had me at hello'."

Coyote Ugly (2000)
Lorelai: "You, of all people, should know the dangers of the Founder's Day punch. Did you learn nothing from Mommy's Coyote Ugly bar dance at last year's Salute to the Quakers festival?"

The Lord of the Rings: The Fellowship of the Ring (2001)
Lorelai: "Does it seem like Frodo is on every fricking channel to you, or is it just me?"

House of Flying Daggers (2004)
Lorelai: "Yes. It was very House of Flying Daggers, but with vomiting."

20.

The Sound of Music (1965)
Logan: "He likes jazz, but not when it gets too experimental, and he hates when they quote My Favorite Things."

Paper Moon (1973)
Rory: "I can't show my face in any stores in New Haven. They think I'm Paper Mooning them."

Chinatown (1974)
Lorelai: "My daughter, my sister, my daughter, my sister, my daughter"

Footloose (1984)
Paris: "Oh, no, Reverend has the town band dancing and singing? I'm really happy."

Hotel Rwanda (2004)
Rory: "Learn a new song, or I am tying you to a chair and putting Hotel Rwanda on again."

21.

Damn Yankees! (1958)
Lorelai says, "Whatever Pola wants, Pola gets." I can't find this one.

22.

The Wizard of Oz (1939)
Zach: "Well, geez, Dorothy, if Tinman and Lion are going to go, I guess I have to go too."

Caged Heat (1974)
The Jezebels (1975)
Lorelai: "Oh, that's good. I mean, not that she's a snob. She can get along with anyone, it's just, it was her first time in a cell, so I didn't want her to be attacked, you know, like in Caged Heat? Or was it Switchblade Sisters? Anyway. I mean, my daughter never gets into trouble. Except, you know, now. But on the whole, the kid is an angel. She goes to Yale."

Festival Express (2003)
Lane: "Okay, okay! I know. It's not perfect. It's not the Festival Express, but it could be really great. What do you say?"

Eternal Sunshine of the Spotless Mind (2004)
Michel: "The memory of those bikers poking each other in the buttocks 'Eternal Sunshine'd out of my mind."

Season Six

1.

The Wizard of Oz (1939)
Willy Wonka & the Chocolate Factory (1971)
Paris: "Yep. Family get-together is like a Lollipop guilt convention. I have to stop myself from asking how it's going at the chocolate factory."

Bob & Carol & Ted & Alice (1969)
Rory: "Very Bob, Carol, Ted and Alice. Minus Bob."

Fiddler on the Roof (1971)
Lorelai: "Oh well...Wonder of wonder, Miracle of miracles. Right?"

Paper Moon (1973)
Lorelai: "Hey, it's only a paper moon dad."

Breaking Away (1979)
Michel: "And I have no intention of catching jock itch on my forearm because Mr. Breaking Away over there can't shower before he invades my den space."

The Blue Lagoon (1980)
Paris: "It's Logan. That Christopher Atkins wannabe is the reason that she's suddenly Blue Laggooning it right out of school."

2.

The Godfather (1972)
Luke: "I'm gonna talk to TJ, but I'm gonna be smart about it, I'm not gonna spook him. I'm gonna be like Michael Corleone dealing with that slimy brother-in-law of his."

March of the Penguins (2005)
Miss Patty: "Honey, go see March of The Penguins."

Star Wars: Episode III - Revenge of the Sith (2005)
Luke: "I mean, they can fly jetpods, but they can't scurry?"

The Graduate (1967)
Rory can be seen watching this film.

3.

The Wizard of Oz (1939)
Michel hums the Wicked Witch of the West's musical intro

The Graduate (1967)
Title reference

Alice Doesn't Live Here Anymore (1974)
Lorelai: "Milk, cream, and sugar's on the table. Flo's got coffee. Who needs a jolt?"

My Left Foot (1989)
Lorelai: "Hey, Luke. I'm just doing my Daniel Day Lewis retrospective for the guys."

The Last of the Mohicans (1992)
Lorelai: "I will find you, no matter how long, no matter how far! I will find you!

Harry Potter and the Sorcerer's Stone (2001)
Gil: "Wash my hair. Hug the kids, set them up in front of a Harry Potter movie, and then do my wife for, like, an hour."

4.

The Lost Weekend (1945)
Lane: "Now you've had it, and soon you'll make up and then this will all be just your lost weekend."

The Godfather (1972)
Brian: "Godmother, huh? Did you make her an offer she couldn't refuse?"

Star Wars: Episode IV - A New Hope (1977)
Zach: "Got to be R2-D2 to understand that thing."

Risky Business (1983)
Lorelai: "Nice sunglasses. Very Risky Business."

Prizzi's Honor (1985)
Lorelai: "In the ads I saw, the Rosie character was calling herself the sheriff, and she was bragging

about her sex life and buying toilet seats. And Angelica Huston directed it. Maerose directed it."

Deuce Bigalow: Male Gigolo (1999)
Lorelai: "If you're watching a Wednesday matinee of Deuce Bigalow, you can yell fire all you want."

Fahrenheit 9/11 (2004)
A poster for this film can be seen in Lane's bedroom.

Mad Hot Ballroom (2005)
Logan: "You can do anything. You just have to believe in yourself. Did we learn nothing from "Mad Hot Ballroom"?"

Riding the Bus with My Sister (2005)
Luke: "Riding the Bus With My Sister."
Lorelai: "Rosie O'Donnell plays a retarded woman who's obsessed with riding the bus, and Andie McDowell is her uptight, big-city sister."

5.

Gunga Din (1939)
Lorelai: "Need water. Gunga din!"

Gone with the Wind (1939)
Michel: "She's been Scarlett O'Hara for two hours. It's sickening."

His Girl Friday (1940)
Rory: "Lacey Boscombe, my right hand, my girl Friday, I could not have done it without you."

The Godfather (1972)
Rory: "I know, but this is business - It's not personal. I should give her that table."

Dog Day Afternoon (1975)
Paris: "So, I started pacing and yelling, 'Attica! Attica!', and then the manager hit a little red button under his desk, so I ran out of there and came right over here. I'm a pauper. I'll be playing a hurdy gurdy on street corners and selling pencils out of a tin cup."

Firestarter (1984)
Lorelai: "Oh, no! Am I a fire starter? I'm a fire starter, aren't I?"

Working Girl (1988)
Just Shoot Me! (1997)
Paris: "So I went to the video store and rented "Working Girl" and the first season of "Just Shoot Me". Got a couple of Wendie Malick bon mots that have already come in handy."

6.

The Godfather (1972)
Kirk: "You know the old saying, cross the Don in the morning, sleep with the fishes in the

afternoon. Plus, Taylor has one of those really fast laser printers."

Bring Me the Head of Alfredo Garcia (1974)
Rory: "Wow, you did it. You brought me the head of Alfredo Garcia."

Norma Rae (1979)
Lorelai: "And I stand up, on the bench, totally Norma Rae, and I write 'Strike' on my town meeting flier, and I hold it up, all defiant!"

Sixteen Candles (1984)
Lorelai: "Then I turned to Taylor, and I said: 'Taylor Doose, if you don't put us back on the map, it will be Molly Ringwald giving her underwear to Anthony Michael Hall and he shows it to a roomful of boys who've all paid a dollar to see it.'"

Welcome to the Dollhouse (1995)
Title reference.

7.

Alice in Wonderland (1951)
Richard: "She's running around, planning tea parties like she's the mad hatter. All she talks about are seating charts and canapes and fund-raisers and that boy."

Girl, Interrupted (1999)
Lorelai: "And so, I come out and I do mad scientist banter, like, 'Hey, who here is from

Bellevue?' and 'Girl Interrupted? Now that's my idea of a feel-good movie'".

March of the Penguins (2005)
Logan: "Huh. Is it me or could the penguins march through here?"

The 40 Year Old Virgin (2005)
Rory: "So, have you seen The 40-year-old Virgin? 'Cause you might like it.

8.

Oliver Twist (1948)
Lorelai: "Bye. Wow, Oliver Twist just kindly asked for a little more gruel, and you kicked him right in the junk."

Sophie's Choice (1982)
Colin: "Finn, watch. Tostingo!"

Scarface (1983)
Lorelai: "Scarface on a soccer field."

Bend It Like Beckham (2002)
Lorelai: "Bend it like Beckham! Oh, so, I dropped Paul Anka off at doggy day care. It was a little scary."

9.

West Side Story (1961)
Lorelai: "Bernardo."
Sookie: "Riff."

Mask (1985)
Lorelai: "No, I can't. The bed is small and really low, perfect for tiny, shrunken limbs that can't be too far off the ground. And then he has this ancient dresser with the original fun-house mirror in it so that when I wake up every morning, and I am at my most visually vulnerable, I'll look in there and think I'm that kid from Mask."

10.

The Wizard of Oz (1939)
Lorelai: "Yeah, well, I get the girls from the Wash & Brush Up company from the Wizard of Oz working for me now."

Willy Wonka & the Chocolate Factory (1971)
Chris: "The Oompa Loompas?"

The Godfather (1972)
Sookie: "Godfather it up for me. Good! Good, good, good. Good, good. Okay. If you can travel back in time and make me not make the veal and ham paté, I'd appreciate it. Talk me out of these things in the future, guys."

Dig! (2004)
Title Reference

Freaky Friday (1976)
Lorelai: "Okay. I'm getting very uncomfortable with the Freaky Friday moment we've got going on here, 'cause it means I have to go to Yale, you

have to run the inn, and oh, God! I don't even like thinking about what it would mean for Luke."

Waiting for Guffman (1996)
Lane: "Very big. Unless it's a 'Waiting for Guffman' thing and the label guys don't show up. Did I just jinx it?"

11.

The Wizard of Oz (1939)
Paris: "Now, Doyle sleeps very deeply, so don't worry about the hours. I, as you know, haven't slept through the night since the first time I saw The Wizard Of Oz - thank you Mum - so I tend to do my crafts in the middle of the night, but the walls are very thick."

Willy Wonka & the Chocolate Factory (1971)
Sookie: "What are you talking about? You have the golden ticket"

Fahrenheit 9/11 (2004)
A poster for the film can be seen in Paris and Doyle's apartment.

12.

My Fair Lady (1964)
Lorelai: "Even with the rain in Spain?"

8 Mile (2002)
Lorelai: "Back to 8 mile?"

13.

Mildred Pierce (1945)
Lorelai: "You totally Mildred Pierced me."

An Affair to Remember (1957)
Logan: "Okay, great. Thursday it is. 7:30. And do not think of backing out, because I will cry and eat a pint of rocky road while watching An Affair to Remember. With Rita Wilson"

Mary Poppins (1964)
Lorelai: "Well, you know, she didn't say it like that, but she said, 'oh! Dinner with Rory! How delightful! Well, spit-spot. Alert the corgis.'

Cabaret (1972)
Lorelai: "Christopher Isherwood. That Cabaret money was burning a hole in his pocket."

The Bridges of Madison County (1995)
Lorelai: "They are the bridges of Madison county, and you are Meryl Streep."

14.

Bullets Over Broadway (1994)
Rory: "Yep. Hey, "Bullets over Broadway."
Solaris (2002)

Lorelai: "Cool. Solaris? There has to be a story in there somewhere."

March of the Penguins (2005)
Lorelai: "They were extras in March of the penguins."

15.

The Sound of Music (1965)
Lorelai: "You've not worn an apron since you saw The Sound of Music and you put one on so you'd look like sister Maria, and you made a big crucifix out of popsicle sticks."

16.

Mary Poppins (1964)
Christopher: "Hi, Mary Poppins."

Network (1976)
Logan: "I'm telling you, we should take this on the road. I see you went with Faye Dunaway in Network."

Invasion of the Body Snatchers (1978)
Lorelai: "If that's your Donald Sutherland Invasion of the Body Snatchers impression, it's a really good one."

The Breakfast Club (1985)
Lorelai: "She is smart. She's Anthony Michael hall in Breakfast Club smart."

Fahrenheit 9/11 (2004)
A poster for this film can be seen on the wall of Paris' apartment.

Brokeback Mountain (2005)
Zach: "I don't mean to get all Brokeback Mountain on you, but we're buds, you know, and I miss you, and you're not gonna believe it, but that kid over there is about to down a whole cup of maraschino cherries."

Saw II (2005)
Doyle: "Last night she decided it would be fun to watch Saw II at 3:00 in the morning."

17.

Psycho (1960)
Lorelai: "Yes like Janet Leigh in Psycho."

Bugsy Malone (1976)
Rory: "I have Bugsy Malone running through my head, especially the scene where Scott Baio buys Florrie Dugger a hot dog and he offers her mustard with onions or ketchup without."

Halloween (1978)
Lorelai: "I mean, where's the Halloween mask? Where's the costume? How can they keep making the same stupid movie over and over and over?"

Star Wars: Episode V - The Empire Strikes Back (1980)

Mrs. Kim: "Don't try, do. 3 1/2 minutes, tops, and radio-friendly."

Friday the 13th (1980)
A Nightmare on Elm Street (1984)
Lorelai: "Okay, but, see, I'm sorry. They did not even come up with a villain. No Freddy, no Jason. The villain is death? How lame is that? Who is seeing this movie?"

Little Man Tate (1991)
Lorelai: "Yeah, she asked you. She called you and I know that traveling across country in a bus full of Little Man Tates has been a lifelong dream of yours."

Final Destination (2000)
Final Destination 2 (2003)
Lorelai asks Rory if she wants to rent and watch the film.

Nanny McPhee (2005)
Final Destination 3 (2006)
Rory: "Fine. Last half of Nanny McPhee, first half of Final Destination 3."

19.

All the President's Men (1976)
Rosemary: "Ooh, how very 'All The President's Men. Exciting."

American Gigolo (1980)
The Bachelorette Party are planning to see this film

Footloose (1984)
Lorelai: "Wow, suddenly Footloose not seeming so silly."

Napoleon Dynamite (2004)
Lorelai imitates Napoleon when she delivers Lane's wedding dress to her, after she has altered it.

20.

Citizen Kane (1941)
The Magnificent Ambersons (1942)
Touch of Evil (1958)
These films are being screened at the Black, White and Read Movie Theater

The In-Laws (1979)
Lorelai: "Serpentine, girls, serpentine."

Endless Love (1981)
Miss Patty: "Is there any other way to sing "endless love"?"

RoboCop (1987)
Logan: "Hey Robocop made a full recovery. Look where that led him."

Harry Potter and the Sorcerer's Stone (2001)
Anna: "It's a rave. Her friends call you Hagrid."

National Treasure (2004)
Lorelai: "Oh, did you steal me the constitution? 'Cause that could be the start of a really dumb movie."

Pretty in Pink (1986)
Lorelai: "All right, girls, um, you're about to meet someone very special to me. Her name is Molly Ringwald."

21.

The Miracle Worker (1962)
Logan: "Helen Keller just signed water, Annie."

The Godfather (1972)
Lorelai: "A sit down what, did you get Clemenza to hide a gun in the bathroom first?"

Give 'em Hell, Harry! (1975)
Bill: "Give 'em hell, Harry."

Broadway Danny Rose (1984)
Lorelai: "No really, I thought you were just doing your best Mia Farrow in Broadway Danny Rose impersonation."

Driving Miss Daisy (1989)
Title reference

Misery (1990)
Logan: "To re-enact their favorite scenes from Misery?"

March of the Penguins (2005)
Doyle: "Penguins. You haven't seen the penguin

movie?"

22.

Mary Poppins (1964)
Logan: "You're gonna break into a chorus of Chim-Chim-Cheree any minute. Kiss me, Mary Poppins."

The Turning Point (1977)
Miss Patty: "Well, uh, I-I don't know. You know, half the time people speak to me, I'm thinking about Baryshnikov. Did you see Turning Point?"

Purple Rain (1984)
Lorelai: "Every now and then, I just feel the need to re-enact certain key scenes from Purple Rain, you know, for a captive audience."

Fatal Attraction (1987)
Rory: "I won't be ignored, Dan."

Shakespeare in Love (1998)
Rory: "Really I thought it was more Gwyneth Paltrow, Shakespeare in love."

Season Seven

1.

Sunset Boulevard (1950)
Taylor: "You run a red light, it's time for your close-up, Mr. Demille. These little wonders are taking over the globe -- New York, Los Angeles, Paris, Singapore."

Winnie the Pooh and the Honey Tree (1966)
Lorelai: "Winnie the pooh band-aids?"

E.T. the Extra-Terrestrial (1982)
Rory: "Hey, maybe it's code. Like I'm his rocket, right? Like I'm his rock, E.T."

The Perfect Storm (2000)
Lorelai: "Yeah, that's me. I'm fast. I'm the perfect storm of caffeine and genetics. Ha-ha."

The Fast and the Furious (2001)
2 Fast 2 Furious (2003)
The Fast and the Furious: Tokyo Drift (2006)
Rory: "Okay, do you remember when you begged me to go see The Fast and the Furious with you, and I said no? And then you begged me to go see The Fast and the Furious 2 with you, and I said no? Then The Fast and the Furious 3: Tokyo Drift came out...

Jarhead (2005)
Lorelai: "No, this is mine. But I wore it with Luke when we went to see Jarhead."

2.

From Here to Eternity (1953)
Lane: "But anyway we decided to re-create the scene in From Here To Eternity."

An Affair to Remember (1957)
Rory: "You know what, mom? If you're heartbroken, rent An Affair to Remember, have a good cry, and drown your sorrows in a pint of ice cream."

The Bridge on the River Kwai (1957)
Lorelai: "Hmm, and that will be followed by an educational video, which includes, but is not limited to, Bridge On The River Kwai…"

Breakfast at Tiffany's (1961)
The Karate Kid (1984)
Mr. Baseball (1992)
The Joy Luck Club (1993)
Shanghai Surprise (1986)
Lorelai: "The Joy Luck Club, Karate Kid, Shanghai Surprise, The Bruce Lee classic Enter the Dragon, the Tom Selleck classic Mr. Baseball, and or Breakfast at Tiffany's."

The Exorcist (1973)
Zach: "Anyway on the second day, I got some parasite, and I've been barfing Linda Blair style

ever since. I'm getting better, but now it looks like Lane's got it."

Speed (1994)
The Lake House (2006)
Liz: "You're living in the same house, man, but you are a couple years apart in the space-time continuum."

Shallow Hal (2001)
View from the Top (2003)
Rory: "You don't have to be perfect. I mean, even Gwyneth Paltrow makes mistakes, like Shallow Hal and that other movie that nobody saw where she played a stewardess. So who's perfect? Nobody. Not even mothers."

4.

Casablanca (1942)
Lorelai: "We can never see Casablanca together. I mean I'm very sorry. I don't care how much I love it, but I will not be responsible for ruining Casablanca."

Jailhouse Rock (1957)
Lorelai: "Whatcha in the mood for? Jailhouse rock? "Folsom Prison Blues?"

The Sound of Music (1965)
Lorelai: "Somewhere in my youth or childhood..."

Christopher: "You must have done something good."

Bullitt (1968)
Lorelai: "So, tell me now. Now! Tell me! Oh, hello, Bullitt."

Driving Miss Daisy (1989)
Dances with Wolves (1990)
Snakes on a Plane (2006)
Lorelai: "No! No! A movie should not just be its title. Driving Miss Daisy didn't all take place in the car, Dances With Wolves wasn't one long wolf dance. But this was nothing but snakes, snakes, relentless snakes, snakes on a plane. Snakes, snakes, snakes on a plane!"

Funny Face (1957)
Lorelai and Christopher watch this film on a date.

5.

Broadway Danny Rose (1984)
Lorelai: "Milton Berle, Broadway Danny Rose, Carnegie deli."

Cinderella
Christopher says Gigi has been watching this

Ghostbusters (1984)
Rory: "Oh, I'd love to wear a middy. And a little sailor hat, like the stay puft marshmallow man."

Dangerous Liaisons (1988)
Lorelai: "Wow, how Dangerous Liaisons of her.

She doesn't call. She doesn't e-mail. Then she sends you a letter with a wax seal that weighs roughly the same as a porterhouse."

6.

Destry Rides Again (1939)
The Lady Is Willing (1942)
Touch of Evil (1958)
Susan: "Touch of Evil, um The Lady is Willing, Destry Rides Again. 'Your husband would rather be cheated by me than married to you.'"

Top Gun (1986)
Kirk: "You inspired me. I look at you, and I think, 'This guy's doing it right. Slave to no master.' You come home at 3:00 in the morning -- no one cares. You want to eat dessert for dinner -- no one cares. You walk around in tube socks and tighty whities -- no one cares. No one cares what you do or where you go. Luke is not looking happy] So, what do you say, Luke? You want to be my wingman, goose to my maverick? 'You never close your eyes anymore when I kiss your lips and there's no tenderness…'

Pleasantville (1998)
Lorelai: "Grass is just not this green -- not outside of Pleasantville, it isn't."

House on Haunted Hill (1959)
Lorelai and Christopher can be seen watching this film.

7.

Casablanca (1942)
Lorelai: "Are you saying we'll always have Paris?"

Funny Face (1957)
Lorelai: "Alright first we have to go to Harry's bar and smoke Gauloises cigarettes and get in a fight about cubism and gesticulate wildly."

The Music Man (1962)
Olivia: "You expect professor Harold hill to move there and sucker everyone into buying band instruments."

Girls Gone Wild on Campus 2 (2003)
Paris: "You really shouldn't be alone at a time like this. Why don't you call your Girls Gone Wild friends? They seem delightful in a - get crazy-drunk in Cancun and flash your breasts - kind of way."

The Dust Bowl (2012)
Lorelai says she could watch this without falling asleep

8.

Norma Rae (1979)
Logan: "'Cause you saw Norma Rae?

An Inconvenient Truth (2006)
April: "Did you not see An Inconvenient Truth?"

The Philadelphia Story (1940)
Luke watches this film while he is waiting in the hospital waiting room.

9.

2001: A Space Odyssey (1968)
Paris: "Space Odyssey -- that's a theme. People dress up like astronauts or apes."

A Brief History of Time (1991)
Luke: "So, what are you up for tonight? I was thinking we could rent A Brief History of Time again. Maybe I'll understand something more than the credits."

Bride of Chucky (1998)
Babette: "I was the Bride of Chucky."
Christopher: "Oh, yeah? Did Morey go as Chucky?"

10.

Duck Soup (1933)
Logan: "Rory and Marty, they used to hang out all the time at Branford and watch Duck Soup."

Rent (2005)
Lorelai: "What about instead of La Boheme, we took our inspiration from Rent - east village, 1985, rickety tables, chipped glassware..."

11.

Christmas in July (1940)
Rory: "Okay hurry back Christmas in July screening in 30 minutes."

Casablanca (1942)
Lorelai: "Casablanca. Casablanca is such a good movie. Casablanca."

How the Grinch Stole Christmas! (1966)
Lorelai: "I didn't let any Christmas happen. I grinched it up so hard, I didn't even let it snow."

Joe Versus the Volcano (1990)
Rory: "Okay. Well, you know, mom, I've been around for a while, too. I remember tom hanks from his Joe Versus The Volcano days."

The Muse (1999)
Lorelai: "You know I need a muse. Perhaps I need 'the muse.' Maybe it would help if Sharon Stone would appear to me in an alarming caftan and coo inspirational words in my ear."

12.

Heathers (1988)
Paris: "Oh, so now she's decided to just ignore you? How very Heathers of her."

Al Capone (1959)
Lorelai can be seen watching this film.

15.

Fahrenheit 9/11 (2004)
A poster for this film can be seen in Rory's apartment.

16.

Dirty Dancing (1987)
Rory: "I'm gonna need you to drive because I have to change in the backseat, "Dirty Dancing"-style. Do you want me to get that?"

A Beautiful Mind (2001)
Lorelai: "I don't want to go all "Beautiful Mind" on you, but according to my calculations..."

17.

Oklahoma! (1955)
A song from this film can be heard playing in the car.

Tuesdays with Morrie (1999)
Lorelai: "Yes, it's our Thursday computer lesson. And it's no "Tuesdays with Morrie."

Hitch (2005)
The Lake House (2006)
Lorelai: "All righty. Looks like our choices are Hitch or The Lake House."

The Pursuit of Happyness (2006)
Lorelai: "Have you seen The Pursuit of Happyness?"
Emily: "Is that the one with Will Smith? He's so attractive."

18.

His Girl Friday (1940)
All the President's Men (1976)
Rory: "Okay, I need to pick out a coat. A trench coat would be too All The President's Men, but my blue coat would be too His Girl Friday."
Rudolph the Red-Nosed Reindeer (1964) (TV Movie)
Rory: "And Rudolph and scab nose."

The Godfather (1972)
Rory: "Yeah, he's basically the Mayor of Stars Hollow and Don Corleone all wrapped up into one."

Star Wars: Episode IV - A New Hope (1977)
Logan: "I mean theoretically, I could make a fortune selling virtual Lightsabers or something on Everquest 2"

19.

Back to the Future (1985)
Rory: "Oh. So new car, huh? You should get a DeLorean like in Back to the Future."

Blades of Glory (2007)
Paris: "Yeah, I'm fine. Trust me, it's not like I've been dying to see Blades of Glory anyway. I'd better get started on my phone calls for the alumni surveys."

20.

The Sound of Music (1965)
Babette and Miss Patty: ""So long, farewell Auf Wiedersehen, goodbye, goodbye!"

Das Boot (1981)
Dead Calm (1989)
Open Water (2003)
Lorelai: "So! Anything could go wrong. You're on a boat in the water in the middle of nowhere. Haven't you seen Dead Calm, Open Water, Das Boot?"

Titanic (1997)
Lorelai: "Titanic, surely you've seen Titanic."

Fahrenheit 9/11 (2004)
A poster for this film can be seen in Lane and Zach's Apartment

House on Haunted Hill (1959)
Lorelai can be seen watching this film.

21.

Anything Goes (1936)
Emily and Richard perform "You're the Top" at Rory's party.

The Unbearable Lightness of Being (1988)
Rory: "What? You're not a big Kundera fan?"
Lorelai: "Uh, no. I'm unbearably light on him."

David Blaine: Above the Below (2003)
Kirk: "I will be suspended 20 feet above the street in a clear Lucite box with no food or water."
Lorelai: "Like David Blaine."

Syriana (2005)
The poster for this film can be seen at Stars Hollow Video.

A Year in the Life

Winter

The Odd Couple (1968)
Lorelai: "Felix!"
Luke: "Oscar!"

This Is Spinal Tap (1984)
Lorelai: "You Spinal Tapped the painting."

The Breakfast Club (1985)
Lorelai: "She learned her language skills via The Breakfast Club."

Trainspotting (1996)
Lorelai: "It had that early American tenement shtetl slash Trainspotting vibe that every mother wants for her little girl."

Saving Private Ryan (1998)
Lorelai: "It'd be like the first 15 minutes of Saving Private Ryan, but at least those guys got to be in France."

The Lord of the Rings: The Fellowship of the Ring (2001)
Lorelai: It's nuts! "Wizard, you shall not pass!" Seriously! Fine! I made a mistake! Are you happy? I gave them the wrong dimensions, and they screwed it up."

Eastern Promises (2007)
Lorelai: "Five nights in a row! I'm looking for a bathroom and then I find one and it's like the Eastern Promises steam room scene, only the stuff on the walls ain't blood."

Rock of Ages (2012)
Lorelai: "Everything's planned and they have Wi-Fi and Rock of Ages and you don't have to bring money."

Les Misérables (2012)
Lorelai: "You should be singing 'I Dreamed a Dream' with a bad haircut while selling yourself to a bunch of French dock workers."

Inside Llewyn Davis (2013)
Emily: "Her traipsing around from one couch to another like she's Llewyn Davis."

Gone Girl (2014)
Paris: "I'll send you a DVD of my top picks. I'll also include a copy of Gone Girl."

Inside Out (2015)
Paul: "It's got the Sadness stickers from Inside Out on it."

Zoolander 2 (2016)
Lorelai: "You're doing yoga in the aisles in cashmere sweatpants while your comfort dog watches Zoolander 2 on his watch."

Batman v Superman: Dawn of Justice (2016)
Rory: "Where would Superman change when he comes to save our town from Ben Affleck?"

Restless Virgins (2013)
Deadly Honeymoon (2010)
Killer Crush (2015)
Mini's First Time (2006)
Accidental Obsession (2015)
Murder in a College Town (1997)
Crimes of the Mind (2014)
Fatal Acquittal (2014)
Not With My Daughter (2014)
Baby Sellers (2013)
Unfinished Betrayal (2013)
The Girl He Met Online (2014)
The Boy She Met online (2010)
Deadly Vows (1994)
Lying Eyes (1996)
Lies He Told (1997)
My Nanny's Secret (2009)
Eastern Promises (2007)
These are all films that Lorelai has recorded on the DVR

Spring

Million Dollar Baby (1941)
Them! (1954)
Giant (1956)
Posters for these films can be seen at the Stars Hollow movie theatre

West Side Story (1961)
Francie: "Take a powder, Baby John."

Beach Blanket Bingo (1965)
Emily: "Well, even Claudia just called him "your guy," like it's a beach blanket movie."

Fiddler on the Roof (1971)
Logan: "It's the Gentile Fiddler on the Roof."

Eraserhead (1977)
Kirk: "Welcome, everyone, to the spring season of the Black, White and Read Movie Theater. I am pleased to present tonight's feature film, Eraserhead."

Star Wars: Episode IV - A New Hope (1977)
Rory: I slept with a Wookiee!"

Scarface (1983)
Lorelai: "Like Scarface?"

Heathers (1988)
Francie: "What's your damage?"

Get Shorty (1995)
Rory: "Get shorty!"

Up (2009)
The Real Paul Anka: "Squirrel!"

Swing Time (1936)
A History of Violence (2005)
Lorelai can be seen watching these films.

Cloud Atlas (2012)
Rory says Naomi's story is no Cloud Atlas

Summer

The Ghost and Mrs. Muir (1947)
Lorelai: "I don't know - Mrs. Muir, find a ghost."

On the Waterfront (1954)
Rory: "I could've been a contender."

Who's Afraid of Virginia Woolf? (1966)
Taylor: "You may know him as the author of a little something called Who's Afraid of Virginia Woolf?"

Fiddler on the Roof (1971)
Babette" "Tevye, move over. There's a new Jew in town."

The Godfather (1972)
Lorelai: "Consigliere of mine, I think it's time you tell your Don what everyone seems to know."

You're a Good Man, Charlie Brown (1973)
Lorelai: "I was Lucy in You're a Good Man, Charlie Brown."

Chinatown (1974)
This film plays at the Stars Hollow theater.

Annie Hall (1977)
Lorelai: "It's from Annie Hall."

The Lion King (1994)
Babette: "Ah! I knew it! Simba, you've been dethroned."

You've Got Mail (1998)
Lorelai: "It has a quote for every circumstance."

There Will Be Blood (2007)
Lance: "It's from There Will Be Blood."
Rory: "The movie?"
Lance: "Mmm hmm. We love everything Paul Thomas Anderson does."

Mamma Mia! (2008)
The song Waterloo is performed in the Stars Hollow Musical.

Wild (2014)
Lorelai: I'm gonna do Wild."

The Jungle Book (2016)
Rory: "Doyle, your review of The Jungle Book took a 20,000-word detour into the history of African colonialism."

Fall

The Wizard of Oz (1939)
Robert: "Now I know I have a heart, because it's breaking."

Snapped (2005)
Lorelai is watching this on her T.V. in the motel

Casablanca (1942)
Rory: "Well, well well. Of all the gin joints in all the world."

Baby Doll (1956)
Miss Celine: "I met him on the set of Baby Doll."

La Dolce Vita (1960)
Logan: "Another La Dolce Vita."

The Sound of Music (1965)
Michel: "Yes, any skeletons in that closet of yours? Drug problems? Cheating scandals? Played Rolfe in The Sound of Music one too many times?"

True Grit (1969)
Sookie: "It's a bear! So, now, you know, Jackson thinks that everything outside is a bear, and he's rigged the entire property with bear traps that blast "Welcome To The Jungle" if you trip them off, and I'm out chasing Cogburn, our rooster, and then voilÃ ! You know, Panama all over again."

The Godfather (1972)

Bugsy (1991)
Emily: "Well, I bought it, and it wasn't even for sale. I just upped and pulled a Bugsy Siegel and made 'em an offer they couldn't refuse."

An Unmarried Woman (1978)
Grease (1978)

Lorelai: "And he took me to the movies. We saw Grease and An Unmarried Woman. Something for me and something for him, he said."

Dawn of the Dead (1978)
Jess: "Diner of the Dead?"

Arthur (1981)
Arthur (2011)
Colin: "First Arthur, now this. They never learn."

The Pee Wee Herman Show (1981)
Lorelai: "Did that nice Pee-wee Herman ever find a lady?"

Yentl (1983)
Finn: "Like Yentl."

The Goonies (1985)
Lorelai: "I hate nature."

Edward Scissorhands (1990)
Rory: "I also wanted to marry Edward Scissorhands and Jerry Orbach from Law & Order."

Sister Act (1992)
Lorelai: "Is Whoopi Goldberg around anywhere?"

The Adventures of Priscilla, Queen of the Desert (1994)
Lorelai: "Priscilla Queen of the Desert or desnudas"

The Lion King (1994)
Lorelai toasts: "To the circle of life!"

Jerry Maguire (1996)
Emily: "Show me the money! Have you seen Jerry Maguire? It was on Starz last night. It's delightful."

The Lord of the Rings: The Fellowship of the Ring (2001)
The Lord of the Rings: The Two Towers (2002)
Lord of the Rings: The Return of the King (2003)
Rory: "And that you had an obsession with Lord of the Rings, that you did a terrible *Sméagol* impression."

The Machinist (2004)
Lorelai: "the thru-hiker looked a little like Christian Bale in The Machinist. She knew how to get all that crap in her pack."

The Hurt Locker (2008)
Lorelai: "it is really packed in there and the minute I open this thing up, it's like The Hurt Locker. No one survives."

Eat Pray Love (2010)
Brenda: "I am so glad I'm doing this. I almost did

Eat, Pray, Love, but my miles were blacked out. So, here I am."

Wild (2014)
Lorelai goes on a Wild inspired hiking trip

It's a Lifestyle.
It's a Religion.

Television

Television in Gilmore Girls

One of the hallmarks of the show was the amount of television shows that are referenced. The girls watch shows, talk about them, and quote them throughout the series as often as they reference books, movies and music.

Some of the *Gilmore Girls'* most important moments happen in the shadow of other important television shows which sit in history as the predecessors of *Gilmore Girls*. Rory and Dean's relationship moves forward after an episode of *The Donna Reed Show* inspires Rory to create a themed date where she gives Dean a "Donna Reed Night". Rory's college applications arrive as her and Lorelai watch re-runs of *The Brady Bunch Hour,* and an episode of *The Twilight Zone* confirms Logan's love for Rory after he moves to London and commences a long-distance relationship with her.

Just as *Gilmore Girls* is the backdrop for many of the life events that fans experience, the following television shows serve as the backdrop for many important Gilmore moments, and should be watched by any fan who wants to be Gilmore'd.

Season One

2.

The Dukes of Hazzard (1979)
Lorelai: "I look like that chick from The Dukes of Hazzard."

The View (1997)
Headmaster Charleston: "Not Oprah, Rosie, or one of the women from The View?"

3.

The New Price Is Right (1972)
Lorelai: "Okay, Bob Barker. Listen - Rory knocks herself out all week at Chilton. Weekends are the only time she has to unwind and have fun."

4.

Saved by the Bell (1989)
Lorelai: "You once told me that you loved Saved by the Bell."

5.

Hee Haw (1969)
Michel: "Hello? Hello? Where is Lorelai? I'm dropping something off. Yoo-hoo, 'Hee-Haw' man, where is Lorelai Gilmore?"

The Oprah Winfrey Show (1986)
Babette: "I saw on Oprah a few weeks ago - she had on couples who lost a child. Most of the marriages when belly up for the pain of it all, even though they loved each other."

6.

I Love Lucy (1951)
Lorelai: "Lucy, I'm home!"

Star Trek (1966)
Lorelai: "No, she has her Vulcan death grip on that one."

The Waltons (1971)
Rory: "I wonder if the Walton's ever did this."

7.

General Hospital (1963)
Lorelai: "Oh, OK, great. I was watching General Hospital the other day and you know, they have a new Lucky 'cause the old Lucky went to play something where he could have a real name. So

the old Lucky had this girlfriend, Liz, who thought that he died in a fire. So then they bring on this new Lucky and you're all like "OK, I know that's not the old Lucky because the new Lucky has way more hair gel issues" but still, Liz was so upset about his supposed death that you could not wait to see them kiss, you know?"
Rory: "When do you have time to watch General Hospital?"

8.

Star Trek (1966)
Rory: "Right, Rich Bloomingfeld. Does he still wear the Star Trek Shirt?"

Wonder Woman (1975)
Lorelai: "Maybe I should put on my red, white and blue leotard and fly the invisible plane over there."

9.

Live! With Kelly and Michael (1988)
Lorelai: "What, Mom? She can make some cash off of it. Become a crazy Oscar Levant kind of celebrity - go on talk shows, heckle Regis."

V.I.P. (1998)
Lane: "Because I have to go home soon and my mom threw out our TV when she caught me

watching V.I.P. So I'm bored and I need some entertainment."

11.

This Old House (1979)
Lorelai: "What can I say - watching someone work makes me hungry. If I hadn't stopped watching This Old House I'd be 500 pounds right now."

Lillehammer 1994: XVII Olympic Winter Games (1994)
Lorelai: "And I'm Tonya Harding. I'm gonna do the whole shoe lace coming untie - nervous break - let me start again act and everything."

13.

The Yogi Bear Show (1961)
Paris: "Before it's dark, they'll have every picnic basket that's in Jellystone Park."

Star Trek (1966)
Rory: "This stuff is like Tribbles!"

Wonder Woman (1975)
Lorelai: "So she was wonder woman."

Joanie Loves Chachi (1982)
Louise: "Oh yes - 6'2... and fiesty. So how's that going? Are you two still Joanie loves Chachi?"

14.

I Love Lucy (1951)
Lorelai: "Do I pull a Lucy Ricardo?"

Mutual of Omaha's Wild Kingdom (1963)
Sookie: "That's very 'Wild Kingdom' of you"

Sex and the City (1998)
Babbette: "Oh great! We've got a kitchen full of food and Morey just got cable so you can watch those four girls talking dirty if you want to."

The Donna Reed Show (1958)
Title Reference
Rory and Lorelai are seen watching the show
Rory recreates the show for Dean

15.

I Love Lucy (1951)
Lorelai: "My father almost hit someone. My father has probably only hit another man in college wearing boxing gloves and one of those Fred Mertz golden gloves pullover sweaters."
Christopher: "Fred Mertz?"
Lorelai: "'I Love Lucy' - Fred Mertz."
Christopher: "Landlord to Ricki, husband to Ethel, I know. It's just a weird reference."

Get Smart (1965)
Christopher: "Employ six individual cones of

silence…Boy the old balcony is still the same isn't it?"

Happy Days (1974)
Christopher: "And you were the girl in the Pinky Tuscadero t-shirt sitting right next to me."

16.

Iron Chef (1993)
Lorelai: "I want to be the Iron Chef."

17.

Sesame Street (1969)
Lorelai: "Trash doesn't actually talk at all unless it's on 'Sesame Street.'"

Lifestyles of the Rich and Famous (1984)
Lane: "I mean there should be a map or a tour guide or Robin Leech or something."

18.

Dawson's Creek (1998)
Rory: "Nietzsche?"
Louise: "Dawson."

19.

Star Trek (1966)
Lorelai: "Well, I don't know exactly what's going on in Rachel's head because I'm not a Vulcan, but from the way she talks about you and the way she smiles when your name comes up, I'm pretty sure that she's serious about staying in Stars Hollow this time."

Charlie's Angels (1976)
Rory: "The original Charlie's Angels. It took us years to get a complete set. You can find the Kate Jackson's and the Shelly Hack's pretty easily. Even the Cheryl Ladd's. But the Farrah Fawcett's and the Jacklyn Smith's are a little harder to come by, but still accessible. The real trick however is to find the Tanya Roberts. We have three."

20.

Mutual of Omaha's Wild Kingdom (1963)
Lorelai: "I wanna play Wild Kingdom."

21.

Soul Train (1971)
Lorelai: "Okay, well, did you date like casual nothing type dating or did you date like get down, soul train kind of a dating?"

Season Two

1.

The Tonight Show (1962)
Lorelai: "Not getting The Tonight Show."

Jeopardy! (1984)
Lorelai: "I'll take any other subject in the world for $200, Alex."

2.

All in the Family (1971)
Lorelai: "You know how in 'All in the Family' when Edith would be yapping about something and Archie would pretend to make a noose and pretend to hang himself or shoot himself in the head?"

Mahha GoGoGo (1967)
Lorelai: "By the time I could get my jaw off the ground, Speed Racer had taken my plate."

The Oprah Winfrey Show (1986)
Luke: "It must have been a really good Oprah."

Home Again with Bob Vila (1990)
Rory: "Funny. I never pictured you as a Bob Vila kind of girl."

The Ren & Stimpy Show (1991)
Louise: "Happy happy, joy joy."

Xuxa (1993)
Lorelai: "Hey, whatever happened to Xuxa?"

3.

Electra Woman and Dyna Girl (1976)
Lorelai: "Well, we are Electra Woman and Dyna Girl."
Max: "ElectraWoman."

4.

The Munsters (1964)
Lorelai: "W.E.B. Du Bois, Yo-Yo Ma. Oh cool! Fred Gwynn!"
Rory: "Who?"
Lorelai: "Herman Munster. Now I'm impressed."

Happy Days (1974)
Rory: "You do realize that all of your college kid jargon comes from 'Happy Days' and the 'Valley Girls' song?"

Behind the Music (1997)
Rory: "Your 'Behind the Music' is gonna be really wild."

5.

Live! With Kelly and Michael (1988)
Lorelai: "He's not going to be subbing for the new dodo on the 'Regis' show anytime soon."

6.

The Brady Bunch (1969)
Lorelai: "Yeah, it's right up there in between old Brady Bunch reruns and the lyrics to Rapture."
Jeeves and Wooster (1990)
Rory: "Why, thank you Jeeves."
BattleBots (2000)
Rory: "Remember Neil Young. Remember that you love me. Remember that I'll be watching BattleBots with you for a month."

7.

Fat Albert and the Cosby Kids (1972)
Lorelai: "Yeah, look Fat Albert. Get me a soda, will you?"

8.

Lost in Space (1965)
Lorelai: "Danger, Will Robinson, danger!"

Star Trek (1966)
Mia: "Star Trek, that's it!"
Rory: "You were a Trekkie?"

9.

South Park (1997)
Paul is wearing a shirt with characters from the show on it

Leave It to Beaver (1957)
Tristin: "Somehow, I'll recover from the great romance between you and the Beav."

The Twilight Zone (1959)
Paul: "The Twilight Zone marathon was on all week"

The Monkees (1966)
Rory: "Hey."
Madeline: "Hey."
Louise: "We're the Monkees".

The Sonny and Cher Show (1976)
Professor Anderson: "And my favorite - the climactic last scene was set during the final days of the Sonny and Cher show."

Wheel of Fortune (1983)
Lorelai: "You know what, Vanna? I'm gonna need a few more vowels here."

Doogie Howser, M.D. (1989)
Luke: "Doogie Howser was a doctor 16"

Martha Stewart Living (1991)
Sookie: "I saw it on Martha Stewart"

Absolutely Fabulous (1992)
Lorelai: "He's never seen Ab Fab"

Inside the Actors Studio (1994)
Lorelai: "You'll have James Lipton asking you what your favorite swear word is"

The Powerpuff Girls (1998)
Lorelai: "Today is the day we finally spring for the Powerpuff Girl shot glasses"

10.

I Love Lucy (1951)
Lorelai: "Hey, did you ever see that I Love Lucy where she goes to Buckingham Palace?"

Def Comedy Jam (1992)
Lorelai: "I'll send him a Def Jam Comedy tape."

Days of Our Lives (1965)
Lorelai: "Like sands through the hourglass, so are the Gilmore's of our lives."

11.

The Honeymooners (1955)
Lorelai: "I swear, one of these days, Alice. Pow! Right in the kisser!"

NFL Monday Night Football (1970)
Lorelai: "Monday night football?"

The Sopranos (1999)
Lorelai: "'Cause I'm Tony Soprano?"

12.

Bewitched (1964)

Lorelai: "Mom, when Dad was talking about the vase, you were pulling a full-on Tabitha"

Star Trek (1966)
Lorelai: "Nothing that came out of your mouth today might, in any universe visited by Kirk or Spock, be construed as constructive"

Taxi (1978)
Rory: "Ooh, we could do a Ruth Gordon film festival. Harold and Maude, Rosemary's Baby, and that really great episode of Taxi"

The Facts of Life (1979)
Lorelai: "It is not going to be fine. It's going to be horrible. It is going to be a bad, depressing Lifetime movie and Nancy McKeon will be playing me. I am Jo"

13.

Monty Python's Flying Circus (1969)
Dean: "I'd do a silly walk, but I'm not feeling very John Cleese right now"

14.

The Twilight Zone (1959)
Lorelai: "This whole morning has been a little Twilight Zone-y"

The Outer Limits (1963)
Luke: "Or Outer Limits-y."
Lorelai: "What?"
Luke: "Great show, just as eerie, same era, but no one ever references it."

Pee-wee's Playhouse (1986)
Rory: "But I also pictured you with Pee-Wee Herman"

Ricki Lake (1992)
Rory: "I feel like I'm on the Ricki Lake show"

Two Fat Ladies (1996)
Rory: "Not Two Fat Ladies again"

15.

Mission: Impossible (1966)
Lorelai: "What, did you break into our house, you got all dressed in black and pulled a Mission: Impossible?"

17.

Charlie Rose (1991)
Lorelai: "Yeah, Taylor, this isn't Charlie Rose"

I Dream of Jeannie (1965)
Rory: "Just assume that Jeannie's gonna get Major Healey out of whatever scrape he's in."

18.

The Andy Griffith Show (1960)
Lorelai: "Gomer said!"

Who's the Boss? (1984)
Lorelai says: "Oh my God. It's Who's the Boss - the later years"

19.

Schoolhouse Rock! (1973)
Jess: "Are we gonna do some of those Schoolhouse Rock! songs?"

ER (1994)
Lorelai: "Honey, let George Clooney talk here, okay?"

The Facts of Life (1979)
Kirk: "Japanese movie? No, I'm sorry, I have the wrong person. Who's the guy who directed all those Facts of Life's?"

Lorelai: "I don't – "

Kirk: "Asaad Kelada, sorry. In my soul I know I am Asaad Kelada"

20.

The Tonight Show Starring Johnny Carson (1962)
Lorelai: "Next time, hold an envelope to your head before you do that"

M*A*S*H (1972)
Richard: "Amazing. You're like the tiny fellow on that Mash program, always anticipating"

Happy Days (1974)
Taylor: "Rory, you don't have to explain a thing to me. I know that there is absolutely no way that you would be involved in something like that if it weren't for that Sal Mineo wannabe, believe me. Chachi, and Chachi alone, will be held responsible for that incident, okay? Good. Now take a peach"

21.

Saved by the Bell (1989)
Lorelai: "Hey, try to seat us next to a celebrity on the Concorde, like Sting or Screech or someone"

22.

Diff'rent Strokes (1978)
Lorelai: "I'm telling you, it's knocking 'whatcha talking 'bout, Willis?' right out of first place"

Season Three

1.

All in the Family (1971)
Rory: "Well, I got to see Archie Bunker's chair at the Smithsonian Museum, so it was a big thumbs up for me."

Politically Incorrect (1993)
Lorelai: "name of the show was Politically Incorrect for God's sake. Didn't anybody read the title? He was supposed to say those things, dammit!"

2.

The West Wing (1999)
Francie: "I'll make her so ineffectual, she'll make Jimmy Carter look like Martin Sheen – do you get me?"

3.

The Courtship of Eddie's Father (1969)
Dave: "Yeah, now their front-man's that kid from the Courtship of Eddie's Father."

The Waltons (1971)
Rory: "Your usual chores, John-boy?"

Holmes and Yo-Yo (1976)
Hee Haw Honeys (1978)
Lorelai: "Yeah, right after "Holmes and Yoyo" and "Hee Haw Honeys." Oh, Rory, get back here! They're in clown suits and headed for the pool."

Family Matters (1989)
Lane: "Yeah, what's next – Urkel joining the Wu-Tang Clan?"

Johnny Bravo (1997)
SpongeBob SquarePants (1999)
Lorelai: "Hmm, so, circle all of them except sports. Oh, they want a picture. How about the one of us sticking our heads through the carved out holes of Johnny Bravo and SpongeBob Squarepants?"

Malcolm in the Middle (2000)
Dave: "Or maybe Malcolm in the Middle fronting for the Butthole Surfers."

The Brady Bunch Variety Hour (1976)
Rory and Lorelai watch this show

4.

The Lawrence Welk Show (1951)
Zack: "Dude, Lawrence Welk cranked louder than this. It's a waste of time."

Leave It to Beaver (1957)
Jess: "Hey, if you're gonna get all Ward Cleaver on me, I gotta go call Eddie and Lumpy and tell 'em I'm gonna be late."

5.

Saturday Night Live (1975)
Lorelai: "Well we are not two wild and crazy guys."

Oz (1997)
Lorelai: "Yeah, apparently Dwight's last home was Oz, and not as in 'The Wizard Of.'"

6.

The Andy Griffith Show (1960)
Jess: "Geez, how Andy Griffith is this town that people get so excited by a car?"

The Patty Duke Show (1963)
Lorelai: "They're cousins, identical cousins…"

Quincy M.E. (1976)
Lorelai: "Not quite. A half hour before I had Rory, I was eating a pepper sandwich and watching TV. You were almost named Quincy."

The 67th Annual Academy Awards (1995)
Rory: "Oprah, Uma."

7.

The Brady Bunch (1969)
Shane: "Who are you, Bobby Brady? Get a life."

8.

Star Trek (1966)

Rory: "You going to smoke that or mind meld with it?"

9.

CBS Evening News with Dan Rather (1981)
Sookie: "And that's the thing. They still say, 'And now the CBS Evening News with Dan Rather.' You see? Dan is still associated with it even though he's off snorkeling or something, just like I'm gonna be associated with the dinner because Bob is substituting for Sookie. Excuse me one minute."

10.

Gilligan's Island (1964)
Rory: "I think I do, Tina Louise."

That Girl (1966)

Francie: "You do not wanna be my enemy, Marlo Thomas."

Fantasy Island (1977)
Jess: "Hey Tatu, just look at the plane, will ya?"

Shields and Yarnell (1977)
Lorelai: "Uh, well, if you like, I could recommend a few places in town. Uh, okay, uh huh, sure. Why don't you talk to your wife and call me back. Okay, bye. Hey, Shields and Yarnell, what's going on?"

12.

Sanford and Son (1972)
Lorelai: "We're Sanford and Son. Yuck, bye bye."

The Powerpuff Girls (1998)
Lorelai: "I wrote it on Powerpuff Girls stationery. Who'd he think was setting him up, Hello Kitty?"

13.

Quincy M.E. (1976)
Young Lorelai watches this show

14.

Inside the Actors Studio (1994)

Rory: "The Holy Barbarians. I mean, what a title. And it's by a Venice Beach beatnik about Venice Beach beatniks, and to top it off, the beatnik who wrote it is the father of the guy that does those Actor's Studio interviews on TV."

The Sopranos (1999)
Lorelai: "Yeah, and then after, he and Paulie are hitting the Bada Bing."

Dr. Phil (2002)
Jess: "Give it a rest, Dr. Phil."

16.

ABC Afterschool Specials (1972)
Paris: "What if he doesn't love me anymore? What if he doesn't think I'm special anymore? How am I going to tell him I didn't get into Harvard? What am I gonna do?"

17.

General Hospital (1963)
Paris: "This isn't General Hospital. I don't deserve General Hospital."

Star Trek (1966)
Fred: "Yeah, but it's just a hobby. We're not Trekkies!"

Family Feud (1976)

Jess: "Well, as they say on the Family Feud - good answer."

Pee-wee's Playhouse (1986)
Rory: "I was more of a Pee Wee Herman kind of gal."

Gumby Adventures (1988)
Paris: "What happened? Harvard was my destiny. I was flipping through Harvard class schedules when you were still delighting to The Adventures of Gumby and Pokie."

Charlie Rose (1991)
Rory: "Okay. Try and make it home in time for Charlie Rose. Billy Joel's on, and he might cry or something.

18.

The Carol Burnett Show (1967)
Lorelai: "Well, put Mrs. Huh-wiggins on the phone. Have her tell me."

19.

The 700 Club (1966)
Rory: "The Gilmore house is partying like it's 1999."
Lorelai: "And here it's At Home with The 700 Club."

20.

The Monkees (1966)

Lorelai: "Exactly. What's next? Stay home and dance around in your underwear to the Monkees' greatest hits night?"

21.

Teenage Mutant Ninja Turtles (1987)
Jess: "It's a little late to throw me a Teenage Mutant Ninja Turtle birthday party."

Cops (1989)
Lorelai: "Now no one's around, but the second I run that light, a police car, four helicopters, the Canadian mounties and the crew of Cops jump out of a dumpster - and I'm toast."

Felicity (1998)
Paris: "Yes. He goes there, and if I go there, it's going to look like I went there just to be with him. Suddenly I'm Felicity without the hair issues and I'm not terribly comfortable with that."

The 75th Annual Academy Awards (2003)
Lorelai: "Every kid in that brochure was awkward and panicked. It looked like the Academy Award audience during Michael Moore's speech."

22.

The Dating Game (1965)
Sookie: "Okay, I've gotta tell you, even with the champagne and the Herb Albert, I've been depressed for days. I couldn't watch the Dating Game anymore."

The Love Boat (1977)
Lorelai: "The Love Boat."
Luke: "What?"
Lorelai: "A cruise is a good spot to get down on one knee."

Season Four

1.

I Love Lucy (1951)
The Dick Van Dyke Show (1961)
Jackson: "Hey, in the old days, the guys would pace back and forth in the waiting room until a pretty nurse in a nice white outfit would come out and say, 'Congratulations - it's a 'insert your chosen sex here'. Ricky Ricardo didn't know, Dick van Dyke didn't know, and by gum, if it was good enough for Rick and Dick, it's good enough for me."

Star Trek (1966)
Lorelai: "Yeah. You better walk really fast, like warp speed Mr. Sulu kind of fast."

Daria (1997)
Rory: "I mean, I've always had time for the town in the past, and now suddenly I don't? Am I changing? I don't wanna change. I don't wanna be the anti-town girl. I'm not Daria."

2.

The Little Rascals (1955)

Rory: "You look like Alfalfa coming to pick up Darla."

The Oprah Winfrey Show (1986)
Lorelai: "Like on Oprah?"

Doogie Howser, M.D. (1989)
Lorelai: "Happy birthday, Doogie."

3.

The Love Boat (1977)
Lorelai: "Redmond, Riley, nice to meet you. I'm Julie, your cruise director. I'm here to help you with your costumes."

The Simpsons (1989)
Louise: "Well, he hopes. Right now, he's totally freaked that The Simpsons are going to be off the air by the time he graduates."

4.

I Dream of Jeannie (1965)
Lorelai imitates Jeannie by folding her arms across her chest and blinking

Queer Eye for the Straight Guy (2003)
Sookie: "You called me! You kept me on the phone for over an hour. I missed the beginning of Queer Eye for the Straight Guy, and by the time I got back, they were all gay."

5.

Lassie (1954)
Lorelai: "Really, Lassie? Why is that?"

Alice (1976)
Lorelai: "Fine. Sorry about that. He's trying to steal the "World's Grumpiest Diner Guy" title from Mel."

Sex and the City (1998)
Emily: "It's bad enough that you haven't taught your daughter how to interact with the opposite sex. You will not dress her up in one of your Sex and the City ensembles and send her out to tell the entire campus, Don't worry. I'll ask you."
Lorelai: "How do you know about Sex and the City?"

Monk (2002)
Lorelai: "Oh, my God. You're beyond monk. You're uber-monk."

7.

The Gumby Show (1956)
Lorelai: "Aw. You might want to check that Gumby/Pokey watch, Kirk."

Afterschool Specials (1972)
Lorelai: "I saw it. It was the same one that boy who couldn't hold it had to use in that after-school special. What was that called?"

Rory: "It's Not Benny's Fault."

8.

At the Movies (1982)
Lorelai: "Well, Siskel's chimed in. What about you?"
Lorelai: "Thus spake Ebert."

Wheel of Fortune (1983)
Richard: "Oh, they talk, I can verify that. One of them kept yelling, 'wheel...of...fortune!'"

Mister Ed (1958)
Jason: "Talking horses?"

9.

Charlie Rose (1991)
Paris: "I saw you on Charlie Rose. You were good."

South Park (1997)
Lorelai: "Yeah, of course I'll get bored, but that's when the South Park impressions kick in."
Emily: "Lorelai, we have invited friends – important people."
Lorelai: "I'm kidding, Mom. I can only do Cartman."

10.

Nanny and the Professor (1970)
Title reference

Happy Days (1974)
Michel: "Fonzie used that bathroom office only intermittently and not for any business for which he was paid. He had use of a private office at the auto shop he worked at, then access to the teachers' lounge where he taught night school part time."

Martha Stewart Living (1991)
Rory: "How'd you do that?"
Paris: "Martha Stewart."

The Daily Show (1996)
Lorelai: "I watched The Daily Show, fell into the best sleep I ever had, woke up, watched Fast Times at Ridgemont High, and had a vanilla-scented jacuzzi bath."

Punk'd (2003)
Michel: "I'm being Punk'd. I know I'm being Punk'd."

11.

Star Trek (1966)
Lorelai: "Really, Kirk and Captain Kirk?"

Sesame Street (1969)

Lane: "I started it when I was six. The day you told me the Cookie Monster was one of the seven deadly sins."

Hart to Hart (1979)
Lorelai: "All those years of watching Hart to Hart are about to pay off."

12.

Lost in Space (1965)
Lorelai: "Yeah. Which means he might be here part of the day tomorrow, so uh, 'Danger, Will Robinson.'"

Star Trek (1966)
Star Trek: The Next Generation (1987)
Jason: "But, it's inevitable. They're gonna see us together someplace, or a traffic report will take pictures of cars on the expressway and we'll be sitting in the car - and then Richard will be watching the news and he will see us, so barring some sort of Star Trek-like cloaking device - which was problematic in every incarnation of Star Trek - I remember Kirk complaining about it, I remember Picard complaining about it - they will see us, and we'll get caught."

Frontline (1983)
Paris: "He TiVos Frontline."

14.

Happy Days (1974)
Paris: "Nice addition, Potsie."

The Kids in the Hall (1988)
Lorelai: "Sookie, for the past six weeks, I have taken every meeting. I have been at the inn round the clock - I haven't had a second for myself - and all I asked for was just one hour to get my hair done, and then two seconds into the shampoo I get a phone call from a guy who sounds like a Kids in the Hall character telling me I have to get to the inn to okay a sink that I wouldn't know how to okay because I don't know what makes it okay. You know what makes it okay, which is why you said you would be there to say whether or not it was okay."

15.

The L Word (2004)
Rory: "How very The L Word."

The Tonight Show Starring Johnny Carson (1962)
Lorelai: "A monk, a trunk, and a skunk."
Luke: "What are you doing?"
Lorelai: "Carnak, although I don't have a punch line. Never stopped Johnny."

Hogan's Heroes (1965)
Christine: "It's so "Hogan's Heroes!" I wonder if I can pull up the floorboards at my house."

Teletubbies (1997)
Christine: "I thought my mom was harsh, but your mom makes the guy from Joy Division look like one of the Teletubbies."

Futurama (1999)
Zach: "Well, maybe you should skip displaying your Futurama action figures. That might open space up a bit."

16.

Nigella Bites (2000)
The show can be seen playing in Rory's room

17.

Joanie Loves Chachi (1982)
Paris: "The Joanie loves Chachi moment."

CSI: Miami (2002)
Rory: "So, the person's David Caruso?"

Joseph Campbell and the Power of Myth (1988)
Rory and Paris rent this and watch it on Spring Break

18.

Petticoat Junction (1963)
Kirk: "I've been up for one and a half days straight. I haven't done that since the Petticoat Junction marathon in '97."

19.

Bewitched (1964)
Lorelai: "Bewitched? I love Bewitched!"

Dynasty (1981)
Lorelai: "Oh, come on. You know why. We were going to tell them when the time was right. Of course, I had no idea we were dealing with the Carringtons. All we needed was a swimming pool and some ball gowns to really end the evening right."

20.

The Flintstones (1960)
Jess: "Oh, I'm having a gay old time."

21.

Monty Python's Flying Circus (1969)

Paris: "Please. They were singing the lumberjack song at the top of their lungs. They're embarrassment-proof. Here."

Queer Eye for the Straight Guy (2003)
T.J.: "The Queer Eye guys are very against old polish."

22.

Late Show with David Letterman (1993)
Lorelai: "There was no waking you up. You were completely out of it. We're talking Farrah on Letterman. Hey."

Season Five

1.

Laverne & Shirley (1976)
Lorelai: "Aw, hey, good timing, Squiggy."

2.

E! True Hollywood Story (1996)
Zach: "She's not the mom, but she's not slutty. That's what this dude Constantine wanted you to believe, right? He was purging the E! True Hollywood Story part of it for his own benefit. Turned the whole thing into Hollywood Babylon, and chicks got the short end."

3.

Queer Eye for the Straight Guy (2003)
Lorelai: "Gee, Carson, thanks."

4.

The Greatest American Hero (1981)
Hep Alien performs the theme song from this show.

Jazz (2001)
Brian: "I have Ken Burns' "Jazz" on DVD, if you're into that kind of thing."

Cribs (2000)
Lorelai: "Cribs," baby. Watch it."

5.

The Addams Family (1964)
Lorelai: "Ah, your Lurch left you in the lurch. Hey, is that where that's from? You know, Lurch on the "Addams Family"? 'Cause he would leave people in the lurch?"

Brian's Song (1971)
Zach: "Well, it's bumming me out. It's reminding me of Billy Dee Williams and cancer. Change it."

The Six Million Dollar Man (1973)
Kyle: "Everybody loves the Bionic Man. That's not me. Mine plays Superfreak."

6.

Star Trek (1966)
Star Wars: Episode V - The Empire Strikes Back (1980)
Doyle: "It is amazing. It's absolutely amazing that I spent all summer in Indiana working my ass off for the Muncie Messenger, and you went from Star Trek Convention to Boba Fett Fan Club

Symposium, and yet, lookie here. The New York Times. Isn't that great, Rory? Aren't you seeing how great it is?"

8.

The Little Rascals (1955)
Lorelai: "You know, it may have choked Artie, but it ain't going to choke me. Some Little Rascals humor there for ya."

The Addams Family (1964)
Finn: "You rang?"

Barefoot Contessa (2002)
Lorelai: "I can, I have powers. Once the Barefoot Contessa was making a soufflé and when it fell, she looked out the TV and said, 'Gilmore, was that you?'

The Daily Show (1996)
This show can be heard in the background

9.

Toast of the Town: Episode #17.19 (1964)
Emily: "I have to tell you, every time I hear Mahler's Seventh Symphony, I get ridiculous, giddy. It's like The Beatles on The Ed Sullivan Show."

Peyton Place (1964)
Rory: "I broke up with my boyfriend this week -- that was fun. In front of a bunch of people at my grandmother's house. And then, because apparently that wasn't enough Peyton Place for me, I have this whole thing going with my dad, who's suddenly back in my life again."

10.

I Love Lucy (1955
Lorelai: "Great! Then, I'll hop a fence and get Richard Widmark to sign my grapefruit."

Buffy the Vampire Slayer (1997)
Rory: "Its eleven o' clock at night. Who are you hoping to hook up with now? Spike and Drusilla?"

11.

Sesame Street (1969)
Lorelai: "And his support group is two and heavily into Sesame Street."

Baretta (1975)
Reverend: "It's too "Baretta."

Total Request Live (1998)
Michel: "I know. I haven't been this excited since Madonna just dropped by Total Request Live."

12.

How the Grinch Stole Christmas! (1966)
Lorelai: "Ooo, the toothpaste world. Is that anything like Whoville?"

Pink Lady (1980)
Charlie Rose (1991)
The Daily Show (1996)
Lorelai: "But Charlie Rose, Jon Stewart, Pink Lady and Jeff?"

Will & Grace (1998)
Lorelai: "Say goodnight, Gracie."
Luke: "Goodnight, Gracie."

The Office (2001)
Rory: "I can't believe you've never seen the Office!"

Dark Shadows (1966)
Sookie: "A few weeks ago I read in the paper that there was going to be an episode of Dark Shadows on, the one where Barnabas is released from his tomb, and I used to love Dark Shadows, and I just suddenly really wanted to see it.:

Teletubbies (1997)
Gigi watches the show.

13.

Cop Rock (1990)

Lorelai: "Yeah, yeah, that's fine. Rory's spending the night. We're having a Cop Rock marathon."

Absolutely Fabulous (1992)
Lorelai: "Ab fab, sweetie darling.

Queer Eye for the Straight Guy (2003)
Lorelai: "Say, aren't you the culture Queer Eye guy?"

14.

The Odd Couple (1970)
Rory: "Um, just what I've seen on T.V. The Odd Couple."

Quincy M.E. (1976)
Rory: "Quincy played it, but he wasn't called Quincy, um, Oscar and Felix. Felix didn't play it. Tony Randall, he cooked for them sometimes."

SpongeBob SquarePants (1999)
Michel: "Like I'm Sponge Boy Big Pants or something? I do not entertain children."

15.

I Love Lucy: Lucy and Harpo Marx (1955)
Marty: "I thought the I Love Lucy episode with Harpo Marx was lame."

Batman (1966)
Sookie: "Apparently Batman's attacking the inn."

16.

Soap (1977)
Rory: "Soap marathon."

Seinfeld (1989)
Lorelai: " She's the serial killer who goes to work and talks about a funny Seinfeld he saw and then goes home and cooks himself a man-flesh sandwich."

Beverly Hills, 90210 (1990)
Lane: "Yes. Jessica Simpson and Donna from 90210."

Reno 911! (2003)
Lorelai: "It's the Reno 911 short shorts. Ooh, disturbing."

17.

Sesame Street (1969)
Emily: "Some flash cards, some Sesame Street characters to sing a song about it?"

The Price Is Right (1972)
Michel: "I was just sitting there, minding anybody's business, and a man came up to me and

asked if I would like to be a contestant on the Price is Right!"

The $10,000 Pyramid (1973)
Sookie: "Boy, that's weird. Jackson's cousin Monty did the Price is Right, and he told us that the contestants had to get up at the crack of dawn, sit in line for hours, with hundreds of tourists, and then show how enthusiastic of a contestant they would be. You know, jumping up and down, screaming and yelling."

The Oprah Winfrey Show (1986)
Lorelai: "Fun. Sure. I get it. Friends with benefits. No problem, I watch Oprah. Okay, so. Are you sure you're cool with this?"

18.

Pippi Långstrump (1969)
Luke: "What is this, still about the Pippi night? The Bop-it? Fine."

The Andy Griffith Show (1960)
Lorelai: "Ah. Can't Sheriff Taylor just let him share a cell with Otis for the night?"

Queer Eye for the Straight Guy (2003)
Paris: "Since the IRS red-foxed my father. The place in Asylum Hill, the Nantucket cottage – even the crack-house in Harlem that we converted

into a co-op was sold to one of the Queer Eye guys."

Summerland (2004)
Andrew: "He's kind of distracted anyway. The whole time I was there he was Tivo-ing through a fresh Summerland."

19.

I Love Lucy (1955)
Lorelai: "That's very Lucy of you. I'll call when I find them. Now rest. Bye."

Who's the Boss? (1984)
Honor: "Oh, my God! I've never heard him call anyone his girlfriend before. Well, Alyssa Milano, but he was ten and in a weird Who's the Boss phase.""

The Amazing Race (2001)
Lorelai: "Ah, if this is the eccentric couple version of the Amazing Race, I think you guys are winning."

Ellen: The Ellen DeGeneres Show (2003)
Luke: "And it will be here waiting for you when you get back. Until then, sit back, relax, and watch Ellen dance around a little. I got work to do."

20.

Deadwood (2004)
Rory: "Yes, with Doyle. And do not mock or make fun, because when Paris is happy, the whole world is happy. But when she's not happy, the whole world is Deadwood."

22.

Get Smart (1965)
Colin: "Yes. Maxwell Smart finally found his Ninety-Nine."

NYPD Blue (1993)
Lorelai: "I was just wondering. Is Rory in the system now? Because I just remember when Sipowicz's son accidentally got arrested because he looked like a drug dealer. Sipowicz was freaked out that the son was going to wind up in the system. And I just wonder, you know, should I be freaked out? And also, what exactly is the system?"

Season Six

1.

Star Trek (1966)
Emily: "Isn't that wonderful? We're just a push button away. Like Star Trek. Hosanna! We're coming in."

Benson (1979)
Michel: "Nope. I am here. I am here and not at the Dragonfly Inn, which I theoretically run, when I'm not busy answering doors like Benson."

2.

Bewitched (1964)
Bewitched (2005)
Lorelai: "Okay, I'm sorry. They screwed up Bewitched. Nicole Kidman, good choice. But that concept?"

The Office (2005)
Lorelai: "That's what she said."

3.

Meet the Press (1947)
Zach: "Every day with him is like being on Meet the Press."

Star Trek (1966)
Lorelai: "Of course, I'd have to leave now and pick up some dilithium crystals on the way to fix the warp drive in my jeep so that I could drive there and back in time to meet the wedding party back at the Inn, but that's doable."

4.

Magnum, P.I. (1980)
Luke: "You need an episode of "Magnum PI", from 1986?"

Knots Landing: Moments of Truth (1981)
Lorelai: "Of course not. That tape is mislabeled. That's A Knots Landing from 1981. All the women are held hostage at gunpoint during Ginger's baby shower, classic."

Please Don't Eat the Daisies (1965)
Lorelai: "Good. Oh! Please Don't Eat the Daisies, seasons two and four. I've been looking for this."

21 Jump Street (1987)
Luke: 21 Jump Street, season one. You do not need this."

America's Castles: Florida's Grand Estates (1995)
Lorelai: Oh, look at that! America's Castles, the special Florida edition. Seen it five times, keeping it."

5.

M*A*S*H (1970)
Rory: "Any incoming choppers, radar?"

The Life and Times of Grizzly Adams (1977)
Lorelai: "Hey, Grizzly Adams. Why are you back? The woods closed or something?"

Rock Star: INXS (2005)
Paris: "I meant the transaction. I'd love a performance review. Come on, be my Dave Navarro."

6.

Today (1952)
Emily: "You're missing Katie Couric."

Scooby Doo, Where Are You! (1969)
Luke: "No, change 'em all. Name 'em after cartoon characters. I'll be on Scooby Doo Lane. It's all the same to me."

Charlie Rose (1991)

Richard: "Far as I could tell. We're missing Charlie Rose."

7.

The Waltons (1971)
Rory: "I wonder if the Waltons ever did this."

My Little Pony Tales (1992)
Luke: "God, that's terrible. It's like drinking a My Little Pony."

8.

The Twilight Zone (1959)
Luke: "It's The Twilight Zone. I do not know what to do here."

Battlestar Galactica (1978)
Rory: "I'm positive that there are at least five of her wandering the property like she's a Cylon."

Doogie Howser, M.D. (1989)
Jess: "You graduate already, Doogie?"

Queer Eye for the Straight Guy (2003)
Lorelai: "Oh. Oh, get one for me, too, please. How about the ceiling? Dark magenta! You've got the queer eye, my friend. Oh yeah!"

9.

The Shining (1980)
Saturday Night Live (1975)
Lorelai: "No. Land shark. Candygram. Here's Johnny. Uh! Luke, open the door!"

CHiPs (1977)
Lorelai: "When I was in fifth grade, I told everybody Erik Estrada was my boyfriend and that we used to make out on his motorcycle."

The Oprah Winfrey Show (1986)
Lorelai: "Uh, books are back. Oprah says. Did we order the new box slips yet?"

Teletubbies (1997)
Lorelai: "I think they enjoyed watching a show for once that didn't have la-la playing the guitar."

Desperate Housewives (2004)
Lorelai: "Oh, my god. Enjoy Wisteria Lane, you major drama queen."

The Comeback (2005)
Lorelai "Yeah, you're giving me a Valerie Cherish, you know, and 'I don't wanna see that!' It's a great show. You should watch it."

11.

Taxi (1978)

Rory: "Why "Taxi" never utilized his musical-comedy skills is astonishing."

Sanford and Son (1972)
Angela's Ashes (1999)
Lorelai: "It's Angela's Ashes".
Rory: "It's basic."
Lorelai: "It's Sanford and Son".

The Twilight Zone: Spur of the Moment (1964)
Lorelai: "What if it's like that Twilight Zone where the woman on a horse is being chased by another woman on a horse who turns out is older her chasing younger her, trying to tell her that she should not run off with the guy she's going to run off with because it will be a terrible, terrible mistake."

12.

Today (1952)
Lorelai: "I saw the beginning of Katie Couric. I don't think I've seen the first five minutes of her in my life. You know, she and Matt Lauer are much more serious in the first half-hour than they are later on."

Columbo (1971)
Megan: "Good job, Colombo."

Smurfs (1981)
Babette: "So, I...I...I got Smurfs and dirty pasta."

The O.C. (2003)
Zach: "Yeah! Yeah! Welcome to the S.H. bitch!"

13.

Laugh-In (1967)
Lorelai: "Rowan? Martin?"

Reno 911! (2003)
Lorelai: "Reno 911!?"

14.

7th Heaven (1996)
Lorelai: "Oh, how very 7th Heaven of you."

16.

Mahha GoGoGo (1967)
Lorelai: "Yeah, okay. Hold on there, speed racer.

Full House (1987)
Schindler's List (1993)
Lorelai: "Shhhhh-indler's list? Oh, Full House. You know, I think the Olsen twins weigh less now than they did on that show. Right. I get it. I don't like it when people talk to me when I'm watching TV either."

Teletubbies (1997)
Lorelai: "Yeah, I'm fun. I like Teletubbies."

Brideshead Revisited (1981)
Title reference

17.

Star Trek (1966)
Lorelai: "Kirk, get out of here. Take your jacket and your dippy Star Trek device and your creepy new career and scram."

Nancy Grace (2005)
Lorelai: "That buffer is my mother's best friend. Take the buffer away and you got Nancy Grace camping out on miss patty's lawn for a month."

18.

This Is Your Life (1952)
Jess: "Yeah, there's a definite 'Jess Mariano, this is your life' vibe here today."

Star Trek (1966)
April: "Grown-ups. You never saw the original Star Trek?"

Animaniacs (1993)
The song from this show is playing on the bus

The Lonely Island: Lazy Sunday (2005)
Lane: "It's all about the Hamilton's, baby."

19.

Rhoda (1974)
Lorelai: "No, only the ones where I look like Rhoda."

Chico and the Man (1974)
Lorelai: "It was Rory's first day of kindergarten, and she insisted on wearing my Chico and the Man t-shirt, which I thought would either elicit confused shrugs or label her as a weird '70s-sitcom kid."

Battlestar Galactica (1978)
Lorelai: "Frakking Céline Dion!"

Dr. Phil (2002)
Zach: "Hey just 'cause I'm married now doesn't mean we're gonna have any Dr. Phil moments."

20.

America's Next Top Model (2003)
Sookie: "you got suddenly very excited to film your audition tape for America's Next Top Model."

Two and a Half Men (2003)
Lorelai: "And yes, that is the guy from Two and a Half Men. All right, enjoy."

21.

Frosty the Snowman (1954)
Lorelai: "If we put that hat on frosty the snowman, he'd be living in Miami right now."

60 Minutes (1968)
Emily: "They'll do a 60 Minutes on that woman one day. Mark my words!"

Marcus Welby, M.D. (1969)
ER (1994)
Emily: "Marcus Welby was handsome, and George Clooney."

Monty Python's Flying Circus (1969)
Rory: "So I guess get up, but super slow. It should look like a Monty Python routine, you're moving so slow."

22.

The Andy Griffith Show (1960)
Taylor: "Oh, forget it...Barney Fife."

The Monkees (1966)
Kirk: "One of the Monkees. Anyway, I'm guessing when word hit the east coast troubadour community, every one of them thought to come to stars hollow for their shot at the big time."

The Sopranos (1999)

Lorelai: "Lynnie, as a psychologist, tell me what do you think of The Sopranos?"

Season Seven

1.

The Twilight Zone: The Long Morrow (1964)
Rory: "And this episode of The Twilight Zone came on -- "the long morrow."

Star Trek (1966)
Rory: "Ugh. What about space?"
Lorelai: "It's the final frontier?"

Happy Days (1974)
Rory: "Chachi, right?"

2.

Leave It to Beaver (1957)
Rory: "And Courtney Love? She's no June Cleaver."

Barefoot Contessa (2002)
Lorelai: "But then I asked myself, 'W.W.T.B.F.C.D.?' And it came to me in a flash. 'I'm gonna make waffles.'"
Rory: "What would the barefoot Contessa do?"

Battlestar Galactica (2004)
T.J.: "Don't underestimate me, Luke. I read. And I watch Battlestar Galactica."

3.

Privileged: All About Friends and Family (2008)
This can be seen playing in Rory's room.

4.

Iron Chef America: The Series (2005)
Lorelai: "Wow! Today's secret ingredient is gourds!"

5.

Sábado Gigante (1962)
The View (1997)
Girlfriends (2000)
Lorelai: "The View? Girlfriends? Sábado Gigante? Who controls this thing, you or Pedro Almodóvar?"

The Brady Bunch (1969)
Rory: "I don't know about you, but most of the Bobby's I know are guys -- Bobby Kennedy, Bobby Brady, Bobby Knight, Bobby Brown."

Danger Mouse (1981)
Rory: "And it'll be like an online version of the Algonquin group, like throwing a party in your head where everyone you've ever wanted to talk

to is there -- Ira Glass, Sofia Coppola, Flaubert, Danger Mouse."

Full House (1987)
Rory: "Adorable is what you say about a Full House rerun."

6.

Laverne & Shirley (1976)
Lorelai: "Hey, let's be Laverne and Shirley."

Antiques Roadshow (1997)
Kirk: "Sometimes when you're watching Antiques Roadshow, you just don't want somebody tickling your arm."

Project Runway (2004)
Lorelai: "Since he got addicted to Project Runway."

America's Next Top Model (2003)
April and Lane can be seen watching this.

7.

60 Minutes (1968)
Zach: "You know, young adults. Not like I'm gonna be smoking a pipe, and she's gonna be all, 'hey, let's watch '60 Minutes.'"

Sesame Street (1969)
Rory: "Yeah, I'm beginning to wonder if he really exists, or if he's just Lucy's Snuffleupagus."

The Real World (1992)
Olivia: "Watching Real World: Denver. Lucy's eating it up with a fork and spoon 'cause boyfriend's working, and you know how much he hates reality TV."

Everybody Loves Raymond (1996)
The bread delivery man thinks that Lorelai and Christopher are joking with him about wanting food, cites "Everybody Loves Raymond" as an example of their American humor.

8.

The Jetsons (1962)
Lorelai: "It's so 'meet George Jetson, his boy, Elroy' -- Leroy?"

9.

The 78th Annual Academy Awards (2006) (TV Special)
Lorelai: "It's very Joaquin phoenix at the Oscars."

10.

Kentucky vs. the University of Alabama, Freedom Hall - Louisville, Kentucky (January 21, 1998).

Christopher and Jackson can be seen watching this game at the bar

Survivor (2000)
Liz: "We've been watching Survivor sometimes, you know, and he does the challenges, you know like standing on one leg or dragging the sandbags around, and he lasts longer than the guys on the show."

11.

Bosom Buddies (1980)
Lorelai: "Honey look, I have been around a long time, okay? I wore leggings the last time they were trendy. I knew Tom Hanks when he was a Bosom Buddy. I have lived, and I have learned."

13.

The Apprentice (2004)
Logan: "Like the Apprentice."

15.

Puppet Playhouse (1947)
Captain Kangaroo (1955)
Lorelai: "Why not a howdy doody or a captain kangaroo?"

16.

Gilligan's Island (1964)
Kirk: "You can be Ginger to Lulu's Mary Ann. Let's lock down dates now. When are you free?"

The Monkees (1966)
Lane: "Mom, I'm fine. Hey, this is fun. Don't they push a bed through the streets in the opening credits of The Monkees?"

Top Chef (2006)
Lorelai: "Oh, my god. Next year, no excuses. We are making you that audition tape for Top Chef."

17.

The Sopranos (1999)
Lorelai: "Hi, dad. Nice threads. Having lunch with Tony Soprano?"

18.

Bozo (1960)
Rory: "Yeah, you joke, but it was very traumatic, okay? I scraped up my whole face. There was a big old scab on my nose the first two weeks of fifth grade. Oh, they called me bozo.

That Girl (1966)
Rory: "What about this? Is it too That Girl?"
Logan: "You can never be too That Girl."

19.

24 (2001)
Lorelai: "Be right back. Yeah, you know how Jack Bauer should torture terrorists? Make them go car shopping with their exes."

20.

Star Search (1983)
Lorelai: "In Canada. She was on Star Search. She dated Dave Coulier. She struggled a lot before Jagged Little Pill."

Top Chef (2006)
Rory: "I like "Top Chef."

21.

Happy Days (1974)
Lorelai: "Not unless he played the Fonz."

A Year in the Life

Winter

Lassie (1954)
Michel: "We could be walking by that well that Timmy fell down, and he'd throw a penny in."

The Price Is Right (1972)
Lorelai: "Is this like The Price Is Right, where if I'm a little under I win, over I lose?"

Doogie Howser, M.D. (1989)
Paris: "Let's just call him Doogie Howser."

Buffy the Vampire Slayer (1997)
Paris: "Tell them you'll pay them back for the semester you spent studying Buffy the Vampire Slayer's effect on the feminist agenda."

The Voice (2011)
Rory: "Don't judge."
Lorelai: "I'm Gwen freakin' Stefani!"

The Sopranos (1999)
Emily: "You have been trying to get me to a therapist ever since you saw that Tony Soprano show."

Spring

Wonder Woman (1975)
Lorelai: "My Wonder Woman stamina and a box of Twinkies."

Law & Order (1990)
Babette:" I brought up a couple of their credits on my phone. Sackovich did Law and Order."

Blue Bloods (2010)
Babette: "Tara Grabowski did an independent movie and a two-episode arc on Blue Bloods."

Outlander (2014)
Lorelai: "Hot in Outlander, but elsewhere And I had you, and rules, and work, and rules."

Summer

Hawaii Five-O (1968)
Several members of the secret street club call out "Five-O!" when Taylor approaches.

Mary Tyler Moore (1970)
Jess: "Very Lou Grant."

The Muppet Show (1976)
Michel: "For our special little muppets, complimentary lollipops."

Matlock (1986)
Emily: "I'm watching PBS, not Matlock."

Thirtysomething (1987)
Babette: "Hey Doll, you now about the Thirtysomething gang, yeah?"

Baywatch (1989)
Lorelai: "Excuse me Mr. Hasselhoff."

The Real World (1992)
April: "Oh, it's like a postcard from The Real World."

Punk'd (2003)
Rory: "Am I being Punk'd?"

Game of Thrones (2011)
Rory: "Woah! Give him a crystal sword, he's a White Walker."

Halt and Catch Fire (2014)
Rory: "I know about it from Halt and Catch Fire, and I didn't watch the show that closely."

The Mysteries of Laura (2014)
Rory: "He gave me a copy of The Mysteries of Laura."

Narcos (2015)
Lorelai: "Is Colombia pissed over Narcos and holding out?"

Les Revenants (2012)
Luke and Lorelai can be seen watching the show.

Fall

I Love Lucy (1951)
Jess: "Lucy Ricardo stumbling out next?"

Doctor Who (1963)
Luke: "Now they sit around for hours catching old episodes of Doctor Who."

Bewitched (1964)
Serena: "Actually, my momma named me after Bewitched."

Law & Order (1990)
Rory: "I also wanted to marry Edward Scissorhands and Jerry Orbach from Law & Order."

Buffy the Vampire Slayer (1997)
Rory: "Oh uh, sorry, it's, uh I was watching a Buffy marathon and some things stick."

24 (2001)
Lorelai: "Chloe, the canisters are already armed, dammit!"

I Live in Two Worlds. One is a World of Books

Books

Books in Gilmore Girls

"I live in two worlds…one is a world of books."

One of Rory's demarcating qualities was her passion for reading, and over the course of the series, the presence of books and literature came to shape the character of the show, and became one of its defining features. Rory's voracious reading life was relatable to book nerds everywhere – sniffing the pages of old books in libraries, carrying books around, and choosing to stay in to read, rather than go to a party. Bibliophiles saw something in Rory, that made them feel that their quiet passion for literature was welcome. Rory was as bookish as bookish can be, particularly in the earlier seasons, and so, readers felt at home in Stars Hollow. For passionate readers and literati watching the show, the books became a way of not only getting to know who Rory is, through what she reads, but a way of bringing the show into our own lives, by reading the books and stepping into the Stars Hollow world.

My first engagement as an online fan of *Gilmore Girls*, was through an internet group I discovered called "Rory's Book Club". The group was a reading discussion forum, which worked through 'Rory's Book List' - a list of books released that included the books Rory was seen reading on the show, or books Rory would thought to have read. The original list was produced for fans, to imitate the kind of set reading list Rory might follow, and included many titles that were not specifically referenced on the show. Since the release of this list, countless modified 'Rory lists' have appeared online, all attempting to compile a list of every book that Rory ever read or discussed, during the original seven seasons of the show. While most of these lists contain around 330 titles, this one comes in at over 400, making it the most complete that I have come across.

Most of us see a little of ourselves in Rory Gilmore, so it seems only natural that conquering this list became a popular goal for fans and book lovers. Countless bloggers have worked their way through the list, posting reviews and discussions about each book as they tick each one off their Rory list. Several public libraries even compiled recommended reading lists based on Rory's reading habits, and it is not hard to see why. The books on these lists are all amazing pieces of work and, in my opinion, should be read by everyone. Rory's taste in literature is broad – she read non-fiction, literary fiction, contemporary fiction, Russian literature, Shakespeare, horror and more - making it the perfect well-rounded reading experience for all ages.

However, this was not enough for many fans. Rory had, by her own admission, "been a resident of Faulkner's Yoknapatawpha County, hunted the white whale aboard the Pequod, fought alongside Napoleon, sailed a raft with Huck and Jim, committed absurdities with Ignatius J. Reilly, rode a sad train with Anna Karenina and strolled down Swann's Way" (3.22). But, fans of the show can experience more than this. The bookish followers of *Gilmore Girls* can immerse themselves in the world of Stars Hollow, by reading not just 'Rory' books, but 'Gilmore' books. For this reason, this list is not 'Rory's Book List', but a *Gilmore Girls* book list. It contains the title of every book that was mentioned, seen, or referenced by every character, in all seven seasons of the show, as well as *A Year in the Life*. In addition, no *Gilmore Girls* book list would be complete without the addition of the *Gilmore Girls* novelization series, Lauren Graham's fiction and non-fiction work, and the other books that have been written about *Gilmore Girls*. This list Is intended to be more than just a list of what Rory read. It is intended to be a complete fan list, for those who wish to absorb the Gilmore world, as they submerge themselves in literature, and in the world of Stars Hollow.

So, go forth and begin your own book reading challenge, and be sure to smell the books before you read them.

Season One

1.
On the Road by Jack Kerouac
Lorelai calls the man at the diner a "regular Jack Kerouac"

The Adventures of Huckleberry Finn by Mark Twain
The assignment in class is based on this book

Rosemary's Baby by Ira Levin
Rory tells Dean that he is like Ruth Gordon

Moby Dick by Herman Melville
Dean tells Rory that he has seen her reading this

Madame Bovary by Gustave Flaubert
Dean tells Rory that he saw her reading this last week

The Little Match Girl by Hans Christian Andersen
Rory asks Lorelai if they are going to go into the Gilmore's house, or re-enact this story

Mistress of Mellyn by Victoria Holt
Rory clears this from her locker

2.
The Hunchback of Notre Dame by Victor Hugo

Lorelai says she is trying to see if there is a hunchback in the bell tower

War and Peace by Leo Tolstoy
David Copperfield by Charles Dickens
Great Expectations by Charles Dickens
A Tale of Two Cities by Charles Dickens
Little Dorrit by Charles Dickens
These are all discussed in the Chilton class

Harry Potter & the Goblet of Fire by J.K. Rowling
Miss Patty says that if her students drop their books, Harry will die and there will not be another instalment

3.

Peyton Place by Grace Metalious
Richard says, "It's Peyton Place!"

A Mencken's Chrestomathy by H.L. Mencken
My Life as Author and Editor by H.L. Mencken
Richard is going to lend Rory these

4.

The Comedy of Errors by William Shakespeare
King Richard III by William Shakespeare
The Sonnets by William Shakespeare
All mentioned when Rory and Lorelai are studying for the Chilton test

Who's Who & What's What in Shakespeare by Evangeline M. O'Connor
This can be seen sitting open on the arm of the couch

The Oxford Complete Shakespeare by William Shakespeare
Rory pulls this out at Lane's

5.

A Room of One's Own by Virginia Woolf
Rory reads this on the bus

Valley of the Dolls by Jacqueline Susann
Lorelai says that Babette's medicine cabinet for Cinnamon looks like something out of this

6.

Ethan Frome by Edith Wharton
The Age of Innocence by Edith Wharton
Lorelai says Edith Wharton would have been proud

7.

The Crucible by Arthur Miller
Lorelai says Luke dresses like someone from this novel

Don Quixote by Miguel de Cervantes
Lorelai calls Dean 'Lothario'

8.

Northanger Abbey by Jane Austen
Rory had Dean read this

Fear and Loathing in Las Vegas by Hunter S. Thompson
Dean asks Rory to read this

Jane Eyre by Charlotte Bronte
Rory asks Dean to read Charlotte Bronte

9.

A Streetcar Named Desire by Tennessee Williams
Rory calls Lane "Blanche"

The Group by Mary McCarthy
Rory is reading this when she is in line for tickets to the dance

The Outsiders by S.E. Hinton
Rory says "just call me Ponyboy"

The Portable Dorothy Parker by Dorothy Parker
Dean reads this at Miss Patty's

10.

The Miracle Worker by William Gibson
Rory says things are still "Miracle Worker" at her house

The Metamorphosis by Franz Kafka
What Rory buys Dean for Christmas

11.

Swann's Way by Marcel Proust
This book features throughout the episode in Max and Lorelai's relationship

Timeline by Michael Crichton
Lorelai refers to the author

The New Poems of Emily Dickinson by Emily Dickinson
Max teaches this in his class

12.

The Unabridged Journals of Sylvia Plath 1950-1962 by Sylvia Plath
Rory is reading this

Hoover's Handbook of American Business 1996 by Gary Hoover
Lorelai is studying with this book for business school

13.

Carrie by Stephen King
Rory says "They've basically just moved off the plan to dump the pig's blood on me at the prom"

Macbeth by William Shakespeare
Rory quotes a line from this

15.
The Compact Oxford English Dictionary by Henry Watson Fowler
Christopher tries to buy this for Rory

16.
Anna Karenina by Leo Tolstoy
Dean and Rory discuss this

The Mourning Bride by William Congreve
Louise quotes this using "hell hath no fury", which is often attributed to Shakespeare

Gone with the Wind by Margaret Mitchell
Rory says her locker is behind "Belle Watling"

17.
Nancy Drew 33: The Witch Tree Symbol by Carolyn Keene
Lorelai says she read this twice

Who's Afraid of Virginia Woolf? by Edward Albee
Rory talks about going to see the Stars Hollow Elementary Production of this

The Bell Jar by Sylvia Plath
Lorelai asks why Rory doesn't just stay home and read this

The Art of Eating by MFK Fisher
Rory reads this at the party

18.

Glengarry Glen Ross by David Mamet
Lorelai says, "What, did David Mamet just stop by?"

Beyond Good and Evil by Friedrich Nietzsche
Louise quotes something, to which Rory reply, "Nietzche?"

Hamlet by William Shakespeare
Trix quotes this

19.

To Kill a Mockingbird by Harper Lee
Lorelai refers to Rune as Boo Radley

The Grapes of Wrath by John Steinbeck
Emily says the girl's fridge is "The Grapes of Wrath"

20.

Ulysses by James Joyce
Rory can be seen reading this

Out of Africa by Isaac Denison
Lorelai says that Rachel wants to read this

The Art of Fiction by Henry James
Max tells his class to read this

21.

My First Summer in the Sierra by John Muir

Walden by Henry David Thoreau
Lorelai talks about these authors as 'loners'

Webster's Dictionary
Lorelai defines Ennui using this (jokingly)

Season Two

1.
Cujo by Stephen King
Lorelai barks, so Max tells Rory to put Cujo on the phone

Mencken's Chrestomathy by H.R. Mencken
Richard is going to lend this to Rory

2.
A Connecticut Yankee in King Arthur's Court by Mark Twain
Lane says, "You'll read about it in my novel, 'A Connecticut Yankee in Pusan'"

Personal History by Katharine Graham
Rory is reading this on the couch

3.
Secrets of the Flesh: A Life of Colette by Judith Thurman
Rory says she lost Lorelai's place in this

Elmer Gantry by Sinclair Lewis
Rory quotes this when Lorelai is sampling cakes

4.
Alice in Wonderland by Lewis Carroll

The name of the bed and breakfast is based on a character from this novel

Tuesdays with Morrie by Mitch Album
Who Moved My Cheese? by Spencer Johnson
Lorelai tells Rory she can skip these

The Meditations by Marcus Aurelius
This book is mentioned in the stoicism class

Mrs. Dalloway by Virginia Woolf
Rory can be seen reading this

Goodnight Moon by Margaret Wise Brown and Clement Hurd
Lorelai says she worked on 'Goodnight Spoon'

Oxford English Dictionary
Lorelai says Rory's copy of this will need its own room

5.
Howl by Allen Ginsberg
Jess takes this from Rory's bedroom and makes notes in the margins

Oliver Twist by Charles Dickens
Rory calls Jess "Dodger"

Rita Hayworth and The Shawshank Redemption by Stephen King
The film of this is referenced

The Adventures of Huckleberry Finn by Mark Twain

Lorelai references this in her conversation with Taylor

The Godfather: Book 1 by Mario Puzo
Lorelai references Fredo

The Mojo Collection: The Ultimate Music Companion by Jim Irvin
Lane reads from this

6.

The Compact Oxford English Dictionary
Christopher has bought this for Rory

Uncle Tom's Cabin by Harriet Beecher Stowe
Emily says she is attending the Harriet Beecher Stowe literacy auction

Who's Afraid of Virginia Woolf? by Edward Albee
Lorelai says "George and Martha" are coming to dinner

7.

Memoirs of a Dutiful Daughter by Simone de Beauvoir
Rory can be seen reading this

The Hunchback of Notre Dame by Victor Hugo
Rory gets in trouble for 'bell-ringing' and Lorelai asks if she thinks she is the Hunchback

Savage Beauty: The Life of Edna St. Vincent Millay by Nancy Milford
Rory's bus book

Snow White and Rose Red by Grimm Brothers
Ivy says that Sandra Day O'Connor being a Puff is folklore like Snow White and Rose Red

The Complete Poems by Anne Sexton
A general reference is made to Anne Sexton. Rory- "Anne Sexton, right?"

The Divine Secrets of the Ya-Ya Sisterhood by Rebecca Wells
Rory calls The Puffs the 'Ya-Ya Sisterhood'

The Last Empire: Essays 1992-2000 by Gore Vidal
Rory's lunch book

The Sound and the Fury by William Faulkner
The Collected Short Stories by Eudora Welty
Other books Rory is trying to fit into her bag

8.
The Catcher in the Rye by J.D. Salinger
Rory says Jess is trying to be Holden Caulfield

To Kill a Mockingbird by Harper Lee
Jess says the town meetings are so "To Kill a Mockingbird"

9.
Macbeth by William Shakespeare

The teacher mentions this in class

Romeo and Juliet by William Shakespeare
The students at Chilton have to act this out in class

The Shining by Stephen King
Lorelai hired the movie of this

The Tragedy of Richard III by William Shakespeare
This is what the Chilton class acted out last year

10.

The Iliad by Homer
Paris is reading this

The Joy Luck Club by Amy Tan
Lorelai says "the Joy-less Luck Club"

The Shining by Stephen King
Lorelai says the Bracebridge Dinner would be like this if they don't invite others

11.

Gone with the Wind by Margaret Mitchell
Lorelai impersonates Vivien Leigh from the film adaptation of this book

Nancy Drew Mysteries by Carolyn Keene
Madeline says that Louise's break up is a Nancy Drew mystery

The Last Empire: Essays 1992-2000 by Gore Vidal
Rory is reading this at Chilton

12.
Madame Bovary by Gustave Flaubert
Richard talks about a first edition of Flaubert

Rosemary's Baby by Ira Levin
Rory wants to have a Ruth Gordon film festival

The Scarecrow of Oz by L. Frank Baum
Summer of Fear by T. Jefferson Parker
Contact by Carl Sagan
These can be seen in Rory's book drawer

13.
The Children's Hour by Lillian Hellman
Lorelai says she wants to read this

The Fountainhead by Ayn Rand
Jess and Rory discuss this over the phone

To Have and Have Not by Ernest Hemingway
Jess says Hemingway would have only lovely things to say about Rory

14.
The Godfather: Book 1 by Mario Puzo
Lorelai and Rory do a 'bit' about a cannoli, in the diner

15.

Franny and Zooey by J.D. Salinger
Jess said he was looking to see if Rory had this

Inherit the Wind by Jerome Lawrence and Robert E. Lee
Letters to a Young Poet by Rainer Maria Rilke
Rory buys copies of these two books at the fundraiser

Notes of a Dirty Old Man by Charles Bukowski
Jess can be seen reading this

Lord of The Rings: The Return of the King by J.R.R. Tolkien
Rory and Dean discuss this

Like Water for Chocolate by Laura Esquivel
Kirk haggles over this book at the fundraiser

16.

Driving Miss Daisy by Alfred Uhry
Lorelai calls her mother Miss Daisy

Frankenstein by Mary Shelley
Jess says Rory has a Frankenstein scowl

On the Road by Jack Kerouac
Jess says he has one word for Kerouac, "edit".

17.

David and Lisa by Dr Theodore Issac Rubin M.D.

The produce proprietor says Taylor has a "David and Lisa" thing happening

Memoirs of General W. T. Sherman by William Tecumseh Sherman
Luke's uncle wants to be buried with this

Rapunzel by Brothers Grimm
Taylor refers to the 'long haired freak' as Rapunzel

18.

Candide by Voltaire
Rory says she finished this

The Bhagavad Gita
Paris says that the class reading is not this

The Dirt: Confessions of the World's Most Notorious Rock Band by Tommy Lee, Vince Neil, Mick Mars and Nikki Sixx
Lorelai can be seen reading this

Waiting for Godot by Samuel Beckett
Lorelai references this in her conversation with Emily

Dr. Dolittle by Hugh Lofting
Michel says Lorelai is a regular Dr. Dolittle

19.

Fletch by Gregory McDonald
Lorelai and Rory take this off their film list

Othello by William Shakespeare
Rory and Jess are studying this

Please Kill Me: The Uncensored Oral History of Punk by Legs McNeil and Gillian McCain
Jess recommends this to Rory

Slaughter-House Five by Kurt Vonnegut
Jess makes notes in this, in class

Sophie's Choice by William Styron
The Wizard of Oz by L. Frank Baum
The films of these are discussed for possible movie night choices

Terms of Endearment by Larry McMurtry
Lorelai references this in her conversation with the nurse at the hospital

The Yearling by Marjorie Kinnan Rawlings
The movie eventually chosen (again!) for movie night

What Happened to Baby Jane? by Henry Farrell
Lorelai says she is not "'whatever happened to Baby Jane?' yet, thank you very much."

20.

Complete Novels by Dawn Powell
Rory says nobody has ever heard of her

The Little Locksmith by Katharine Butler Hathaway

Lorelai buys this for Rory and gives it to her as they walk through town

21.
Emily the Strange by Roger Reger
Rory says she is a friend to the disenfranchised

High Fidelity by Nick Hornsby
Jess says the record store is right out of this

Essentials of Economics, 3rd ed., Bradley R. Schiller
Lorelai is studying this

Rebecca of Sunnybrook Farm by Kate Douglas Wiggin
Lorelai references Shirley Temple's portrayal in the film version of this

The Graduate by Charles Webb
The film of this is in Lorelai's gift basket

The Jumping Frog by Mark Twain
The Lottery by Shirley Jackson
Lorelai: "I don't know, didn't they feed lead to our jumping frog or something?"
Rory: "Oh yeah, right after they stoned the woman who won the lottery."

The Portable Nietzche by Fredrich Nietzche
What Color is Your Parachute? by Richard Nelson Bolles
Included in Lorelai's gift basket

The Electric Kool-Aid Acid Test by Tom Woolf

Jess is reading this

22.
Brigadoon by Alan Jay Lerner
Christopher was counting how many references Lorelai had about this

Girl, Interrupted by Susanna Kaysen
Lorelai thinks Sookie's aisle song is too much like this film

Inferno by Dante
Rory refers to the fourth rung of hell

The Story of My Life by Helen Keller
The Miracle Worker by William Gibson
Lorelai references the film, and play when she talks about Annie Sullivan, by the water pump

Season Three

1.

A Bolt from The Blue and Other Essays by Mary McCarthy
Rory is holding this on the couch

Pomeranian: An Owner's Guide to a Happy Healthy Pet by Happeth A. Jones
This is sitting on the girls' coffee table

The Divine Secrets of the Ya-Ya Sisterhood by Rebecca Wells
Lorelai says "ya-ya!"

2.

A Confederacy of Dunces by John Kennedy Toole
Jess is reading this at the diner counter

Freaky Friday by Mary Rodgers
Lorelai wants to 'pull a Freaky Friday'

The Legend of Bagger Vance by Steven Pressfield
Watching the film of this put Lorelai to sleep

3.

Dead Souls by Nikolai Vasilevich Gogol

Rory says this is her thing right now

Harry Potter and the Sorcerer's Stone: Harry Potter - Book 1 by J. K. Rowling
Carol says that kids want to go to Harvard after reading this

Henry IV, Part 1 by William Shakespeare
Henry IV, Part 2 by William Shakespeare
Henry V by William Shakespeare
Macbeth by William Shakespeare
The Merry Wives of Windsor by William Shakespeare
These are all referenced in the lunch time trivia

The Bell Jar by Sylvia Plath
The Unabridged Journals of Sylvia Plath 1950-1962 by Sylvia Plath
General author reference

The Manticore by Robertson Davies
Rory answers a trivia question

4.

We Owe You Nothing- Punk Planet: The Collected Interviews edited by Daniel Sinker
Jess is reading this at the start of the episode

5.

Marathon Man by William Goldman
Lorelai says her date with Peyton was Marathon Man kind of painful

The Wizard of Oz by L. Frank Baum
Lorelai says that "Dwight's last home was Oz, and not as in 'The Wizard Of.'

Visions of Cody by Jack Kerouac
Jess has this in his hands when he is walking with a drenched Rory

Letters of Ayn Rand edited by Michael S. Berliner
Rory is reading this on her bed

6.
Deenie by Judy Blume
Lorelai says she read this when she had Rory

The Electric Kool-Aid Acid Test by Tom Woolf
Taylor accuses Babette of drinking electric Kool-Aid

To Kill a Mockingbird by Harper Lee
The town loner is referred to as a 'Boo Radley'

7.
The Fountainhead by Ayn Rand
Jess is reading this at the dance

8.
Love Story, Erich Segal
Lorelai says Luke shouted "finally!" at the end of the film version of this

Oliver Twist by Charles Dickens

A Christmas Carol by Charles Dickens
A Tale of Two Cities by Charles Dickens
Great Expectations by Charles Dickens
Emily makes a general author reference

9.
How the Grinch Stole Christmas by Dr. Seuss
Lorelai says that Luke is the Grinch

The Hunchback of Notre Dame by Victor Hugo
Lorelai asks Sookie where Quasimodo is

10.
Babe by Dick King-Smith
Lorelai uses a line from this at Friday night dinner

Gidget by Frederick Kohner
Francie references this

Stuart Little by E. B. White
Jess says Clara is like Stuart Little

The Art of War by Sun Tzu
Rory says she has read this

The Outbreak of the Peloponnesian War by Donald Kagan
Lorelai buys this for Richard

11.
Eloise by Kay Thompson

Paris references this when talking about the suggestion box

Julius Caesar by William Shakespeare
Paris calls Rory 'Brutus'

The Great Gatsby by F.Scott Fitzgerald
Lorelai says Joe has been 'Great Gatsby pining'

The Diary of Virginia Woolf, Volume 4: 1931-1935 edited by Anne Olivier Bell
Rory has this on her tray when the paper dart is thrown

12.

Macbeth by William Shakespeare
Lorelai says that being cold, wet, and smelly are her three favorite things after the witches from this

13.

Moby Dick by Herman Melville
Jess recommends this to Kirk

Myra Waldo's Travel and Motoring Guide to Europe, 1978 by Myra Waldo
Selected Hotels of Europe
Lorelai receives these from her parents

The Rough Guide to Europe, 2003 Edition
Europe Through the Back Door, 2003 by Rick Steves

Rory buys these

Nickel and Dimed by Barbara Ehrenreich
Lorelai is reading this in the hospital

The Divine Comedy by Dante
Jess is reading this at the diner counter

Hidden Romantic Gems of the Restaurant World
Luke is reading this in the diner

14.

Encyclopedia Brown: Boy Detective by Donald J. Sobol
Lorelai says that she came up to borrow a book, and Jess says if it isn't this, it narrows it down

Gone with The Wind by Margaret Mitchell
Lorelai calls Rory 'Rhett'

The Holy Barbarians by Lawrence Lipton
Rory uses this to bribe Jess into Friday night dinner

Guys and Dolls by Jo Swerling and Abe Burrows
Miss Patty says she was in the on-stage version of this

Lord Jim by Joseph Conrad
Emily references this

15.
Backlash: The Undeclared War Against American Women by Susan Faludi
Lorelai asks Rory, "Where do you think the Susan Faludi's of the world came from?"

Moliere: A Biography by Hobart Chatfield Taylor
Richard references this

Othello by Shakespeare
Rory says there is cute jealous and then Othello

The Adventures of Huckleberry Finn by Mark Twain
The Jumping Frog by Mark Twain
General author reference

Hockey for Dummies by John Davidson
Kirk is holding this at the hockey game

16.
I'm With the Band by Pamela Des Barres
Lorelai is reading this on the couch

The Brontes by Juliet Barker
Rory is reading this on the couch

Into the Woods by Stephen Sondheim
Paris teases Brad about his involvement in the stage production of this

17.
The Raven by Edgar Allan Poe

This is recited at the Poe Society event

In Search of Lost Time by Marcel Proust
Paris refers to this

20.

Eleanor Roosevelt by Blanche Wiesen Cook
Rory is reading this on the bus

One Hundred Years of Solitude by Gabriel Garcia Marquez
Jess is reading this on the bus

Stepford Wives by Ira Levin
Lane refers to this

21.

Basic Writings of Nietzsche by Friedrich Nietzsche
Lorelai and Rory are reading this at Weston's

Naked Lunch: The Restored Text, William S. Burroughs
Jess has this in his hand at the bookstore

The Lovely Bones by Alice Sebold
Emily claims that her book club is reading this

22.

Pinocchio by Carlo Collodi
Title reference

Season Four

2.

Secrets of the Flesh: A Life of Colette by Judith Thurman
The Collected Stories of Eudora Welty by Eudora Welty
The Second Sex by Simone de Beauvoir
The Apocalyptics - Cancer and the Big Lie: How Environmental Politics Controls What We Know About Cancer by Edith Efron
The Diary of Virginia Woolf, Volumes 1, 3-5 edited by Anne Olivier Bell
These can be seen on the bookshelf in Rory's dorm

3.

Atonement by Ian McEwan
Rory is reading this

Haiku, Volume 2: Spring by R.H. Blyth
Rory is putting this into her bag

Mommie Dearest by Christina Crawford
Sookie says she is Mommie Dearest

4.

Northanger Abbey by Jane Austen
Rory is reading this in the gazebo

5.
Cujo by Stephen King
Lorelai calls Luke Cujo

Snows of Kilimanjaro by Ernest Hemingway
Tender is the Night by F. Scott Fitzgerald
These are mentioned in Rory's class

The Sun Also Rises by Ernest Hemingway
Trevor and Rory are both holding a copy of this

Little House on the Prairie by Laura Ingalls Wilder
Sookie says she loves this

6.
The Sun Also Rises by Ernest Hemingway
Rory reads this under her study tree

7.
1984 by George Orwell
Sookie thinks Lorelai is referencing this when she is referring to the year

The Bible
Kirk read this

10.
Valley of the Dolls by Jacqueline Susann
Wuthering Heights by Emily Bronte
Jason says he has these in his collection

Contemporary Political Fiction

Asher holds this up in class

11.
The Old Man and the Sea by Ernest Hemingway
Lane is holding this
The Bright of Martydom (fictional text)
Jane: One Woman's Harrowing Journey to God (fictional text)
Lane has covers made up to look like these books, for smuggling CD's in and out of the house
Punk: The Definitive Record of a Revolution by Stephen Colegrave and Colin Sullivan
Can be seen on Lane's bed

12.
Secrets of the Flesh: A Life of Colette by Judith Thurman
Rory is holding this when she is on the phone

Billy Budd and Other Tales, Herman Melville
Jess is holding this when he gets out of the car

13.
Lies and the Lying Liars Who Tell Them by Al Franken
Jess is reading this in the bookstore

The Gnostic Gospels by Elaine Pagels

Title reference

Billy Budd and Other Tales, Herman Melville
Jess has this in his back pocket

14.
Gulliver's Travels by Jonathon Swift
Paris refers to the Brobdingnagians
Sophie's Choice by William Styron
Sookie refers to this

15.
The Andy Warhol Diaries edited by Pat Hackett
Lane puts this into her drawer

Tender is the Night by F Scott Fitzgerald
Rory reads this in class

16.
Alice's Adventures in Wonderland by Lewis Carroll
Lorelai says the white rabbit ran past

The Crimson Petal and the White by Michel Faber
Emily says she has to finish this for her book club

17.

The Price of Loyalty: George W. Bush, the White House, and the Education of Paul O'Neill by Ron Suskind
Rory is reading this at the beach

Monsieur Proust by Celeste Albaret
Rory reads this on spring break

19.

The Trial by Franz Kafka
Asher mentions this in class

Jaglon by Asher Fleming (fictional text)
The book that Asher is signing

Points of View by W. Somerset Maugham
Richard is reading this

20.

You Deserve Love by D. Sherber
Book and audio tape combo that Luke and Jess are using

21.

You Deserve Love by D. Sherber
Book and audio tape combo that Luke and Jess are using

On the Contrary by Mary McCarthy
Can be seen on Luke's bookshelf

Season Five

1.

Say Goodbye to Daisy Miller by Henry James
Title reference, and Rory references the title

Gigi by Collette
Emily says their European trip will be just like this

2.

A Room with a View by E.M. Forster
Rory shows Lorelai the film version of this and claims it's her Europe trip with Emily

The Da Vinci Code by Dan Brown
Brian and Zach discuss this in the diner

3.

The Pursuit of Love & Love in a Cold Climate by Nancy Mitford
Emily can be seen reading this

5.

The History of the Decline and Fall of the Roman Empire by Edward Gibbon
Richard can be seen reading this

***Swann's Way* by Marcel Proust**

***Plutarch's Lives, volume 1 or 2* by John Dryden and Arthur Hugh Clough**
These can be spotted on Richard's coffee table

6.
The Armies of the Night: History as a Novel, the Novel as History; The Executioner's Song by Norman Mailer
This is on Norman Mailer's table, and Sookie can be seen reading it

The Curious Incident of the Dog in the Night-time by Mark Haddon
Rory is holding this when she talks to Logan

7.
The Iliad and The Odyssey by Homer
Luke has to read these, since he told Richard he likes "Greeks"

9.
A Confederacy of Dunces by John Kennedy Toole
Marty is reading this

A Girl from Yamhill, Beverly Cleary; Like Water for Chocolate by Laura Esquivel
Can be seen in Rory's' dorm room

Peyton Place by Grace Metalious

Rory says "if that wasn't Peyton Place enough for you"

Less than Zero, Bret Easton Ellis
Lorelai says that this is Andrew McCarthy's second best

10.

Yoga for Dummies by Georg Feuerstein and Larry Payne
Kirk reads this

Charlie and the Chocolate Factory by Roald Dahl
Lorelai refers to Willy Wonka

How we are Hungry by Dave Eggers
Rory has a poster of this

12.

My Lai 4: A Report on the Massacre and Its Aftermath by Seymour M. Hersh
The Nancy Drew Series by Carolyn Keene
Rory and Logan reference both of these in their conversation about meeting Seymour Hersh

14.

Sherlock Holmes by Arthur Conan Doyle
Paris refers to Holmes

15.
A Heartbreaking Work of Staggering Genius by Dave Eggers
Rory is reading this in bed

16.
Catch-22 by Joseph Heller
Demons by Fyodor Dostoevsky; translated by Richard Pevear and Larissa Volokhonsky
Pushkin: A Biography by T.J. Binyon
The Naked and the Dead by Norman Mailer
The Executioner's Song by Norman Mailer
Frida by Hayden Herrera
A Clockwork Orange by Anthony Burgess
Bad Dirt by Annie Proulx
The Last Word by Graham Greene
Lolita by Vladimir Nabokov
The Master and the Margarita by Mikhail Bulgakov
A Moveable Feast by Ernest Hemingway
Of Human Bondage by W Somerset Maugham
Theatre by W Somerset Maugham
One Hundred Years of Solitude by Gabriel Marcia Marquez
The Town and the City by Jack Kerouac
Brave New World by Aldous Huxley
Zorba the Greek by Nikos Kazantakis
The Princess Bride by William Golding
These can be seen in the bookstore when Rory and Lane are talking

Leaves of Grass by Walt Whitman
Richard and Emily give the Greek version of this to Rory

Saving the Queen by William F. Buckley Jr.
Can be seen on Lorelai's bookshelf

17.
Angels in America by Tony Kushner
Rory and Logan talk about this play

He's Just Not That Into You by Greg Behrendt and Liz Tuccillo
Lorelai says that there are multiple copies in the Inn library

Social Origins of Dictatorship and Democracy by Barrington Moore Jr.
Rory is reading this when Robert comes over

Nature's Metropolis: Chicago and the Great West by William Cronon
Can be seen on Rory's bookshelf

Clifford the Big Red Dog by Norman Bridwell
A copy of this was left at the inn

18.
Summer of Fear by T Jefferson Parker
Can be seen on Rory's bookshelf

19.
Huckleberry Finn by Mark Twain

The Catcher in the Rye by J.D. Salinger
Death of a Salesmen by Arthur Miller
Gone with the Wind by Margaret Mitchell
Howl by Allen Ginsberg
Lord of the Flies by William Golding
Of Mice and Men by John Steinbeck
To Kill a Mockingbird by Harper Lee
Ulysses by James Joyce
These can be seen on a banned books poster on her wall

The Invitation by Oriah Mountain Dreamer
Can be seen in Paris' room

20.
Ethics by Spinoza
The professor discusses this book in class

Written in Blood by Dianne Fanning
Laroose Wine by David Cobbold
The Wine Bible by Karen MacNeil
Haiti: State Against Nation: Origins and Legacy of Duvalierism by Michel-Rolph Trouillot
Written in Blood: the Story of the Haitian People 1492-1995 by Nancy Gordon Heinl, Robert Debs Heinl
Rory has these sitting in a pile during class

The Crisis by David Harris
Firewall by Lawrence E. Walsh
Can be seen in Rory's room

The Persian Puzzle by Kenneth M Pollack
Can be seen in Rory's room

Taken Hostage: the Iran Hostage Crisis and America's First Encounter with Radical Islam by David Farber
US Foreign Policy and the Iran Hostage Crisis by David Patrick Houghton
Can be seen in Rory's room

22.
The Iliad by Homer
Lorelai says Rory returned this late to the library once

Season Six

4.

The Lion, The Witch, and the Wardrobe by C.S. Lewis
Rory references this in her conversation with the priest

November of the Heart by LaVyrle Spencer
Can be seen on Rory's coffee table

Revolution from Within by Gloria Steinem
Can be seen at the Inn library

7.

Matisse the Master: A Life of Henri Matisse by Hilary Spurling
Richard reads this

8.

The Subsect by Jess Mariano (fictional text)
Jess comes to give Rory a copy of his debut novel

The History of Tom Thumb by Anonymous
Rory references this

9.

The Shining by Stephen King

Lorelai says "Here's Johnny" when she has her had stuck in the door

The Human Factor by Graham Greene
Can be seen at the Inn library

10.
Beowulf by unknown
Lorelai says she started reading this, after Rory recommended it

Martha Stewart Living, Holidays: The Best of Martha Stewart Living
Luke has this on his table

Chronicles of Narnia by C.S. Lewis
Christopher refers to Narnia

11.
Deenie by Judy Bloom
Anna says April read this

A Christmas Carol by Charles Dickens
Rory refers to Scrooge

It Takes a Village by Hilary Clinton
Paris refers to this

One Day in the Life of Ivan Denisovich by Aleksandr Solzhenitsyn
Paris refers to this

As I Lay Dying by William Faulkner
Native Son by Richard Wright

Can be seen on Paris' banned books poster

Blind Faith by Joe McGinniss
Flavor of the Month by Olivia Goldsmith
Can be seen on Paris and Doyle's bookshelf

13.
The Big Love by Sarah Dunn
The Sisters: The Saga of the Mitford Family by Mary S. Lovell
The Dirt: Confessions of the World's Most Notorious Rock Band by Mötley Crüe
Lorelai is picking these up off the floor

Charles Darwin, On the Origin of Species
Can be seen on Lorelai's table

14.
Robert's Rules of Order by Henry Robert
Joni references this when Paris has been voted out

All the Pretty Horses by Cormac McCarthy
Logan is reading this

The Scarlett Letter by Nathaniel Hawthorne
Rory refers to the lead character in this

No Man is an Island by John Donne
Paris says no man is an island, but "this woman is"

15.

The Year of Magical Thinking by Joan Didion
Rory is reading this at Martha's Vineyard

History of the Peloponnesian War by Thucydides
Rory has lost this and needs it

Trouble in Our Backyard: Central America and the United States in the Eighties by Martin Diskin
Can be seen on Rory's bedside table

16.

Sailing Alone Around the Room: New and Selected Poems by Billy Collins
Lorelai is reading this

17.

Charlotte's Web by E.B. White
Lorelai wants Luke to put a spider near a talking pig

Chrysanthemum by Kevin Henkes
Flavor of the Month by Olivia Goldsmith
These can be seen behind Paris

Quiller Bambo by Adam Hall
Can be seen on Luke's bookshelf

18.

The Da Vinci Code by Dan Brown
Jess says his book is not exactly this

20.
Harry Potter by J.K. Rowling
Anna refers to 'Hagrid'

Harold and the Purple Crayon by Crockett Johnson
April says she is obsessed with this

The New Way Things Work by David McCauley
Present for April

22.
Stalin: A Biography by Robert Service
Rory is reading "that Stalin Biography"

Season Seven

1.
In Cold Blood by Truman Capote
Can be seen on Rory's shelf

All the Pretty Horses by Cormac McCarthy
Rory goes through Lorelai's bag

Walden by Henry David Thoreau
Rory references this when she is on the couch with Lorelai

Hammerhead Sharks: Demons of the Deep
Possibly fictional. Lorelai puts it in her Luke pile

3.
Delta of Venus by Anais Nin
Lady Chatterley's Lover by D.H. Lawrence
Sexus by Henry Miller
Story of O by Pauline Reage
Rory is researching this in the bookshop

Charlotte's Web by E.B. White
Rory says this is one of her favorite books

5.
Life of Samuel Johnson by James Boswell
Is referenced in conversation with Logan

Mutiny on the Bounty by Charles Nordhoff and James Norman Hall
Discussed at the Yale Daily News

7.
Poems by Alfred Lord Tennyson
Rory says she can recite Charge of the Light Brigade

Madeline by Ludwig Bemelmans
Gigi's favorite book

8.
Iron Weed by William J. Kennedy
Is referenced in the argument with Logan

9.
American Steel by Richard Preston
Thunder by James Grady
Rory unpacks this

12.
R is for Ricochet by Sue Grafton
S is for Silence by Sue Grafton
Sookie said she read these on her ski trip

The Skin of Our Teeth by Thornton Wilder
Lucy is reading this

13.

A Monetary History of the United States by Milton Friedman
Richard's bedside book

Absolute Rage by Robert K Tanenbaum
Rory brings this for Richard

14.

Eva Luna by Isabel Allende
Rory recommends this to her teacher

The House of the Spirits by Isabel Allende
Rory discusses this with the new teacher

Gender Trouble by Judith Butler
Paris is looking for this in the bookstore

15.

The Vanishing Newspaper by Phillip Meyers
Mitchum recommends to this to Rory, who has already read it

21.

The Unbearable Lightness of Being by Milan Kundera
Lorelai references this title

A Year in the Life

Winter

Leaves of Grass by Walt Whitman
Elements by Euclid
In the Shadow of Young Girls in Flower by Marcel Proust
Points of View by W Somerset Maugham
The History of the Decline and Fall of the Roman Empire by Edward Gibbon
The Complete Works of William Shakespeare by William Shakespeare
Orations of American Orators
History of the Peloponnesian War by Thucydides
Quoted, or seen at Richard's funeral

Trainspotting by Irvine Welsh
Lorelai says Rory's Brooklyn apartment had a Trainspotting vibe

The Lord of the Rings by J.R.R. Tolkien
Lorelai refers to the Arganoth

Nancy Drew by Carolyn Keene
We can see the complete series in Rory's room

When Everything Changed by Gail Collins
Rory references Gail Collins

The Adventures of Huckleberry Finn by Mark Twain
Go Set a Watchman by Harper Lee
Lorelai says she is looking for a Huckleberry Finn prequel

On the Road by Jack Kerouac
Lorelai says Rory is 'on the roading it'

The Life-Changing Magic of Tidying Up by Marie Konde'
Emily declutters her life based on this book

Cyrano de Bergerac by Edmond Rostand
Lorelai says, "Cyrano?"

Mathematical Principles Of Natural Philosophy By Isaac Newton
Luke was reading it to keep up with April

Spring

The Art of War by Sun Tzu
Paris says it's kill or be killed

Consider the Lobster by David Foster Wallace
This is referenced in Rory's meeting

Death of a Salesman by Arthur Miller
Rory references Willy Loman

Cloud Atlas by David Mitchell
Rory references this

The Portable Dorothy Parker by Dorothy Parker
Paris references this

Outlander by Diana Gabaldon
Lorelai references this

First Folio by William Shakespeare
Naomi references this

The Oresteia: Agamemnon; The Libation Bearers; The Eumenides by W.B. Stanford
Logan refers to this

Summer

Wild by Cheryl Strand
Lorelai wants to 'do Wild'.

Anna Karenina by Leo Tolstoy
Rory reads this by the pool

Who's Afraid of Virginia Woolf? by Edward Albee
Taylor says he was mentored by Albee

Game of Thrones by George R.R. Martin
Brandon says "Yes Khaleesi!"

Understanding Power by Noam Chomsky
April says she met Noam Chomsky

I Feel Bad About My Neck: And Other Thoughts on Being a Woman by Nora Ephron

Rory references this when talking to Ethel

Tevya the Dairyman and the Railroad Stories by Sholem Aleichem
Babette References this

Fall

The Picture of Dorian Gray by Oscar Wilde
Lorelai says, "There's a picture of you in the attic that Dorian Gray is consulting copyright lawyers about"

My Struggle by Karl Ove Knausgaard
Jess is reading this

Eat, Pray, Love by Elizabeth Gilbert
One of the women says she was going to do this, instead of Wild

Macbeth by William Shakespeare
The unicyclist in the Life and Death Brigade scene quotes from this

Glengarry Glen Ross by David Mamet
Lorelai asks Emily when she became a Mamet play

Call of the Wild by Jack London
Lorelai references this

Little House in the Big Woods by Laura Ingalls Wilder

Sookie references this

Alice's Adventures in Wonderland by Lewis Carroll
The wedding has touches of this as a theme

The Wizard of Oz by L. Frank Baum
The Life and Death Brigade goodbye scene is a reference to this

Other Gilmore Girls Related Books

18 and Life on Skid Row by Sebastian Bach
Brothers on Life by Matt Czuchry and Mike Czuchry
Coffee at Luke's: An Unauthorized Gilmore Girls Gabfest by Leah Wilson
Downpour by Nick Holmes
Eat Like a Gilmore: The Unofficial Cookbook for Fans of Gilmore Girls by Kristi Carlson
Eat Like a Gilmore: Daily Cravings by Kristi Carlson
Eat Like a Gilmore: Seasons by Kristi Carlson
Fast Talk & Faith: A 22-Day Devotional Inspired by Gilmore Girls
Gilmore Girls: A Cultural History by Lara C. Stache, Rachel Davidson
Gilmore Girls and the Politics of Identity: Essays on Family and Feminism in the Television Series by Ritch Calvin
Gilmore Girls: Like Mother, Like Daughter (Book 1) by Catherine Clark
Gilmore Girls: I Love You, You Idiot (Book 2) by Cathy East Dubowski
Gilmore Girls: I Do, Don't I? (Book 3) by Catherine Clark

Gilmore Girls: The Other Side of Summer (Book 4) by Helen Pai
Grandma Told Me So: Lessons in Life and Love by Carla McCloskey
In Conclusion, Don't Worry About It by Lauren Graham
Living in an Alien Body – Surviving Stroke by Carla McCloskey
No Mistakes: A Workbook for Imperfect Artists by Keiko Agena
Talking as Fast As I Can by Lauren Graham
The Women of Amy Sherman-Palladino by Scott Ryan
Someday, Someday, Maybe by Lauren Graham
Silly Lop by Biff Yeager
Smokey the Cat by Biff Yeager
The Gilmore Girls Companion by A. S. Berman
The Original Valerie's Cat Eye sCream by Valerie Campbell
Screwball Television: Critical Perspectives on Gilmore Girls by David Lavery and David Scott Diffrient
Fast Talk & Faith: A 22-Day Devotional Inspired by Gilmore Girls by Mary Carver
You've Been Gilmore'd!: The Unofficial Encyclopedia and Comprehensive Guide to Gilmore Girls and Stars Hollow by Taryn Dryfhout

Eternal Damnation is what I'm Risking for My Rock n Roll

Music

Music in Gilmore Girls

The world of the *Gilmore Girls* and Stars Hollow is packed with cultural references, of which music is a large part. So many artists and songs are referenced throughout the series that including a music section was essential, and accounts for as large a chunk of this book as the other lists.

Two key artists became fan favorites – Carole King who wrote the show's theme tune, "Where You Lead", and Sam Phillips who created the "la-las" which defined so much of the show's aesthetic. While the theme song frames each episode, and fans can sing along with that familiar feeling of 'home' at the start of each episode, the "la-las" brought out the emotions in the characters, and allowed viewers to relate to the feelings that were bound up with the girls' experiences. Some of the most important moments in the series are ensconced within music. Lane's first kiss with Dave Rygalski, Lorelai's first dance with Luke at Liz's wedding, and Logan's departure for London, would not have been the same without it. Faye Woods points out that both King's theme song and Sam

Phillips' ongoing score "contribute to the patina of Stars Hollow as a utopian idyll little touched by contemporary life."[3] *Gilmore Girls* would not have been the same without the music of these two amazing women. Lorelai and Rory would not have been the same without them.

While Rory has a rather heterogenous taste in music, Lorelai's taste is somewhat stuck in the 80s when she was a teenager, and Lane's focus is on 'Rock and Roll' and anything that 'Mojo' recommends. The musical tastes of the younger characters in the series like Lane, and Rory, were somewhat eclectic, and opened my eyes to a much wider catalogue of music. Artists such as PJ Harvey, The Shins, and Wilco all became regulars on my playlists, making me feel like I was a part of the Stars Hollow world when I could not watch the show. Many of these songs, particularly the work of Sam Phillips, served as the background inspiration that I wrote and complied this book to. This music list reflects the diverse range of songs and artists that can be heard or are referred to in the dialogue.

While there are far fewer music lists available online than there are for books or films

---

[3] Faye Woods, "Generation Gap? Mothers, Daughters and Music," in *Gilmore Girls: The Politics of Identity*, ed. Ritch Calvin, (Jefferson, NC: McFarland & Company Inc., 2008), 129.

mentioned on *Gilmore Girls,* a few attempts have been made. The main problem I have found with other lists is that they often only list the music that is heard or played in the show, but not the music that is referred to in the show. This list, attempts at least, to be exhaustive, and, remains deeply relevant, even after the end of the show.

Season One

1.

"There She Goes" by The La's
First song on the show. Plays as the show opens. Lorelai is seen crossing the street on her way to Luke's Diner.

"Ballet Waltz #3" by Herman Beeftink
Plays at Miss Patty's during her ballet class

"I Try" by Macy Gray
After Lorelai and Rory fight about Dean, they both go into separate rooms and turn this song on

"Wendy" composed by Wesley Yang & Gavin McNett
Plays while Rory is cleaning out her locker on her last day at Stars' Hollow High

"Heartland" by George Strait
Plays when Rory and Lorelai are walking home, and pass Lane who is on the hayride.

"Where the Colors Don't Go" by Sam Phillips
Plays as Lorelai looks at the pictures on her mantelpiece and realised that she will have to ask her parents for the money to fund Rory's enrolment at Chilton. Also plays at the end of her meeting with Emily and Richard.

"My Little Corner of the World" by Kit Pongetti
Plays at the end of the pilot, when Lorelai and Rory are having coffee at Luke's Diner.

"Baby One More Time" by Britney Spears
Rory looks at her Chilton kilt, and says "I'm going to be in a Britney Spears video?"

2.

"I'm the Man Who Murdered Love" by XTC
Lane runs to the Gilmores with the new XTC CD. Lorelai and Rory follow her into the house where she puts this song on.

"I Don't Know How to Say Goodbye to You" by Sam Phillips
Plays while Lorelai and Rory are driving through Stars Hollow

"Stars and Stripes Forever" by John Phillip Sousa
Miss Patty's dance class rehearse their baton twirling to this song

"Man, I Feel Like a Woman!" by Shania Twain
The mother of the brides pays Drella to play this on the harp

3.

"La Casa" by Graham Preskett/Mauricio Venegas
Plays at Miss Patty's, during the twins' dancing lesson

"Teach Me Tonight" by Sammy Cahn and Gene De Paul
Morey plays this on the piano after he finds Cinnamon

"Man! I Feel Like a Woman!" by Shania Twain
"We Are Family" by Sister Sledge
"A Kiss to Build a Dream On" by Louis Armstrong
Plays at the twins' double wedding

"Here They Go" by Sam Phillips
Cue during the episode

4.

"My Darling" by Wilco
Plays while Lorelai wakes after falling asleep in the middle of her Shakespeare study session with Rory

"Iron Man" by Black Sabbath
Drella plays this song on her harp

"Wendy" by Wesley Yang and Gavin McNett

Lane is listening to this in her closet when Rory calls her from her car

5.

"Truly Truly" by Grant Lee Phillips
Plays in the background, when Dean apologizes to Rory for bugging her

"Time Bomb" by Rancid
Plays when Lane is dancing in Rory's room

"I Thought About You" by Johnny Mercer and James Van Heusen
Morey plays this – Cinnamon's song – on the piano

6.

"What a Wonderful World" by Louis Armstrong
Plays at Rory's second birthday party, while the party guests are trading Rory anecdotes

"Happy Birthday" by Altered Images
Plays when Rory discovers that Emily sent birthday party invitations to her peers at Chilton

"Why Does it Always Rain on Me?" by Travis
Plays when Emily and Richard arrive at the Gilmore house for Rory's birthday party

"This Old House" by Brian Setzer Orchestra

Plays while Rory is opening presents at her second birthday party

"The Lathe of Heaven" by Scott Abels, Aaron Owens, Matthew W. Parker, David Fuentes, Brian Dixon
Plays when Luke arrives at the party with ice

"Like a Virgin" by Madonna
Lorelai says that she convinced Emily to have the string quartet play this at Rory's birthday

7.
"Ballo, e canto de' villanelli" by Antonio Vivaldi
What Miss Patty's class dances to when Lorelai and Rory pass them

"Through the Eyes of Love (Theme from Ice Castles)" by Marvin Hamlisch and Carole Bayer Sager
Rory says that this makes Dean cry

8.
"Someone to Watch Over Me" by Rickie Lee Jones
Plays when Lorelai and Max are out in the snow, and Luke sees them together

"Pictures of You" by The Cure

Lane is listening to this son in Rory's room after she touches Rich Bloomingfeld's hair

9.
"We're All Light" by XTC
Plays after Rory and Dean arrive at the dance, while Louise flirts with Dean

"Fade Into You" by Mazzy Star
Plays straight after the first song, when Rory and Dean dance

"Sometimes Always" by Jesus and Mary Chain
Plays while Paris tells Rory that Jacob is her cousin

"Mixed Business" by Beck
Plays when Jacob and Rory are talking

"Thirteen" by Big Star
Plays when Dean is walking through Stars Hollow with Rory

10.
"Santa Claus is Coming to Town" by Tony Bennett
In the background at Emily's Christmas party when Rory first arrives

"Christmas Wrapping" by The Waitresses
Play's while Lorelai tries to order food

"Happy X-Mas" by John Lennon and Yoko Ono
Plays when Lorelai and Rory get food at the hospital

"Thanks for Christmas" by XTC
Plays in Luke's Diner, when Lorelai gifts Luke his new cap

11.
"Livin' La Vida Loca" by Ricky Martin
Sookie sings this in Lorelai's kitchen

"Everlong" by The Foo Fighters
Lane asks Todd if he has heard the acoustic version of this

12.
"Earn Enough for Us" by XTC
Plays prominently during the morning routine sequence

"God Only Knows" by Claudine Longet
Rory and Lane listen to this song which disturbs Lorelai, who is studying

"Holding on to the Earth" by Sam Phillips
Plays in Rory' room, when her and Lane are preparing for their double date

13.
"Walk Like an Egyptian" by The Bangles

Lorelai references this when she gives Rory and her Chilton peers the concert tickets

"Hero Takes a Fall" by The Bangles
The Bangles perform this song during the concert

"Eternal Flame" by the Bangles
The Bangles perform this song during the concert

"I'm Gonna Make You Love Me" by the Jayhawks
Playing at the party where Lorelai finds Madeline and Louise

14.

"Sunday Best" by Grant Lee Phillips
The Troubadour is singing this song when Rory steps off the bus to meet Dean

"Flower Girl in Bordeaux" by Esquivel
Playing when Dean arrives for Donna Reed night

"Johnny Angel" by Shelley Fabares
Rory's choice of dining music for the Donna Reed dinner

"Beautiful Dreamers" by Grant Lee Phillips
Sung by the Troubadour when Lorelai and Luke are taking the paint cans off the truck

"Tambourine Man" by William Shatner
"Lucy in the Sky with Diamonds" by William Shatner

Rory talks about getting these on CD for Lorelai

15.
"Suppertime" by Clark Genser
Lorelai and Christopher sang this when they were kids

16.
"Heavenly" by Grant Lee Phillips
The Troubadour sings this at the Firelight Festival

"Oh My Love" by John Lennon
Plays when Dean shows Rory her car

"Mockingbirds" by Grant Lee Buffalo
The Troubadour sings this at the Firelight Festival

17.
"What Do I Do" by Sam Phillips
Plays when Lorelai goes to visit Max

"Where It's At" by Beck
Playing at Madeline's when Rory and Lane arrive

"Ms. Jackson" by Outkast
Henry and Lane dance to this song

"Everyday I Write the Book" by Elvis Costello
Plays at the party

"From Red to Blue" by Billy Bragg
Lane and Henry slow dance to this song

"Crystal Lake" by Grandaddy
In the background when Rory and Tristan kiss

"Zombie" by The Cranberries
Lorelai says her voice is like "that annoying Cranberries song"

18.
"It's the Life" by Grant Lee Buffalo
Sung by the Troubadour, as he passes the flower shop

19.
"Child Psychology" by Black Box Recorder
Rory and Lane listen to this in Rory's bedroom

21.
"Honey Don't Think" by Grant Lee Buffalo
The Town Troubadour sings this when Lane and Rory walk past him in the town

"Swan Lake" -- Ballet -- Ste Op. 20a: Sea in the Moonlight by Tchaikovsky
Can be heard at Miss Patty's ballet class

"Sadness Soot" by Grant Lee Phillips

The Troubadour sings this before being interrupted by whistling

"One Line" by PJ Harvey
Plays when Rory and Dean make up

"Everybody Needs a Little Sanctuary" by Grant Lee Phillips
The Troubadour sings this, and is joined by the rival troubadour

"My Little Corner of the World" by Yo La Tengo
Closes the scene, and the episode

Season Two

1.
"I Found Love" by the Free Design
Plays as the episode opens

"I'll Be Your Mirror" by The Velvet Underground
This is playing in Lane's closet when she's on the phone to Rory

"Sadie, Sadie" by Barbra Streisand
Title Reference

2.
"Spring Released" by Grant Lee Phillips
This is playing at Max and Lorelai's wedding shower

"Love Will Keep Us Together" by Captain and Tennille
Miss Patty's tap class performs to this song

"One Fine Day" by The Chiffons
Playing while Lorelai goes to the diner to find Luke

"Until the Real Thing Comes Along" by Dean Martin
Plays at the wedding shower

"Love Is Everywhere I Go" by Sam Phillips
Plays as Max and Lorelai dance

3.
"Get Happy" by Judy Garland
A drag queen can be seen lip-syncing this song at Lorelai's bachelorette party

"True" by Spandau Ballet
Plays in the background while Emily talks about the lead up to her wedding with Richard

"Church of the Poison Mind" by Culture Club
Michel dances to this song at the drag club

4.
"Perfect Situation for a Fool" by Jai Josefs
Plays on the radio when Lorelai is driving

"L-O-V-E" by Irving
Plays when Rory and Lorelai are in the college dormitories

"Gypsies, Tramps, and Thieves" by Cher
The Bed and Breakfast guests are singing this when Rory and Lorelai are talking upstairs

5.
"This is Hell" by Elvis Costello

Plays when Jess walks out into the streets of Stars Hollow

"Girl From Mars" by Ash
Plays at the end of the episode, when Jess walks away from Rory

"Act of Love" by Neil Young
"Fuckin' Up" by Neil Young
Lane, Dean and Rory watch Neil Young's Rock & Roll Hall of Fame induction

6.
"Du Hast" by Rammstein
Plays when Christopher pulls up with his new car

"The Way You Look Tonight" by Frank Sinatra
The song Dean and Rory are learning to dance to at their lessons with Miss Patty

"Thank Heaven for Little Girls" by Maurice Chevalier
Plays at the debutante ball

"Jubilee" by Grant Lee Buffalo
Sung by the troubadour as the Gilmore group pass him after the debutant ball, back in Stars Hollow

7.
"Looks Like We Made It" by Barry Manilow

Rory sing this to tease Lorelai who had been listening to Barry Manilow

"Know Your Onion" by The Shins
Rory is listening to this song through her headphones when the guidance counsellor approaches her in the Chilton cafeteria

"Girls Just Wanna Have Fun" by Cyndi Lauper
The runway music for the Chilton mothers, as they walk the catwalk

"It's Alright, Baby" by Komeda
Plays at the close of the episode, as Rory listens through her headphones in the Chilton cafeteria

8.
"Nothin' is For Sure" by Grant Lee Phillips
Sung by the troubadour as Lorelai and Mia pass him after the town meeting

10.
"Human Behavior" by Bjork
Plays when Lorelai and Rory ride home and see their snowman ruined

11.
"Whatever Will Be, Will Be (Que Sera Sera)" by Doris Day

Playing when Lorelai wakes up and goes outside, falling through her porch

"One Step Beyond" by Madness
Plays during the cheerleader's routine

"Be True To Your School" by Grant Lee Phillips
Sung by the troubadour after the pep rally

12.

"A Foggy Day in London Town" by Frank Sinatra
Plays on Emily and Richard's stereo, when Richard returns home from Stars Hollow

"Rockin with the Rhythm of the Rain" by The Judds
Lorelai says all three are fine, like a Judd's song

14.

"Legal Man" by Belle and Sebastian
Plays during the CD drop off montage

15.

"Price Yeah!" by Pavement
Jess sleeps to this music

"What A Wonderful World" by Joey Ramone

Plays at the end of the episode, when Luke knocks a hole in his apartment to start renovations

"It's a Small World" by Robert and Richard Sherman
Lorelai says her voice is like this song going around and around in people's heads

16.
"Deora AR Mo Chroi" by Enya
Plays when Lorelai is having her facial, before Emily enters

"I Can't Give You Anything But Love, Baby" by Jimmy McHugh
Plays in the background of the bar when Lorelai and Emily first arrive

"Come Fly With Me" by Frank Sinatra
Plays at the bar

"Fly Me to the Moon" by Frank Sinatra
This is playing when Emily is asked to dance

"Someone to Watch Over Me" by Frank Sinatra
The song Emily dances to, before panicking and leaving the dance floor

"Stayin' Alive" by The Bee Gees
This is playing at the bar when Lorelai and Emily argue

17.
" Wake Me Up (Before You Go Go)" by Grant Lee Phillips
Sung by the troubadour when Lorelai and Rory pass on the way to the diner

"Jeannie" Theme from I Dream of Jeannie by Buddy Kaye and Hugo Montenegro
Playing in the background when Rory goes to Luke's apartment to find Jess

19.
"Car Song" by Elastica
Plays when Jess and Rory are driving back from getting ice cream

"White Lines" by Grandmaster and Melle Mel
The song Kirk dances to in his film

20.
"Heavy Metal Drummer" by Wilco
Plays in Sophie's Music store

"Hava Nagila" a Jewish folk song
The little Rabbi statue dances to this song when Rory takes the money out from under it

21.
"52 Girls" by B-52's

Plays while Lorelai celebrates her graduation at home, with a drink

"Dance This Mess Around" by B-52's
Plays while Rory talks to Jess on the phone

"O'Oh" by Yoko Ono
Plays while Jess and Rory are walking through New York

"Monkey Gone to Heaven" by the Pixies
Playing in the background of the record store in New York

22.
"I Can't Get Started" by Ella Fitzgerald
Sookie plays this at the beginning of the episode when she's trying to pick a wedding song. Also plays at the close of the episode, at her wedding.

"You're Just in Love" from Call Me Madame
Morey plays this for Miss Patty and Babette to sing as a duet at the piano, at Sookie's wedding

"Walking After Midnight" by Patsy Cline
Kirk sings this at Sookie's wedding, while Morey plays it on the piano

Season Three

1.
"Those Lazy Hazy Crazy Days of Summer" by Nat King Cole
Can be heard throughout the episode, as part of the Stars Hollow festival

3.
"Baby Face" by the Brady Kids
Can be heard on the Brady Bunch episode that Lorelai and Rory are watching

"Smile" by Grant-Lee Phillips
Played by the troubadour at the end of the episode

"Tiny Cities Made of Ashes" by Modest Mouse
Can be heard in Rory's room at the start of the episode

"I Wanna Be Sedated" by the Ramones
Can be heard at the Gilmore's while Lane is working on her advert

"Big in Japan" by Tom Waits
Playing in Carol's room while she gets ready

4.
"London Calling" by The Clash

Lane's ban rehearses this song

"Funky Days are Back Again" by Cornershop
Rory has this song on when she is talking to Lane on the phone

"Naima" by John Coltrane
Lane has this song on when she is talking to Rory on the phone

"Hello Dolly" by Louis Armstrong
Lorelai sings this over the phone to Luke

"Love Burns" by BRMC
Can be heard on Jess' radio when Lorelai is there

"Margaritaville" Jimmy Buffett
Lorelai asks Luke to sing this

"Cities in Dust" by Siouxsie and the Banshees
"I Don't Mind" by Slumber Party
Plays while Lane is having her hair coloured

5.
"Midnight at the Oasis" by Maria Muldaur
This plays when Rory touches the clock at Dwight's

"Space Odity" by David Bowie
Lorelai sings a bit of this song

6.
"Everybody Have Fun Tonight" by Wang Chung

"Who's That Girl?" by White and Schogger
"Fingersnap" by Chucho Merchan
Plays during the baby shower

"Baby Face" by Bennie Davise and Harry Akst
Rory sings the karaoke version

7.
"In The Mood" by Glenn Miller
This song opens the episode, and plays during the dance marathon (fifth)

"Sing Sing Sing (With a Swing)" by James Horner Prima
This song opens the dance marathon

"Walkin' My Baby Back Home" performed by the Swingin Deacons
The second marathon song, played at the six-hour mark

"I Can't Give You Anything But Love" performed by the Swingin Deacons
The third marathon song

"By the Beautiful Sea" performed by the Swingin Deacons
Plays during the run-around

"String of Pearls" by Glenn Miller
Plays during the marathon, when Sookie and Lorelai are talking

"These Foolish Things" performed by the Swingin' Deacons
Plays during the Rory and Dean break up

"Gonna Fly Now" Theme from Rocky by Bill Conti
Plays during Kirk's victory lap, into the end of the episode

8.
"Then She Appeared" by XTC
Plays during Rory and Jess' first kiss

9.
"Man Who Sold the World" by David Bowie
Dave plays this, before starting his hymn. Plays again when he kisses Lane outside

10.
"Fillmore Blues" by Chuck Berry
Rory gives this to Richard for his birthday

"Louie Louie" by Richard Berry
Played by the Stars Hollow marching band

"Without a Net" composed by Ken Hiatt
Played by the Stars Hollow marching band, while Jess and Dean are talking

11.
"Bad Moon Rising" by Creedence Clearwater Revival
Plays at Sookie and Jackson's

12.
"Ave Maria" by Franz Schubert
Dave plays this at the Kim wedding

13.
"99 Luftballons" by Nena
Lorelai listens to this song in the waiting room, while she is in labor

"Easter Parade" by Judy Garland
Lorelai sings this song up the stairs, when she is going to install the DVD player for Emily

14.
"In a Young Man's Mind" by the Mooney Suzuki
Plays in the bands car when they stop at the lights

"One For My Baby" by Frank Sinatra
Miss Patty sings this in her show

15.
"A Mighty Fortress is Our God" written by Martin Luthor

The band rehearse this in the garage. A discussion is had about the meaning of the lyric 'Bulwark'

"The Star-Spangled Banner" by Francis Scott Key
Miss Patty and Babette sing this at the game

"Amazing Grace" by John Newton
The band play this

"I Get Around" by The Beach Boys
Lorelai quotes this song to Jess

16.
"Prologue Into the Woods" from the musical Into the Woods
Paris sings this to tease Brad

18.
"Happy Birthday" by Mildred J. Hill and Dr. Patty Smith Hill
The Gilmore's sing this to Lorelai

19.
"Magic Moments" by Perry Como
The party guests are singing this at the Gilmore's

"La La" by Shark Quest
Can be heard on the radio at the party

"Fell in Love with a Girl" by The White Stripes
"White Riot" by The Clash

Played by the band

"Calling All Enthusiasts" by Radio 4
Can be heard on the stereo at the party

"Saccharine" by Sunday's Best
Can be heard at the party, when Jess and Rory are talking to Lindsay and Dean

"Why" by North Green
Can be heard at the party, when Lane is on the phone to her mother

"Dance To The Underground" by Radio 4
Can be heard at the party, during Jess and Dean's brawl

20.

"Wind Beneath My Wings" by Bette Midler
Lorelai sings this to Rory

"The Candy Man" by Sammy Davis, Jr
Taylor sings this when announcing his store

"Semper Fidelis" by John Phillip Sousa
The marching band plays this during the funeral

"Suffragette City" by David Bowie
Jess and his father nod their heads to this song

21.

"Pipeline" by The Chantays
Plays as soon as Jess hits L.A.

"Catch a Wave" by the Beach Boys

Plays while Jess is standing on the beach

"Mockingbirds" by Grant Lee Buffalo
Can be heard while Jess is waiting in the house

"Los Angeles" by X
Can be heard in the background of the food stand

"One Way or Another" by Blondie
Plays while Jimmy and Jess are talking

22.

"Peace Train" by Cat Stevens
The town troubadour sings this

"Mexican Shuffle" by Herb Alpert and the Tijuana Brass
Jackson puts this on for the celebration with Lorelai

"Pomp and Circumstance" written by Edward Elgar
Plays during graduation

"Cherish" by The Association
Brad sings this during his speech

Season Four

1.
"When You Tell Me That You Love Me" by Diana Ross
Plays in the ballroom dance videos

"The Girl From Ipanema" by Fantastic Strings
Can be heard in the beauty supply store

2.
"Tell Her What She Wants To Know" by Sam Phillips
Plays when Rory and Lorelai are saying goodbye

"Bright Future In Sales" by Fountains Of Wayne
Plays when Lorelai is inviting everyone to the dorm suite

3.
"Don't Mug Yourself" by The Streets
"I Do The Rock" by Time Curry
These can be heard at the Yale party

4.
"The Weakest Shade Of Blue" by The Pernice Brothers

Plays when Rory is sitting in the gazebo

5.
"Shadow Dancing" by Andy Gibb
This is on the radio in the Jeep while Lorelai avoids her mother

"Rusholme Ruffians" by The Smiths
Plays during the laundry room scene at the end

7.
"Head On" by Jesus And Mary Jane
Lanes band play this

"The Entertainer" by Billy Joel
The tune on Sookie's baby pager

8.
"The Boat Ashore" by Michael Roe
Song sung at the end when Rory is writing her review

9.
"Yale Bulldog Chant" by Cole Porter
This is the chant that Richard joins in, at the Harvard-Yale game

"The Whiffenpoof Song" by the Whiffenpoofs
Richard sings this in a circle at the tailgate party

"Nookie" by Limp Bizkit

Brennon is playing this on the air guitar in the diner

11.
"Crazy Beat" by Blur
Lane's band practices this song

12.
"Shy Boy" by Bananarama
Plays on Lorelai's stereo

13.
"Mona Lisa" by Grant Phillips
The troubadour plays this at the firelight festival

17.
"So Says I" by The Shins
"The Laws Have Changed" by The New Pornographers
Playing in the night club

"Suspended from Class" by Camera Obscura
Can be heard in the background when the girls are drinking punch

"Step Into My Office Baby" by Belle and Sebastian
Can be heard while Rory and Paris are watching The Power of Myth

"Get Yourself Together" by Tahiti 80
Plays before the banana eating contest

"Agrophobia" by Incubus
Plays when the girls are at the beach

18.

"Windy" by The Association
Plays when Dean stops Rory in the street

"In My Honey's Lovin' Arms" by Robert Mitchum
Plays when Lorelai and Jason are drinking

19.

"Time Bomb" by Rancid
Hepalien's cover for their gig

"Happy Kid" by Nada Surf
Plays after Hepalien

20.

"Relax" by Frankie Goes To Hollywood
The male stripper performs to this song

"Jacqueline" by Franz Ferdinand
Plays while Rory is packing up at Yale

"Too Shy" by Kajagoogoo
Plays at Liz and TJ's wedding

"In a Big Country" by Big Country
"The Little Ol' Beggar's Bush" by Flogging Molly
Play while Rory is out with Graham

"Reflecting Light" by Sam Phillips
Luke and Lorelai dance to this during the wedding

22.

"Lily is a Passion" by Grant Lee Phillips
Town Troubadour plays this when Rory and Lorelai are in town

"Satellite of Love" by Lou Reed
Plays when Dean comes to the house

Season Five

1.

"If I Could Write" by Sam Phillips
Plays while Emily and Rory are preparing for their Europe trip

"Candy Man" by Sammy Davis, Jr
Rory chooses this as her and Dean's song

2.

"Fell in Love With a Girl" by the White Stripes
Lane's band plays this

"This Town" by The Go-Go's
Spoken by Lorelai when the Cider Mill Parade comes through

"Chimacum Rain" by Linda Perhacs
Plays when Rory is outside Dean's house, looking into the sky

3.

"Lily-A-Passion" by Grant-Lee Phillips
Plays while Luke and Lorelai are on their date

"The Best Is Yet To Come" by Tony Bennett
Plays when Emily is dining on her own

"Crazy" by Patsy Cline

Referenced by Lorelai while Emily and Richard argue at dinner

4.

"Science vs. Romance" by Rilo Kiley
Lane plays this to Rory over the phone

"My Happy Ending" by Avril Lavigne
Clara plays this loudly, annoying Dean in the next room

"Greatest American Hero - (Believe it or Not)" by Joey Scarbury Jackson's favourite song, which Lane's band plays

"Star Spangled Banner" by Francis Scott Key, John Stafford Smith, and Springfield Digital Orchestra
Played by Lane's band during the performance

"Slow Hands" by Interpol
Can be heard playing in the background in the band's apartment

"Happy Days Are Here Again" by Guy Lombardo
Can be heard at Luke's during the victory party

5.

"Superfreak" by Rick James
Can be heard at Kyle's when Rory visits

"Maggie's Farm" by Bob Dylan
Plays on Kyle's phone

"Pippi Longstocking" by Astrid Lindgren
Lorelai and Rory sing this when the movie starts

6.
"Stand By Your Man" by Tammy Wynette
Dean says that Taylor was singing this song

"Manic Monday" by the Bangles
Lorelai sings this when she is at Christopher's house

7.
"As time goes by" Made famous by Sinatra
The Life and Death Brigade sing this at the camp

"My Melancholy Baby" By Dorsey Brothers & Their Orchestra
"The Music Goes Round And Round" by Frank Froeba & His Swing Band
"Diga Diga Doo" by Mills Brothers with Duke Ellington
All played during the Life and Death Brigade gathering

"Burning Down the House" by Talking Heads
"Crosseyed And Painless" by Talking Heads

Plays during the movie Lane and Zach watch on their date

8.

"Mein kleiner grüner Kaktus" by the Comedian Harmonists
Plays during Friday night dinner on the patio

"Come On-A My house" by Rosemary Clooney
Lorelai puts this song on at Luke's

"In the Cool Cool Cool of the evening" by Rosemary Clooney
Can be heard at Luke's when TJ arrives

"I'll Dance At Your Wedding" by Vic Damone
Can be heard during Luke and Lorelai's dinner

"Kiss Me" by Vic Damone
Plays when Lorelai is talking to Rory on the phone

"Down" by Pidgeon
Playing in the pool house

9.

"Symphony No. 7 in E minor ("Song of the Night")" by New York Philharmonic with Henry Grossman
Emily talks about this on her date with Simon

"Starcrossed" by Ash

Can be heard when Rory is studying with Marty

"Roam" by The B52s
Marty says that Rome is the name of a B52s song

10.

"The Coffee Song" By Bob Hilliard & Richard Miles
Miss Patty Sings this at her party

"Robots" by the Futureheads
Plays when Rory and Anna meet Marty in the pub

"Drunk" by North Green
Plays when Rory and Marty are leaving the pub looking for Anna.

11.

"Winter Wonderland" by Bing Crosby
Lorelai says that Crosby is warming up his pipes because of the snow

12.

"Can't Stand Me Now" by the Libertines
Plays at the pub when Rory and Logan meet to swap research

"Six Months In A Leaky Boat" by Split Enz

Plays at the bar when Logan returns the research to Rory

"In a Gadda Da Vida" by Iron Butterfly
Gil asks Kyon if she knows this song

13.
"It's a Good Day" by Peggy Lee
Plays at Emily's bachelorette party

"Wedding Bell Blues" by The 5th Dimension
Plays during Richard and Emily's first dance

"Moon River" by Audrey Hepburn
Luke and Lorelai dance to this at Emily and Richard's wedding

14.
"Tequila" by Los Lodos
Plays when Lorelai arrives back in Stars Hollow

"Under The Boardwalk" by Bette Midler
Caesar sings this in the diner

"Do That There" by Lyrics Born
Plays during Logan's Poker Game

"Dust That Dreams of Brooms" by Aveo
Plays when Rory arranges her date with Logan

15.

"Do You Love Me" from "Fiddler on the Roof"
Sang by Kirk and young girl in the production

16.
"You Can't Hurry Love" by The Concretes
"Hong Kong Garden" by Siouxsie and the Banshees
Plays during Lane and Zach's romantic dinner

"The Man That Got Away" by Judy Garland
Lorelai is playing this and wallowing, when Luke arrives

17.
"Stuck In The Middle With You" by Stealer's Wheel
Plays when Rory and Robert enter the party

"Woo Hoo" by 5.6.7.8's
Plays at the Quentin Tarantino party

"You Never Can Tell" by Chuck Berry
Finn and his date dance like Vincent and Mia from Pulp Fiction

"Let Your Ya Be Ya" by Ranking Roy
"Ja Glory" by Toots Bombarde
"Lively Up Yourself" by The Family Zigag
Lorelai reads this off the back of Luke's CD

18.

"Symphony No.1 in D Major, Titan, Movement IV" by Gustav Mahler
Plays while Paris is moping in her room

"Pleasant Valley Sunday" by The Monkees
This can be heard in the music store when Lane goes to see Sophie

"Too Much Love" by LCD Soundsystem
Plays when Zach and Lane are arguing about shopping

"Buff Right"
Plays in the diorama at the Twickham Museum

"Aquarius" by The Fifth Dimension
Playing when they enter the 60s section of the diorama

19.

"Suburban Homeboy" by Sparks
Can be heard when Rory goes over to Logan's to break up with him

20.

"Walking On Sunshine" by Katrina And The Waves
Paris sings this in the dorm

21.

"Oblivious" by Aztec Camera
Can be heard in the Limo with Luke and Lorelai

22.
"Mama Tried" by Merle Haggard
Sung by the Town Troubadour

"Big Blue Buzz" by Ric Menck
Zach plays this while Lane is talking about band practice

"Chain Gang" by Sam Cooke
Lorelai puts this on the stereo in the kitchen when joking about Rory's crime

"I Think It's Gonna Rain Today" by Claudine Longet
Plays when Rory is unpacking her belongings and moving into Emily and Richard's pool house

Season Six

1.

"Pre-owned heart" by Grant Lee Phillips
The troubadour sings this

"Freaking Out" by Graham Coxon
"Ant Music" by Adam and the Ants
Plays at Rory's party

"Funkytown" by Lipps Inc.
Lorelai says they are going to Funkytown

2.

"Begin the Beguine" by Cole Porter
This is the tune on Richard's cell phone

"Saddest Quo" by Pernice Brothers
This can be head playing in Lorelai's jeep

3.

"Hanging On The Telephone" by Blondie
Hep Alien cover

"A String of Pearls" by Glenn Miller
Plays in Rory's dance class

"Folsom Prison Blues" by Johnny Cash

Rory says she "shot a man in Reno"

"Wicked Witch Theme" (From The Wizard of Oz)
Michel sings this when Paris arrives at the Inn

4.

"Twin Cinema" by the New Pornographers
Plays when Rory enters the pool house and finds the guys are there

5.

"We've Got Magic To Do" by Stephen Schwartz
"Swan Lake, Op. 20, Suite 3 - Danse des petits cygnes" by Herbert von Karajan with the Berliner Philharmoniker
"Koyaanisqatsi" by Philip Glass
These play at Miss Patty's recital

"Bei Mir Bist du Schon" by The Andrew Sisters
"Don't Go Sit Under The Apple Tree" by The Andrew Sisters
"I'll Be With You In Apple Blossom Time" by The Andrew Sisters

These songs are played by the trio at the fundraising party

7.

"Seventh Son" by Mose Allison
"l Ways True To You In My Own Fashion" by Blossom Dearie?
"Everything I've Got (Belongs to You)" by Blossom Dearie
These songs play at the birthday party

"It's De-lovely" by Cole Porter
Lorelai says "it's de-lovely"

8.

"Hang Down Your Head Tom Dooley" by Kingston Trio
Sung at the pub by the folk singer

"All My Life" by The Point
Plays at the pub

"Russian Rhapsody" by The Ossipov Balalaika orchestra, Nikolai Kalinin
Plays during the DAR tea

9.

"The Sound of Silence" by Simon and Garfunkel
Lorelai can't hear any sound and says "okay…Simon, Garfunkel"

"Saturday Night's Alright" by Elton John
Lorelai says she hears it's good for fighting

10.

"Blankest Year" by Nada Surf
Plays before the band's fight

"Pennies from Heaven" by Louis Armstrong
"Eye of the Tiger" by Paul Anka

"Roxanne" by The Police
"My Sharona" by The Knack
"Eleanor Put Your Boots on" by Franz Ferdinand
Zach things that songs with a female name in the title are Hep Alien's best shot at radio airplay, because it worked for these bands and their songs

"Fly Away" by Lenny Kravitz
Lorelai doesn't understand where he gets all his money from, after only one hit song

"Ring of Fire" by Johnny Cash

Babette cut a record of her cats meowing this song

11.

"Jolene" by Dolly Parton
Rory says she and Lorelai saw aa drag queen performance of this

13.

"Hurt So Good" by John Mellencamp
Lorelai references this song when she bumps into Luke

"Ice Ice Baby" by Vanilla Ice
Lorelai says "Ice Ice Baby" when talking to Rory on the phone

15.

"Zydeco Boogaloo" by Buckwheat Zydeco
"Early in the Morning by Buckwheat Zydeco
The Zydeco band play this for their audition

"Bette Davis Eyes" by Kim Carnes
"Take My Breath Away" by Berlin
These songs play in the gym

"Hot Blooded" by Foreigner

Lorelai references this song

16.

"(Take Me) Riding In My Car" by Woody Guthrie
Zach sings this with his banjo

"Kool Thing" by Sonic Youth
Plays when Rory is getting dressed

"Hollaback Girl" by Gwen Stefani
"Hava Nagila" a Jewish folk song
Gil and Brian sing this at the Bar Mitzvah

"Bluebird" by The Rosebuds
Plays in the pub when Rory and Doyle are drinking

17.

"Side Streets" by Saint Etienne
Plays in Anna's store

"What More Can I Say" by Kurt Cobain
Plays during the transition from Zach and Mrs. Kim to Rory and Lane

18.

"The Elements Song" by Tom Lehrer
Kids on the bus singing.

"Angst in My Pants" by Sparks
Plays when Lorlelai is circling the wedding dress

19.

"Around the World" by Daft Punk
Michel dances to this at the Inn

"Don't Know Why (You Stay) by The Essex Green
Can be heard in the house when the girls crash the boys' party

"Wedding March" by Felix Mendelssohn
Plays at the second wedding

"Heart of Glass" by Blondie
Plays at the wedding reception in the square

"I'm a Believer" by The Monkees
Hep Alien Cover

"Endless Love" by Lionel Ritchie and Diana Ross
Lorelai supposedly sang this when she was drunk

20.

"40 Years" by House of Freaks
Sang by the Troubadour

"Our Lips Are Sealed" by The Go-Go's
Playing when the girls go into the beauty shop

"I Won't Grow Up" by Rickie Lee Jones
"Tropical Ice-Land" by The Fiery Furnaces
"Pretty In Pink" by The Psychedelic Furs
These songs play at the birthday party

"Castle Of Spirits" by Parvaneh Butterfly & Jonny Franco
The girls sing this at the slumber party

"Slung-Lo" by Erin McKeown
Plays in Anna's store

21.

"Me and Julio Down By The School Yard" by Paul Simon
The Troubadour sings this

"A Whiter Shade Of Pale" by Procol Harum
Plays in the bar

22.

"Amazing Glow" by Joe Pernice

Sang by the first Troubadour

"Perfume" by Sparks
Played by the Troubadour with the keyboardist

"Lost Volvo" by Mary Lynn Rajskub
Sang by the troubadour in front of the diner

"Beanbag Chair" by Yo La Tengo
This plays while Taylor is talking to the postman

"What a Waste" by Sonic Youth
Band plays this in front of the gazebo

"A Beaver Ate My Thumb" by Daniel Palladino
Played by the trio when Taylor is leaving

"Taking Pictures" by Sam Phillips
Sam Phillips performs this as one of the Troubadours

"Don't Sleep on the Subway" by Petula Clark
Plays at Logan's party

"Last Train to Clarksville" by The Monkees
Kirk wonders if Neil Young still sings this song

Season Seven

1.

"We Are the Champions" by Queen
Sookie sings this after winning to Michel in arm wrestling

"Bette Davis" Eyes by Kim Carnes
Lorelai says Logan and Bette Davis both have expressive eyes

2.

"20th Century Girl" by Pizzicato Five
Plays in the background of 'Crazy Asia'

4.

"The Perfect Crime 2" by The Decemberists
Can be heard in the apartment when Rory brings the Olivia and Lucy home

"Funny Face" by Fred Astaire
Plays at the beginning of the film

"'S Wonderful" by Audrey Hepburn & Fred Astaire
Plays at the end of the movie and the end of episode when Lorelai & Christopher kiss.

"Folsom Prison Blues" by Johnny Cash
"Jailhouse Rock" by Elvis Presley
"Chain Gang" by Sam Cooke
Lorelai asks Emily if she wants to listen to any of these songs

"Something Good" from The Sound of Music
Christopher and Lorelai reference this in their conversation

5.

"18 And Life" by Skid Row
Plays in Christopher's car on the way to Friday night dinner

"Who Will Save Your Soul" by Jewel
"Come on Feel The Noize" by Slade
"Songbird" by Kenny G
"Come a Little Bit Closer" by Jay and the Americans
These songs play on the way back from Friday night dinner

6.

"You've Lost That Loving Feeling" by The Righteous Brothers
Kirk sings this

"Living On A Prayer" by Bon Jovi
Sung by an A cappella group at the Yale event

"Zombie Jamboree" by The Kingston Trio
Lorelai says her and Christopher almost ran into an acapella group singing this

7.

"Ce petit coeur" [This Small Heart] by Francoise Hardy
"L'anamour" [The Anamour] by Jane Birkin
These songs play in the background in Paris

"Selling Yourself Short" by What Made Milwaukee Famous
Can be heard when talking to Olivia on the phone.

"You and Me" by Daniel May
Plays when Chris and Lorelai arrive at the restaurant

"What A Time It Was" by Daniel May
Plays in the background during Chris and Lorelai's dinner

"Lullaby" by Johannes Brahm
"Purple Rain" by Prince
Lorelai said she sang these to try and go to sleep

9.

"It's Getting Hot In Herre" by Nelly
Doyle & Paris practice their 2002 dancing

"Work It" by Missy Elliot "
Plays at the party

"Get The Party Started" by Pink
Paris & Doyle dance to this song

"When The Saints Go Marching In" by The Dixieland All Stars
Played by the band during the Knit-a-thon

"Video" by India Arie
Plays while Rory and Marty talked on the couch about how they met

10.

"We Wish You a Merry Christmas"
"Deck the Halls"
These songs play at the end of the fight

"The Joker" by Steve Miller Band
Plays in the bar that Chris is at

11.

"Angels We Have Heard on High"

Christopher sings this around the house

"I'll Be Home For Christmas" by Bing Crosby
Plays while Lorelai finishes the letter and mails it

13.

"Maggie Blues" by Bing and Gary Crosby
Rory plays this for Richard

14.

"My Heart Will Go On" by Celine Dion
Zach plays an acoustic version on his guitar for Chin-Chin's funeral

"Diamond Dogs" by David Bowie
Zach wants to sing this for Chin-Chin's funeral

"My Heart Belongs to Daddy" by Marilyn Monroe
"My Heart Belongs to Me" by Barbra Streisand
"My Heart Belongs to You" by Jim Brickman
"My Heart Stood Still" by Ray Conniff
Lorelai sees all of these chord charts at the music store

"Tears in Heaven" by Eric Clapton
"I Will Always Love You" by Dolly Parton

Zach tries to sing one of these instead of Celine Dion

15.

"Making Noises" by The SqueeGees
TJ plays this in Luke's apartment

"Happy Birthday" by Concrete Blonde
Plays in Logan's apartment

16.

"B-A-B-Y" by Rachel Sweet
"All Fired Up" by Tralala
"Happy Song" by Milkshake
"I Would Go" by Smoosh
These songs all play at Lane's baby shower

"Hush, Little Baby" (Mockingbird song)
Zach sings this

"Mambo Italiano" by Dean Martin
Miss Patty says she will never forget this

17.

"Oh, What A Beautiful Morning" by Rogers & Hammerstein
Emily plays this in her car

"Conscience Clean (I Went to Spain)" by Pernice Brothers
Plays during the dinner with Luke, Zach and Lane

"On the Road Again" by Willie Nelson
Lorelai asks if Emily is Willie Nelson

18.

"My Favourite Letter" by Stephen Lang
Plays in the maze

"Raise the Spirit" by Grant Lee Phillips "
The Troubadour sings this in the maze

19.

"To Go Home" by M. Ward
Plays in the bar

20.

"Boys Don't Cry" by The Cure
Plays when Lane is putting the babies down

"So Long, Farewell" by Rogers & Hammerstein
Babette and Miss Patty sing this when Lorelai leaves the diner

"Friendship" by Judy Garland and Johnny Mercer
"Fever" by Peggy Lee
Miss Patty and Babette sing these at KC's

"Tell Her What She Wants to Know" by Sam Phillips
Plays when Lane and Zach are going to KC's

"Do You Really Want to Hurt Me?" by Culture Club
Kirk sings this at KC's

"I Will Always Love You" by Dolly Parton
Lorelai sings this at KC's

"Jagged Little Pill" by Alanis Morrissette
Lorelai talks about this in the diner

21.

"You're The Top" by Cole Porter
Emily and Richard sing a modified version of this to Rory at her party

"Pomp and Circumstance"
Plays at graduation

"I Will Always Love You" by Whitney Houston
Luke says the song Lorelai sang at KC's was this

22.
"The Neutral" by Sonic Youth
"Pink Steam" by Sonic Youth
These play when Lane and Rory are talking on the porch

"How to Dream" by Sam Phillips
Plays when Rory sleeps

"Celebration" by Kool and the Gang
"ABC" by Jackson 5
Plays at the party

"Inside Out" by Mighty Lemon Drops
Plays when Luke and Lorelai kiss

A Year in the Life

Winter

"Cat's in The Cradle" by Harry Chapin
Lorelai sings this while she complains about Rory only being in town for a day

"Winterglow" by Grant-Lee Phillips
The Troubadour sings this in the town square

"Genius of Love" by Tom Tom Club
Plays while Lorelai and Rory discuss the Brooklyn apartment

"Top Of The World" by The Carpenters
Kirk sings this as he drives

"Time" by Tom Waits
Plays during the Richard's funeral scene

"Bye Bye Blackbird" by Peggy Lee
This song is one of Richard's favorite songs

"Archives" by Louise Goffin
Sung by the busker as Taylor leaves the diner

"I'm The Man" by Joe Jackson
Hep Alien rehearse this

"Valley Winter Song" by Grant-Lee Phillips
The Troubadour plays this

"Here You Come Again" by Dolly Parton
Plays at the end of the episode

"I Dreamed a Dream" by Anne Hathaway
Lorelai says Rory should be singing this with a bad haircut

"Ave Maria" by Franz Schubert
Emily was surprised that Lorelai didn't have a pizza delivered during this

Spring

"William Tell Overture" by St. Olaf Orchestra
"Hiding in The Trees" by Mindcleaner
"Piano Sonata No. 2 in B Minor, Op. 35: III. Marche funèbre: Lento" by Vitalij Margulis
Theme from "Terms of Endearment" by Michael Gore, Arr. Mark Northam
These songs are in Kirk's film

"Takin' Care of Business" by Bachman-Turner Overdrive
Plays while Idea show Luke and Emily a potential location for franchising

"Lonesome Street" by Blur
Plays when Lorelai and Rory are looking for cronuts

"Pick Yourself Up" by Fred Astaire & Ginger Rogers
Plays during Lorelai's movie

"Amazing Grace" in Korean
Mrs. Kim has this performed at her food festival stall

"Ironic" by Alanis Morisette
Lorelai references this in therapy

Summer

"Summer" by Charlotte Hatherley
Plays at the pool

"Bubbles: by The Free Design
Plays while Lorelai and Rory walk around town with parasols

"A Cockeyed Optimist" by Rogers and Hammerstein
Violet sings this when Taylor comes out to praise her

"These Boots Are Made For Walkin'" by Nancy Sinatra
Plays while Rory and Lorelai deliver the Stars Hollow Gazette

"I Feel The Earth Move" by Carole King
Sophie plays this on the piano

"Waterloo" by ABBA
The Stars Hollow Musical ends with this song

"Unbreakable" by Daniel and Amy Sherman-Palladino, Jeanine Tesori
Violet performs this

"Working on Building Stars Hollow" by Daniel and Amy Sherman-Palladino, Jeanine Tesori
"What's There Not To Love About Stars Hollow?" Daniel and Amy Sherman-Palladino, Jeanine Tesori

"Love Revolution" by Daniel Palladino, Jeanine Tesori
The Rap Song by Daniel Palladino
These songs are al in the Stars Hollow Musical

Fall

"With A Little Help From My Friends" by Joe Anderson and Jim Sturgess
Plays during the Life and Death Brigade scene

"Gotango" by Olof Roter
Plays at the tango club

"Botch-A-Me (Ba-Ba-Baciami Piccina)" by Rosemary Clooney
Colin Announces that he has purchased the tango club and that it will only play music by Rosemary Clooney.

"Some People" by Bernadette Peters and William Parry
Emily turns this one and then looks at the brochure

"So Long, Farewell" by Rogers and Hammerstein
Michel sings this to Damon

"Reflecting Light" by Sam Phillips
Lorelai and Luke's wedding song

"Where You Lead" by Carole King
Plays at the end

'Relax" by Frankie Goes to Hollywood
Lorelai has organised a flash mob for the wedding to this song

"Charma Chameleon" by Boy George

Miss Patty is going to swap the flash mob song for this

The Whole Town Should be Medicated

Stars Hollow

The Town of Stars Hollow

Founded in 1779, two different legends seek to explain the naming of Stars Hollow (1.4, 5.18). However the town was settled, it only takes an episode or two of the show before most fans are hooked on this charming small town in New England, with its colorful cast of quirky characters, and the 18th century-style gazebo which marks the center of the town. Johns and Smith argue that Stars Hollow is "the backbone around which the show is built", and Beail even goes so far as to suggest that the town of Stars Hollow "is as important to the narrative as any of the characters or plot devices".[4]

---

[4] Erin K. Johns and Kristin L. Smith, "Welcome to Stars Hollow: Gilmore Girls, Utopia, and the Hyperreal" in *Gilmore Girls and the Politics of Identity: Essays on Family and Feminism in the Television Series*, ed. Calvin, Ritch (Jefferson, North Carolina : McFarland & Company, Inc., 2008), 23.
Linda Beail, "The City, the Suburbs, and Stars Hollow: The Return of the Evening Soap Opera." In *You've Come A Long Way, Baby: Women, Politics, and Popular Culture*, ed. Goren Lilly J., (Kentucky: University Press of Kentucky, 2009), 108.

This small town, packed with annual events and 'To Kill a Mockingbird' style town meetings, is the holy grail for any Gilmore fan. Fans (myself included) have been chasing the 'real' Stars Hollow since they first saw the show. Visiting Washington Depot (the town that inspired Stars Hollow), the set at Warner Bros. Studios, or sitting in gazebos drinking coffee are among favorite activities for those who would rather be in the fictional town, than anywhere else.

Some of the things that make Stars Hollow such a magical place include its history, the warmth of the vibrant, endearing residents, and the charm of the events which give it such a rich, cultural footprint. Each event is put on by the coming together of the townsfolk, who all know each other by name, and who all helped to raise Rory. Like Disneyland, the town lights up for Christmas, holidays, and the change of season, encouraging individuals and business owners to join in on the fun. For a population of less than 10,000, there is certainly a lot to do, and the Gilmore girls never seem to be bored, or lonely. Diffrient calls Stars Hollow "the embodiment of the American Dream" and argues that the town meetings "further mythologize the idyllic American small town". It's no wonder that we continually chase it, and watch Gilmore Girls to have a vicarious experience of it.[5]

---

[5] Diffrient, "Introduction," xxv.

This section contains a directory of the businesses that inhabit Stars Hollow which are marked only by their first appearance. Despite Stern's claim that "Throughout the run of the series, 16 small businesses are identified", this list contains more than 100.[6] This section also contains all of the Stars Hollow events which take place throughout the series. This will be followed by Kirk's resume, which outlines all of Kirk's jobs, tales from the town, and finally, a list of episodes where you can watch town meetings, and watch the town troubadour perform.

The appeal of Stars Hollow is obvious to anyone who has watched more than an episode of *Gilmore Girls*. It is quaint, nostalgic, and seems to abide by its own social, and cultural rules. According to Rawlins, "Stars Hollow provides a utopian sphere where everyone engages in the ceaseless flow of knowledge and exchange of culture, regardless of their socioeconomic status or educational capital."[7] Like so many others, I

---

[6] Danielle M. Stern, "It Takes a Classless, Heteronormative Utopian Village: Gilmore Girls and the Problem of Postfeminism," *The Communication Review*, 15:3, (2012), 172.
[7] Justin Owen Rawlins, "Your Guide to the Girls: Gilmore-isms, Cultural Capital, and a Different Kind of Quality TV." In *Screwball Television: Critical Perspectives on Gilmore Girls*, ed. Diffrient David Scott and Lavery

found myself a Stars Hollow, complete with small diner and town gazebo, where I can go to feel like an honorary Gilmore for the day. For those that are still searching, or who can't make it to a Stars Hollow, hopefully this section will help you to channel some of that nostalgic, Stars Hollow vibe.

David (Syracuse, NY: Syracuse University Press, 2010), 54.

Stars Hollow and Gilmore Girls Business Directory

Al's Pancake World (1.2)
Antonioli's Restaurant and Pizzeria (1.8)
Baco's: Sporting Good Store (AYITL: Summer)
Birch Grove Spa (2.16)
Beat Records (7.5)
Black, White, and Read Bookshop/Theatre (1.8)
Bootsy's Newsstand (2.1)
Buff Rite Inc. (5.18)
Butchery (5.1)
Café Coffee (5.17)
CBGB (4.11)
Chez Zinjustin (7.6)
Chilton Academy (2.2)
Churchogogue (1.15)
Cider Mill (5.2)
China Garden (4.9)
Colonial Museum (5.9)
Dante's inferno (3.21)
Damen's (6.5)
Dell's Bar (6.19)
Doose's Market (1.2)
Dragonfly Inn (1.19)
Dynasty Makers (AYITL: Winter)

Eastside Dental (AYITL: Summer)
Fair Game Video and Arcade (4.15)
Farmer's Market (2.17)
Ferme (7.7)
First National Bank (2.11)
Fred's Dry Cleaning (6.8)
Gabby's Flower Shop (1.8)
Gallery (1.20)
Gelston House (1.2)
Goodwill (6.6)
Groove Yard Music (5.17)
Gypsy's Garage / Hewes Brothers (1.17)
Hair Salon (5.17)
Halfway House Café (AYITL: Fall)
Harry's Bar (7.7)
Harry's House of Twinkle Lights (2.17)
Hockey Rink (2.15)
Homeless Pets on the Net (1.11, 6.2)
Household (1.18)
Hungry Diner (2.20)
Independence Inn (1.1)
Jackson's Produce (1.2)
Jojo's Burgers (5.5)
John Skinner Medical Centre (7.13)
KC's Tavern Bar and Grill (1.8)
Kim's Antiques (1.1)
Kirk's Diner (7.2)
Kirk's Doggy Daycare (6.8)
Kirk's Pedi Cab (4.17)
Kirsten's (5.14)
L'Aprge (7.7)

Le Chat Club (1.20)
Lena's Stationery (5.2)
Lila's Café (7.9)
Lisa's Beauty Parlor (6.6)
Luger's Bait and Tackle (6.8)
Luke's Diner / William's Hardware (1.1)
Madison House (6.18)
Malin DSL (1.2)
Mailboxes, Etc. (4.19)
Marry Mimi's Bridal Shop (2.2)
Mediterranean Delight (4.15)
Miniature Golf (6.6)
Miss Patty's Dance School (1.1)
Momo's Tyres (AYITL: Winter)
Mongolian Grill (4.15)
Museum of Rocks that Look Like Famous People (6.6)
Muskie's (1.1)
Nancy's Cottage of Calico (3.9)
No Fish Today (1.5)
Old Place Gambling Hall (6.6)
Once Upon a Bookstore (1.8)
Ooober (AYITL: Winter)
Paris Fashions (1.1)
Posey's (AYITL: Winter)
Post Office (1.11)
Pretty Pastures (AYITL: Fall)
Quest Copying (6.17)
Radio Shack (4.15)
Record Breaker (2.5)
Renaissance Fair (5.1)

Recycling Centre (1.17)
Rich Man's Show Bar and Grill (6.14)
Sally's Florist (4.18)
Salvation Army (6.6)
Samantha Leigh's Bakery (1.8)
Samuel Mudson's Apothecary (6.6)
Sandeep's (2.16)
Sandee Says (AYITL: Spring)
Sears (4.15)
Seaspray Motel (4.17)
Sophie's Music (2.20)
Something Old, Something New Bridal Shop (6.11)
Sniffy's Tavern (5.3)
Stamford Eagle Gazette (5.19)
Stars Hollow Animal Hospital (1.5)
Stars Hollow Bank (1.5)
Stars Hollow Baby (7.16)
Stars Hollow Beauty Supply (3.4)
Stars Hollow Books (1.15)
Stars Hollow Chamber of Commerce (AYITL: Summer)
Stars Hollow City Council (1.16)
Stars Hollow Dairy (6.22)
Stars Hollow Elementary School (2.17)
Stars Hollow Fire Department (1.21)
Stars Hollow Gazette (4.3)
Stars Hollow High School (1.1)
Stars Hollow Library (2.15)
Stars Hollow Middle School (6.8)
Stars Hollow Municipal Pool (AYITL: Summer)

Stars Hollow Museum (5.18)
Stars Hollow Party Supply (5.15)
Stars Hollow Pharmacy (5.02)
Stars Hollow Security (4.4)
Stars Hollow Shoe Repair (5.10)
Stars Hollow Swimming Pool (AYITL: Summer)
Stars Hollow Retirement Home
Stars Hollow Video (2.12)
Stars Hollow Visitor Center (6.6)
Suddaby's (6.6)
Taco Barn (4.9)
Taylor Doose's Old-Fashioned Soda Shoppe and Candy Store (3.3)
Teriyaki Joe's (1.19)
Teriyaki Tokyo (4.15)
Tilman Farm (7.6)
The Autobody Shop (1.21)
The Binser Corp (6.6)
The Cheshire Cat (2.4)
The Linen Closet (7.2)
The Hartford Courant (7.4)
The Chimney Sweep (6.19)
The Good Neighbor Pharmacy (1.5)
The King's Head Inn (AYITL: Fall)
The Learning Center (3.11)
The Radio Station (5.16)
The Road Crew (5.16)
The Secret Bar (AYITL: Spring)
Tricky's Dry Cleaners (2.10)
Truncheon Books (6.18)
Vintage Clothing (1.20)

Walmart (3.17)
West Hills Market (4.9)
Weston's Bakery (1.1)
Winkie's Restaurant (7.17)
Yale Bookstore (4.19)
Yale University (4.2)
Yummy Bartenders (6.19)

According to Luke, Stars Hollow also has "twelve stores... devoted entirely to peddling porcelain unicorns" (2.5)

Stars Hollow Town Event Guide

Arbor Day Festival (2.17)
Book Club (5.16)
Buy A Book Fundraiser (2.15, AYITL: Spring)
Charity Rummage Sale (1.13)
Christmas Caroling (1.10)
Connecticut Bike Race (5.22, 6.1)
Com Com Boom (AYITL: Spring)
Cornucopia Can Drive (1.7)
Easter Egg Hunt (4.18)
Edgar Allen Poe Society 'Readings of Poe' (3.17)
End of Summer Madness Festival (3.1, AYITL: Summer)
First Annual Stars Hollow Gay Pride Parade (AYITL: Spring)
Harvest Festival (AYITL: Fall)
Hay Bale Maze (7.18)
Hayride (1.1)
Hodges Sports Club (AYITL: Spring)
Kirk in a Box (7.21)
Miss Patty's Grand Recital (6.5)
Monique Ashwell Bakery (AYITL: Spring)
Movie Night In The Square (2.19)
Snowman Contest (2.10)

Spring Fling Festival (7.18)
Stars Hollow Autumn Festival (2.8, 3.9)
Stars Hollow Bid-On-A-Basket Festival (2.13)
Stars Hollow High Pep Rally (2.11)
Stars Hollow Spring International Food Festival (AYITL: Spring)
Stars Hollow Winter Carnival (3.10)
Stars Hollow Winter Festival (2.10, AYITL: Winter)
Tennessee Williams Lookalike Competition (3.7)
The 24-Hour Annual Dance Marathon (3.7)
The Annual Stars Hollow Founders Firelight Festival (1.16, 4.13)
The Christmas Pageant (1.10)
The Festival of Living Art/Pictures (4.7)
Stars Hollow Loves Pasquale Day (4.20)
The Old Muddy River Bridge Knitathon (7.9)
The Revolutionary War Reenactment (1.8, 5.11)
The Stars Hollow Musical (AYITL: Summer)
Wicca Convention (6.18)

Stars Hollow Winter Carnival

Includes:
Crazy Psychic From Woodbury
Ice Bowling
Throw a Snowball at a Band Geek
Homemade Desserts
Popcorn
Sno Cones
Icicle Ring Toss
Pretzels
Hot Cider
Milk Bottle Toss
Sponsor a Letter
Cotton Candy
Funnel Cakes
Tarot Card Readings
Hot Dogs
The Amazing Doggy Swami
Fresh Pastries
Warm Glogg
Polar Petting Zoo

(3.10, 6.12, AYITL: Winter)

Stars Hollow Spring International Food Festival

Includes:

Swedish Meatballs
Peruvian Salted Papas
Indonesian Rice Porridge
Korean Food
- Galbi
- Bibimbap
- Bulgogi
- Sikhye

Spanish
- Sangria
- Paella

AYITL: Spring

Kirk's Jobs

Any *Gilmore Girls* fan will tell you that while we love Lorelai and Rory, it is the unusual cast of townsfolk that make the show what it is. Of these characters, there is one, in particular, whose awkward nature and one-of-a-kind personality, has won us over. He is the "Ubiquitous juggler of odd jobs".[8]

This character is not only unique, but is one of Stars Hollow's most peculiar residents because of his dedicated work ethic and his ability to acquire the extraordinary amount of jobs he has had over the course of the show.

Kirk's jobs have become one of the iconic features of *Gilmore Girls* and is deserving of a list of its own. Over the course of seven seasons and *A Year in the Life*, we saw Kirk working at more than 50 different jobs, and trying to acquire several more, "despite his obvious inability to keep a job and his general weirdness".[9] Stars

---

[8] David Scott Diffrient, "Introduction: "You're about to Be Gilmored"." In *Screwball Television: Critical Perspectives on Gilmore Girls*, edited by Diffrient David Scott and Lavery David, Xv-Xxxvi. New York: Syracuse University Press, 2010. Xxxv.

[9] Sara Morrison, "Your Guide to the Real Stars Hollow Business World," in *Coffee at Luke's: An Unauthorised*

Hollow's most colorful character, Kirk (or Mick, as he also goes by), is known for being the most employed resident of Stars Hollow.

Kirk works so much, that toward the end of season five, he claims to have had 15,000 jobs and saved almost $0.25 million. In this same episode, Kirk also tells us that he has been working for 11 years. This means Kirk held down an average of 3.74 jobs <u>per day</u> up until this moment. While 15,000 jobs seems a bit excessive, Kirk's jobs form an integral part of his identity.

However, Kirk's career is far more mysterious than a number game. The ambiguity around Kirk's work history remains, with so many questions left unanswered. Does Kirk have a closet with all of his old work uniforms in it? Does he keep getting fired from these jobs, or does he quit? Does he file his own taxes? While you might expect Kirk to be settled into a job in his 40s, *A Year in the Life* also showed him moving from job to job, in true Kirk-style.

When Kirk isn't dressed up as a hot dog, delivering swans, making a film or driving a pedicab, he is actively pursuing new roles, usually in an unorthodox manner. He has crashed

---

Gilmore Girls Gabfest, ed. Jennifer Cruise, Leah Wilson (Dallas: BenBella Books, 2007), 86.

Lorelai's staff meeting, run a real estate business out of a condemned building, and offered to jump out of a plane, all in the name of building his resume and earning some cash. The following lists all of the jobs that Kirk has held, as well as the jobs he attempted to land, but failed.

Kirk Gleason
Resume

- DSL Installer (1:2)
- Swan Delivery Man (1:3)
- Assistant Manager, Doose's Market (1:5, 4:21)
- Daisy Delivery Man (1:21)
- Coordinator, Max and Lorelai's Engagement Party (2:2)
- Photographer, Historic First Street Walk (2:3)
- Mechanic (2:7)
- Actor, Bracebridge dinner (2:10)
- Termite inspector (2:11)
- Video Store Attendant (2:12)
- Independent Filmmaker (2:19)
- Skincare Salesman, Hay There Product Line (3:1)
- Photo Delivery Man (3:2)
- Spy for Town Selectman Taylor Doose (3:3)
- Server, Weston's Bakery (3:10)
- Shop Assistant, Beauty Shop (3:12, 4:1)
- Director, Miss Patty's Show (3:14)
- Announcer, Stars Hollow Hockey Game (3:15)
- Mailman (3:16)
- T-shirt Designer and Salesman (3:17)

- Moving Assistant, World's Largest Pizza (3:18)
- Mold inspector (3:22)
- Security Alarm Installer (4:4)
- Mailbox salesman (4:6)
- Planner, Firelight Festival (4:13)
- Dog Walker (4:15, 6:8)
- Pedicab Driver (4:17)
- Planner, Stars Hollow Annual Easter Egg Hunt (4:18)
- Clerk, Mailboxes Etc. (4:19)
- DJ, Liz and TJ's Wedding (4:21)
- Firewood Delivery Man (4:22)
- Poller, Town Selectman campaign (5:4)
- Movie Theater Attendant, Black, White and Read Bookstore (5:5, 5:14)
- Flyer Distribution, Dragonfly Inn (5:6)
- Salesman, Bath and Shower Adhesive (5:10)
- Town Ribbon Collector (5:17)
- Souvenir Salesman, Old Man Twickham (5:18)
- Tow Truck Operator (5:22)
- Ring Salesman (6:1)
- Physical Therapist (6:1)
- Representative, Board of Tourism (6:6)
- Coordinator, Winter Carnival (6:12)
- Sample Distributor, Taylor's Olde Fashion Soda Shoppe (6:13)
- Realtor (6:17)
- Owner, Yummy Bartenders (6:19)

- Home Movie Setup, April's Birthday Party (6:20)
- Driver, Stars Hollow's First Stop Light (7:1)
- Owner/Operator, Yummy Bartenders (7:2)
- Owner / Operator, Kirk's Diner (7:3)
- Organizer, Knit-a-thon (7:9)
- Wrapping paper Salesman (7:10)
- Flower Delivery Man (7:14)
- Minotaur, Stars Hollow Town Meeting (7:18)
- Maze Guard, Hay Bale Maze (7:18)
- Stars Hollow Town Sash Maker (7:22)
- Ooo-ber Driver (AYITL, Winter)
- Wedding Planner, Luke and Lorelai's Wedding (AYITL, Fall)
- Glogg Seller (AYITL: Spring)

Attempted

- Photographer, Lorelai and Max's Wedding (2:3)
- Shop Assistant, Sophie's Music Shop (2:20)
- Manager, Taylor's Olde Fashioned Soda Shoppe (3:3)
- Shop Assistant, Luke's Skateboard and Bottle Shop (3:3)
- Skydiver, Taylor's Olde Fashion Soda Shoppe (4:1)

- Kitchen staff, Dragonfly Inn (5:12)
- Receptionist, Dragonfly Inn (5:12)
- Manager, Luke's Diner (6:18)

The Story of Stars Hollow
(1.16)

This, boys and girls, is the story of true love. A beautiful girl from one county; a handsome boy from another. They meet and they fall in love. Separated by distance and by parents who did not approve of the union, the young couple dreamed of a day that they could be together. They wrote each other beautiful letters. Letters of longing and passion. Letters full of promises and plans for the future. Soon the separation proved too much for either one of them to bear. So, one night, cold and black with no light to guide them, they both snuck out of their homes and ran away as fast as they could. It was so dark out that they were both soon lost and it seemed as if they would never find each other. Finally, the girl dropped to her knees, tears streaming down her lovely face. "Oh, my love. Where are you? How will I find you?" Suddenly, a band of stars appeared in the sky. These stars shone so brightly they lit up the entire countryside. The girl jumped to her feet and followed the path of the stars until finally she found herself standing right where the town gazebo is today. And there waiting for her was her one true love, who had also been led here by the blanket of friendly stars. And that, my friends, is the story of how Stars Hollow came to be, and why we celebrate that fateful night every year at about this time.

The Story of Faye Wellington and Art Brush
(5.3)

Faye owned a flower shop and Art owned a candy store and they fell madly in love about ten years ago. Big romance! And for a while it all worked very synergistically - flowers and candy seemed like a perfect match. Until Art met Margie - the fudge queen. The whole town split - right down the middle. Suddenly, you could buy flowers, or you could buy candy. Valentine's day was a nightmare. Eventually, the hostility forced Art to move. Faye never married. She stopped making candy. It was very sad. And those storefronts were empty for a year. Noone wanted to be there.

We think Faye still lives in the caves above the Clancy's Mill. We can't prove it, but every so often we hear Delta Dawn playing over and over.

Sniffy's Tavern: A Story of Love
(5.3)

Maisy Fortner and Bertram 'Buddy' Linds met at a high school basketball game. She was playing, he was not. They fell in love, got married. Buddy went to work at a dairy and Maisy worked at the school, but they dreamed to someday own a restaurant so that all their friends and family could come and eat, and visit and laugh with them every single day. One day—Sniffy—their beloved dog, ran away. Maisy and Buddy searched high and low for him. Finally, they stumbled past a dilapidated old tavern that had been boarded up for years. They heard a dog howling. They forced open the door and there was Sniffy, stuck under a fallen beam. Maisy and Buddy pulled Sniffy free and rushed him to the vet where he immediately went into emergency surgery. Four hours later...Sniffy was dead.

Who Has Your Mail?
(4.4)

Lorelai and Rory Gilmore -----------> Miss Patty/Gypsy
Babette --------------------------------> Andrew
Norma ----------------------------------> The Deli
Taylor ----------------------------------> ?
Andrew ---------------------------------> Gypsy
Gypsy ----------------------------------> Lorelai and Rory
Al ---------------------------------------> Lorelai and Rory

The Battle of Stars Hollow
(5.11)

The year – 1779.

The location – Stars Hollow.

Fortune turning point when our brave town militia learned that a powerful British general was riding through the area to rejoin his troops and wage a decisive battle. It inspired an idea.

First, the militia went off to block the high road.

The British general had no choice but to take the only path or road on this snowy day. The road through Stars Hollow.

Soon a scout arrived to warn of the general's coming.

And then the general arrived.

Then a brave woman put herself in harm's way and emerged to distract the general.

This simple, common woman whose livelihood defied laws of morality but acting in a fashion which God would forgive her, led the British general to the warmth of her boudoir. She saved Stars Hollow.

The British general was kept occupied long enough for Lafayette's troops to ambush his men – a decisive victory for the colonists.

Stars Hollow Liberty Bell
(2.20)

The bell at Stars Hollow was cast in 1780 to celebrate the first anniversary of the town. The bell cracked the first time it was rung and weighed 2080 pounds. The strike of the bell is E-flat. On June 6, 1944, when Allied forces landed in France, the sound of the bell was broadcast to all parts of the country.

Stars Hollow vs. Jess Mariano
(2.8)

- Stole the "Save the Bridge" money
- Stole Pierpont from Babette's garden
- Hooted on of Miss Patty's dance classes
- Took a garden hose from Fran's yard
- Set off the fire alarm at Stars Hollow High
- Controls the weather
- Wrote the screenplay to *Glitter*

Stars Hollow Specials

Troubadour Episodes

1.16, 1.18, 1.21
2.2, 2.8, 2.11, 2.17
3.3, 3.21
4.13, 4.22
6.21
7.18
AYITL: Winter

Town Meetings

1.8, 1.21
2.8, 2.17
3.3, 3.6, 3.22
4.4, 4.7
5.3, 5.4, 5.9
6.6, 6.12
7.5, 7.18 , 7.21, 7.22
AYITL: Spring, Summer

It takes years of training to eat the way we do

Eating Like a Gilmore

Food in Gilmore Girls

As we have seen already, there is a lot to love about *Gilmore Girls*, and a lot of lists to work through, if you want to live a life that is steeped in the Gilmore and Stars Hollow world. Having read, watched, and listened to everything that you can, it is now time to turn your focus to food, and the girls certainly worked their way through a lot of it.

With a mother who either cannot cook, or doesn't care to (it is likely a combination of both), the girls had to survive on vending machine burritos, instant mac and cheese, and Pop Tarts. This unrealistic diet of Lorelai and Rory's is arguably one of the most controversial and questioned themes of the show. Diffrient points out that "the Pop-Tart-popping protagonists are able to be gluttonous without ever having to cope with the consequences of uninhibited eating".[10] How can they eat like that, and stay in such great shape? Apparently, doctors call it "The Lorelai Paradox" (5.17). This, of course, has been attributed to the

---

[10] Diffrient, "Introduction," xxx.

fact that "although food tends to be abundant, characters are rarely shown eating it."[11]

Even one watch through of the show will reveal that a few key foods create the backdrop for many of the events which take place in the girls' lives. Chinese food is ordered the night that Lorelai has a fight at her house with her father (2.12), and cherry danishes mark the severity of the rift between Lorelai and Luke (2.5). Burgers and fries at Luke's often come before, or after, significant events in the lives of Lorelai and Rory, and if the lettuce in the burger left it's essence behind, then they consider themselves as practically having eaten a salad. Lorelai even cites the humble Pop Tart as the key to her emancipation from her parents, stating that her first one tasted like "freedom and rebellion and independence"(7.3). In the same way, pizza has been through it all with the *Gilmore girls*, including break-ups, 'wallowing', birthdays, first dates, and the Lorelais' first night at college.

While their everyday eating habits consist of these junk-food staples, there are also special occasions which require a bit more thought.

---

[11] Susannah B. Mintz and Leah E. Mintz, "Pass the Pop-Tarts: The Gilmore Girls' Perpetual Hunger." In *Screwball Television: Critical Perspectives on Gilmore Girls*, ed. Diffrient David Scott and Lavery David (Syracuse, NY: Syracuse University Press, 2010), 236.

Thanksgiving consists of four turkey dinners, and movie nights (especially classics like *Willy Wonka*, cannot be undertaken without "massive amounts of junk food" (1.7). Red Vines, marshmallows, jelly beans, peanut butter, and cookie dough are all essentials for a Gilmore night in. In the spirit of living like *Gilmore Girls*, many fans have taken to preparing for re-watches, and watch parties in the same way. Pinterest features many pictures of table spreads which would make the girls' proud.

Of course, no other food element comes close to being as impacting, or as important, to the girls as coffee. Lorelai is on her sixth cup of the day when we meet her in the pilot, and the drink becomes so ubiquitous (is that the word?) as the series goes on, that it could almost be considered a character in itself. Max and Lorelai start dating, and break up, over coffee (1.5, 1.11), Rory has a mental breakdown when she can't visit the coffee cart at Yale anymore (6.11), and Luke waits patiently in the background of Lorelai's life with a coffee pot in hand, hoping she will realize that they belong together.

This section starts with a list of what I have called the "Quintessential Gilmore Foods". This is a quick list of the foods that we have come to know, and to associate with *Gilmore Girls* and Stars Hollow. From 'the devil's starchy fingers' to pudding, this list will sum up the Gilmore eating experience. Some of these foods may only have been eaten, or referenced once, but true fans will understand the significance of them. This is followed by a list of everything that the girls eat throughout the show. Finally, is a selection of menu's that include all of the food items that are eaten on the show, at places like Luke's, the Inn, and Friday night dinners, cataloguing the rest of the foods eaten, or referred to in the show.

So, go forth and live the Gilmore dream by eating like one. Because, like any true Gilmore girl, my philosophy is that If eating cake is wrong, I don't want to be right.[12]

---

[12] *Gilmore Girls,* 2.3

Quintessential Gilmore Foods

- Coffee (bonus if it's in an I.V.)
- Pizza
- Mallomars
- Red Vines
- Milk Duds
- Pudding
- Cake
- Indian Food
- Chinese Food
- Tacos
- Burritos
- Mashed Banana on Toast
- Mac and Cheese
- Cherry Danish
- Fries (the devil's starchy fingers)
- Burgers
- Ice cream
- Donuts
- Pop Tarts
- Hamburger Helper
- Pie
- Pancakes
- Santa burger

- Zima
- Desert Sushi

Season One

1.
Coffee
Sugar, dairy and wheat free muffins and tea
White wine
Salad
Orange juice
Cheeseburgers and fries
Champagne, lamb, potatoes, red wine (and beets?)
Chilli fries

2.
Rediwhip
Coffee
Peach
Pizza

3.
Red wine and cassoulet
Coffee
Iced tea and rolls
Cheeseburger
Chocolate cake
Blueberry shortcake
White wine

4.
Coffee
Pie

5.
Steak and green beans
Coffee
Apple
Punch
Burger, fries and salad
Iced Tea?

6.
Red wine
Pudding
Apple
Coffee
Birthday cake
Shirley Temple (black)
Shirley Temple
Rory-face birthday cake

7.
Coffee and muffins
Leftover Chinese
Marshmallows, jellybeans, chocolate kisses,
cookie dough, peanut butter, sugar stick with dip,
Red Vines
Pizza
Popcorn and spray cheese

8.
Hot dogs and soda
Rocky road cookies
Pizza with extra parmesan
Coffee
Soda

9.
Salad with avocado, rolls
Tacos with hot sauce, burritos
Mashed banana on toast
Coffee

10.
Coffee
Bagged lettuce with ranch dressing
Santa burger
Chicken, carrots, mashed potatoes, rolls

11.
Osso Buco
Squab, peas, and white wine
Coffee
Tea
Soda
French fries
Pizza
Chicken, peas, mashed potatoes

12.
Coffee
Pop Tarts
Rolls
Martini

13.
Coffee
Pop Tarts

14.
Pepperoni Pizza and Salad
Bordeaux wine, potato dish and bread
Beer
Ritz crackers with Easy Cheese, steak, green beans, mashed potatoes, and "lime fantasy supreme" (green Jell-O and cool whip)
Three-egg omelette, goat cheese, and pancetta
Coffee
Candy
Chinese
Fruit from Doose's to ward off scurvy

15.
Coffee
Pie
Martini's and soda
Asparagus and potatoes
Brown Liquor

16.
Coffee
Hamburger Helper
Red wine
Gin
Three different types of pasta, and a meatball to go
Pot roast and carrots
Tea and chocolate cake

17.
Coffee
Chocolate chip pancakes, extra heavy on the chocolate with whipped cream on top
Cheese and pepperoni pizza with extra parmesan
French soda
Chocolate chip cookie dough ice cream
Pizza

18.
Carrots (and something green)
White wine, cheese, spiced nuts
Carrots, green beans, meat
Coffee
Clown-shaped doughnuts
Frozen chocolate cake
Rabbit (and something orange)
Brandy

19.
Artichokes, salad, rolls (and mashed potatoes?)
French toast with bacon, extra crispy
Pancakes with two eggs over easy
Coffee
Orange muffin with cinnamon glaze
A raspberry
Raspberry jam
Popcorn
Cake
Pie, ice cream with hot fudge

20.
Coffee
Sugar-cinnamon pretzels
Eggs
A lamb sandwich
Strudel
Pizza

21.
Cornflakes and milk
Fries
Vanilla wafers with seltzer water
Chocolate-covered espresso beans
Ring Pops
Hot dogs and fries

Season Two

1.
Blueberry muffins
Coffee
Roqufort puffs
Salad
Tater Tots, chicken fingers
White wine and soda
Beefaroni and Twinkies

2.
Salad with "lemony" dressing
Coffee
Entrée that looks like a tiny hat
Martinis
Assorted pastries

3.
Sample wedding cakes - mocha-crunch cream
and raspberry
Carrots
Garlic bread and something else made by Max
Chocolate cake
Coffee
Blueberry pancakes
Steak and baked potatoes
Ice cream cones

Shirley Temple and Long Island Ice Tea
Mixed nuts

4.
Fuzzy Certs
Scones
Coffee
Burgers
Ice cream

5.
Eggs
Doughnuts (chocolate, cinnamon, and sprinkles)
Coffee
Pot Roast, four different kinds of salad, chicken wings, mashed potatoes, grilled cheese, and garlic bread
Cherry Danishes

6.
Pancakes, and French toast
Coffee
Kung Pao chicken and egg rolls
Martinis
Burgers and fries

7.
Coffee
Muffins
Diet Coke

Sandwich, broccoli, fruit salad, and soda
Grilled corn, peppers, rolls, salad
Cake and tea

8.
A meal by Emily's new cook (corn, salad, potatoes?)
Coffee
Raspberry cake, a rum ball
A cupcake
Eggs, sausage, toast, fruit salad

9.
Burrito
Coffee
Burgers, salad and fries

10.
Rolls, roast chicken, rice, green beans
Coffee
Soup, salad

11.
Coffee
Soda, sandwich
Salad, mixed fruit
Chips
Ice cream
White wine

12.
White wine, Coke
Red wine, rolls, carrots, green beans, potato, rice
Coffee, grapefruit, banana pancakes with a side of bacon
Chinese – egg foo young, garlic chicken

13.
Homemade granola, wheatgrass juice, soy, chicken taco's
Meatball hero's, chips
Four types of pesto, three desserts, edible pretzel with goat cheese filling, Pineapple cranberry chutney
Stale Pop Tarts and a Slim Jim
Pizza
Coffee, burgers

14.
Popcorn, chips
Apple juice, leftover Halloween Candy
Toast, cereal with fruit
Coffee

15.
Pancakes with a side of pancakes
Ice Cream and Reddi-whip
Egg rolls, garlic chicken, kung pao chicken, Szechwan chicken, chicken in brown sauce

16.
Coffee
Cucumber water
Indian takeout
Fries, mac and cheese, salad
Peanuts, shrimp cocktail, vodka martinis, steak
Ice cream

17.
Mushroom soup
Eggs on toast
Scrambled eggs on toast
Hamburger, strawberry ice cream with chocolate sauce
Coffee with cream and sugar

18.
Pot roast, potatoes, salad, and bread
Chocolate
Omelette with jack cheese
French toast
Rolls

19.
Some sort of berry mixture
Marshmallows
Six Pop Tarts, bagel dogs, Cheese Nip
Brownies
Broccoli?

A biscuit
Pie
Coffee
Ice cream cones

20.
Coffee
White wine
A peach
Soda
Cheeseburger
Perrier and champagne
A doughnut

21.
Scrambled eggs, bacon, toast, coffee, and fruit salad
A scone and tea
Margaritas
Graduation cake, filled with two pounds of crushed chocolate-covered espresso beans
Hot Dogs

22.
White wine and coke
Salad and rolls
Eggs, toast, and fruit

Pancakes
Coffee
Chocolate doughnut, doughnut with sprinkles
A Jordan almond
Icing
Tiki drink

Season Three

1.
Bacon, eggs, pancakes, and coffee
Kosher bacon
White wine
A doughnut

2.
Pancakes, fried eggs, side of bacon
Chicken-noodle soup with a side of mashed potatoes
Coffee
Rice Krispies, marshmallows, and milk in a bowl
Raspberries
Cheeseburger, fries, onion rings, and a cherry coke
White wine
Mac and cheese, Tater Tots, pizza rolls, chilli bean soup, cake

3.
Soda
Coffee, pancakes, bacon
Scotch
Doughnuts
Iced tea
Potatoes, chicken, rolls
Water

4.
Hamburgers
Rice Krispies

5.
Coffee
Pizza and cheesy bread
Merlot, pork, potatoes, rolls
Something unidentifiable at Luke's
Soda, white wine, and cheese

6.
Ice cream
Mojitos
Potato salad
Cake

7.
Coffee
Pancakes and bacon
Chicken, asparagus, rolls, and white wine
Pizza and coke
Faux egg-salad sandwiches

8.
Doughnuts
Coffee
Chocolate
Coke

"Sand dabs"
Burger and fries
Tacos

9.
A pop tart
French dip with extra fries
Cherry pie
Tofurkey
Turkey, stuffing, mashed potatoes rolls, vegetables
Martini
Salad
Coffee
Rolls

10.
Pizza
Coffee
Blueberries
Unidentifiable snack in a foil container

11.
Wine
Coffee
International grab-bags
A sandwich, chips, and soda

12.
Peas, carrots, mashed potatoes (and chicken?)
Coffee and doughnuts

13.
Scotch
Coffee
Martini
Roast, rolls, carrots
A sandwich

14.
Steamed spinach, rolls, (stuffing?) poultry, and white wine
Coffee
Chips, pretzels, melba toast, and bagel bites
Salad and prime rib
"One of everything" at Al's

15.
Coffee
Rolls, pork, peas, potatoes, and pie
Jack omelette with bacon on the side
Blueberry muffin
Hot dogs
Chinese food

16.
A KitKat

Coffee
Martini
Pizza

17.
Coffee

18.
Johnny Marzetti IV
Bagels
Chocolate cake with individual vanilla cupcakes on top
"The world's biggest pizza...almost"
Coffee
A gigantic bowl of macaroni and cheese
Chocolate milk
Another large cake

19.
Coffee

20.
Coffee
Pancakes, bacon, fruit salad, orange juice

21.
Cherry pie
Coffee
Pop-Tart, orange juice

Soup, salad, pizza, and ice cream with rainbow sprinkles

Season Four

1.
Cocoa
Biscotti
Coffee
Rolls, chicken, cheese plate, soufflé

2.
Sausage wrapped in a pancake wrapped in bacon
Balinese, Singaporean, German, Chinese, Japanese, Indian, Mexican, and pizza
Ice cream
Coffee

3.
Marshmallow cookies
Muffins
Coffee
Fries
Tortilla chips

4.
Coffee
Fries
Ice cream – Butter brittle crunch and chocolate chocolate chocolate

5.
A waffle and hash browns
Pizzas
Coffee
Fries, pumpkin pie, whipped cream, a burger with double cheese, Chinese food, beer
Meringue cookies

6.
Potatoes, carrots, roast, rolls, red wine, and mini lemon bundt cakes
Broccoli tarts

7.
Burgers with mustard and fries
Coffee

8.
Broccoli, white wine, rice (and salmon?)
A coffee mint
Coffee
Lobster Thermidor

9.
Pumpkin Pancakes with homemade cinnamon butter
Coffee
Salad, bread, Coke
Potatoes, roast, roll, red wine

Cheese omelette (extra cheddar, no jack), two bacons, two sausages, sourdough toast
Rye toast
Fig Newtons
Alcohol from the "fun flask"
Bloody Mary's
Mac and cheese, Pringles, and chip dip

10.

A pizzelle and earl grey tea
Rolls and something else unidentifiable
Marzipan
Pizza
Coffee, orange juice, scrambled eggs, bacon
Carrots, beef, rolls, red wine, salad

11.

Coffee, a muffin, and onion rings
A doughnut
Mashed potatoes, meatloaf, and corn
Pie

12.

Coffee
Muffin
A Coke, salad, macaroni and cheese, green beans
A martini
Hot chocolates

13.
Coffee and Pop Tarts
Cherry Danish
Hot cocoa
"Possibly beef in some sort of cream sauce"

15.
Coffee
Pretzels
Mexican, Moroccan, sweet and sour pork, corn dogs, pizza, a McDonald's burger and fries, fried cheese, "some wrap thing", soda, iced tea, Orange Julius, root beer
Coffee
Pie

16.
Escargot, white wine, bread
"something with cheese!"
Coffee
Martini
A soda

17.
Fruit loops
Coffee
French toast, bacon and syrup
Pizza, Lay's potato chips, Pepsi
Chips

18.
Rolls, potatoes, meat, salad
Cheesecake and coffee
Brandy
Vodka

19.
Coffee and cherry Danish
Martini
Soda
Pastry

20.
Coffee
Barbecue sandwiches, marshmallows, Twizzlers, Nutter Butters, pizza, chips
Chicken chow mein, Pop Tarts, carrot sticks

21.
Salad, chicken Kiev, salad, white wine, rolls
"Funky monkey"
Mixed plate of wedding food - grapes and corn
Beer

22.
Mac and cheese
Coffee

Duck, rolls, red wine, fruit and ice cream
Bread and salad

Season Five

1.
Iced tea
Bread

2.
Coffee and a doughnut
A triple espresso
Soda
Root beer
Potato chips, pizza with steak sauce, Chinese

3.
Martinis, coke, Hungarian cheese
Fennel-potato soup with a touch of chilli, rolls, white wine
Scrambled eggs with cheddar cheese, a side of half bacon, half sausage and a side of fruit for both
Coffee
Champagne
Marshmallows
Unidentifiable drink

4.
Eggs, bacon, blintzes, coffee

Tomato

5.
Peas, chicken, rice, and coffee
Boysenberry pie with ice cream, hot-fudge sundae, grapefruit
Chili burgers, fries, popcorn, soda
Beer

6.
Coffee
Nachos and a slushie
Pizza

7.
Vodka martinis
Unidentifiable dish at Emily's
Champagne

8.
Meat skewers
Martini and soda
Carrots, bread, potatoes, chicken, salad, white wine
Blueberry muffin and coffee
Chicken, carrots, peas
Sandwiches -Chicken salad, tuna salad, ham, something grey
Chips and soda
Lamb and artichoke stew, penne with pesto and

potatoes, roasted garlic with rosemary focaccia, tomatoes stuffed with breadcrumbs and goat cheese, ricotta cheesecake, amaretto cookies, and coffee
Wine
Baby carrot
Champagne

9.
Fruit salad?
Unidentified hor d'oeuvres
Soda
Frozen pizza with cheese in the crust
Scotch neat
Wine, bread, and pork chops brined in a salt water-bourbon solution
Coffee and pie
Potato chips
Popcorn

10.
Pie and brownies
Caviar
Coffee

11.
Coffee
A martini and a soda
Milk and cookies
Tequila

12.
Coffee
Toblerone
Champagne

13.
Doughnuts and Coffee
Pancakes, pop tarts, marshmallows, Tater Tots and a pizza tower
Potstickers
Rum and coke
Unidentified alcohol
Champagne

14.
Fruit Loops, Chex, Captain Crunch
Tollhouse cookie dough, chocolate-covered matzo, blue and red Twizzlers, three different types of Pop Tarts, chocolate cookies, chocolate chip cookies, marshmallows, Doritos, three different type of cereals

15.
Chicken, pasta, broccoli, carrots, and coke
Ice Cream
Coffee
Leftovers

Pretzels of the world -San Francisco sourdough,
German pumpernickel, chocolate-covered swiss,
and wasabi nuggets
Pizza and sodas
Beer, fried shrimp, Chinese food

16.
Coffee
Roast duck and strawberry shortcake
Pie and two rum balls
Cheeseburger
Scones
Chinese food

17.
Mocha-chocolate-caramel Swirlaccino with
whipped cream
Coffee
Cocoa puffs
Burger and fries
Doughnut
Goose
Harry and David fruit
Ice cream

18.
Trail Mix with the raisins, dried cranberries
Coffee
Fruit 'N' Oats, Sugar Rice Pops, and a third cereal
Founder's Day punch

19.
Hard tacos, soft tacos, curly fries, straight fries, spicy fries, a beef burrito
Orange soda
Club soda
Soup

20.
A meat and pasta dish
Burger, rare with cheddar cheese and BBQ sauce on the side, fries
Banana-cream pie
Coffee
An Altoid
Soft-shell crab amandine and wild rice, roll, white wine
Gin martini with an onion
Club soda
Roast, rolls, avocado salad with beet dressing
Coffee and baked apples
Unidentifiable dish Sookie is testing

21.
Marshmallows dipped in chocolate fondue
An apple
A MoonPie, DingDong, and Orange Crush

22.
Doughnut

Bread
Pop Tarts
Coffee

Season Six

1.
Zima
Coffee, pastries
Beer

2.
Beer
Packed lunch

3.
Shredded wheat, coffee, muffins
Fruit
Chicken
Mimosa's

4.
Coffee
Salmon Puffs
Fries

5.
Red wine, squash, beef, vegetable medley
Coffee

6.
Coffee, scooped bagel with cream cheese and jam

Grapefruit
Coffee

7.
Assorted cakes
Chicken
Pot roast, rolls, salad, Irish butter
Chocolate chip pancakes with whipped cream
"The Rory", birthday cake

8.
Coffee
Scotch, brewski, burger

9.
Red wine
Muffins, croissants, fresh fruit, scrambled eggs
Coffee
French toast, soda
Burgers -butter burgers, burgers with Jackson's famous rub, chicken and dumplings, salad, red wine
Coffee
Burgers, fries, onion rings, donuts, ice cream

10.
'Everything' from Luke's
Huge array at the Dragonfly Inn (looks like everything on the menu)
Coffee

11.
Coffee, cake
Fries with ketchup

12.
Coffee
Glazed doughnuts
Harry and David pears
Chinese food

13.
Coffee
Giant marshmallows covered in chocolate sauce
Double cappuccinos
Red wine and a sub sandwich
Martinis
White wine, rolls, salad
Passion fruit sorbet
Sherry

14.
Endive salad, rolls, white wine, and something
with a red wine reduction
Pizza with Tater Tots on top
Apple and cherry turnovers
Strawberry Pop Tarts
Coffee
Shrimp
Gin martinis
Soup

15.
Orange juice and a scone
White wine, salad, lobster, broccoli, mashed potatoes, bruschetta
Coffee and pastries

16.
Eggs and blueberry pancakes
Water
Champagne
Bar nuts, unidentifiable alcohol

17.
Chinese food
Coffee
Mac and cheese (pasta a la Sookie), mini hot dogs (bratwurst), taquitos (bellini's), chilli fries, red wine
Coffee, burger and fries

19.
Tequila shots, chips, candy

20.
Coffee
Chinese Takeout

21.
Spaghetti and meat balls, bread, red wine

22.
Seafood chowder, red wine

Season Seven

1.
Coffee

2.
Coffee, orange juice, toaster waffles with butter, chocolate syrup, syrup, whipped cream, syrup, and M&M's
Fortune cookies
"Dessert sushi" - Tootsie Roll-marshmallow-Twizzlers roll; Butterfinger-Junior Mint-chocolate-chip-Jujubes roll; Oreo-Red Hot sashimi

3.
Martini
White wine, rolls, and potage au cresson
Pop-Tarts, Fruit Loops
Muffin
Coffee
Chocolate brownie

4.
Milk Duds, Sour Patch Kids, and Twizzlers
Coffee
Mints, other unidentifiable candy

Popcorn and biscotti

5.
Fritos and ginger ale
Duck, short ribs, Gazpacho, a "cheese pie thing" and a "2003 red something" wine
Lunchables
Champagne and a "bread plate"
Salad with pears, rolls, red wine, lamb, and rhubarb pie

6.
Café au lait and a croissant
Coffee
Red wine, rolls, French food, creme brulee, and cognac
Doughnuts

7.
Champagne

8.
White wine, bread, escargot, salad
Coffee

9.
Champagne, lamb, bread
Coffee
Upside down tequila slammer with a twist

10.
Coffee
Meatloaf with extra gravy, mashed potato and vegetables
Indian – basmati and vindaloo

11.
Coffee
Popcorn, cookies
Candy canes, candy cane coffee, uncandycane coffee coffee, pie

12.
Quail mazatlan with tequila cactus sauce
Coffee
Muffin tops - apple cinnamon walnut, lemon poppy seed, apple spice, double chocolate chip
Muffin bottom pie
Water
Mac and cheese, salad, roll

13.
Coffee, sandwich
Milk Duds
Burgers, sandwiches, salad, pie, chocolate chip cookies, fish fillets, fish taco's, lobster roll, tuna fish sandwiches, fried fish, fish sticks

14.
Coffee

15.
Seabass, bread, green beans, carrots, lemon dill sauce
Amuse bouche
Vodka

16.
Blue icing from a cupcake

17.
Lobster, shrimp, hot dog
Champagne
Chocolate cake
Mrs. Field Cookie, Nutter Butters, crackers, mini doughnuts

18.
Coffee
Paella, red wine
Pie with vanilla ice cream

19.
Coffee
Chicken nuggets
Muffin
Beer and pretzels

Cantaloupe, orange juice, toast, cereal

20.
Martinis
Coffee
A sandwich, mac and cheese
French toast with extra cinnamon
A cosmopolitan and club soda
Scrambled eggs
Fries and a soda

21.
Coffee, doughnut, muffin
Champagne
Fruit and oats cereal

22.
Soup, bread, and white wine
Coffee
Tea

A Year in the Life

Winter

- Coffee
- Taco's
- Mac and Cheese, parmesan cutlets
- Tater tots
- Powdered sugar mini-doughnut
- Red wine.
- Eggs, toast.
- Green pea congee, fried shallots, spring onions, and chili oil with abalone
- Martinis with olives,
- Scotch
- Crudité
- Unidentifiable casserole
- Coffee
- Sprinkles off a single donut.
- Fluke carpaccio with lime and chilis
- Cheeseburger
- Bourbon
- Unidentified grain alcohol

Spring

- Bibimbap
- Paella
- Vietnamese suckling pig
- Wine and assorted sandwiches
- British lunch, featuring $300 wine and fries
- Profiteroles
- Linguini with meatballs
- Wine
- Coffee
- Yano's Burgers
- Chinese takeout
- Sausage
- Popcorn
- Chocolate cake
- Soup and sandwiches
- Scotch
- Hot dogs, chips, Funyuns, and Pepsi
- Bloody Mary
- Crodough Cake
- Hot dogs
- Pot roast, mashed potatoes, and a banana split

Summer

- Salad, garlic bread (and macaroni and cheese?)
- Popcorn
- O-So strawberry soda
- Dry gin martini and tequila with salt
- Scotch
- Burgers
- Strawberry milkshake
- Coffee
- Pop Tarts
- Chinese, Greek, and Italian takeout
- Hot dogs
- Tea
- Crab puffs
- Gimlets with Russian vodka

Fall

- Freeze-dried meatballs, chili mac, and spaghetti
- Franzia
- LeanCuisines
- Various snacks, and assorted other alcohols
- Champagne
- Martinis
- Steak
- Unspecified alcoholic beverage with two limes
- Pop-Tarts, Chinese takeout, ice cream, Red Vines, and coffee
- Cookies in tiny wrappers
- Coffee
- Sherry
- '69 Dom Perignon
- Wedding cakes
- Sookie's fat-free magic granola
- Unspecified soup
- Pop Tarts
- Pizza
- Doughnuts
- Wine

Independence Inn

Angel Wings with Dipping Sauce (1.6)
Baked Alaska (1.13)
Blueberry Shortcake (1.2)
Champagne (2.12)
Chocolate Bomb (3.20)
Chocolate Cake (1.2)
Graduation cake with chocolate covered espresso beans (2.21)
Handkerchief Pasta with Brown Safe and Butter Sauce (1.4)
Homemade Ice cream (1.2)
Hothouse Tomato Salad with Assorted Fresh Herbs (1.4)
Lobster (2.1)
Lobster Bisque (1.4)
Low-fat Whole Wheat Blueberry Pancakes (2.9)
Maple Syrup Snowflakes (1.8)
Meatloaf with Mashed Potato, Stuffing, Carrots and Corn on the Cob (2.8)
Mini Orange Biscuits with Honey Mustard Ham and Cheddar Sauce (1.6)
Mushroom Soup (2.17)
Oatmeal Cookies (1.1)
Orange Glazed Muffins with Warm Cinnamon Butter (1.19)
Risotto (1.4)
Rocky Road Cookies (1.8)

Stuffed Fried Squash Blossoms (1.11)
Three Egg Omelette with Goat Cheese and Pancetta, Cooked in a Sherry Olive Oil (1.14)
Waffles with Peach Sauce (1.1)

Dino's

Soft Taco's
Hard Taco's
Curly Fries
Straight Fries
Spicy Fries
Beef Burrito

Sandeep's Menu

Garlic Naan
Samosas
Chicken Vindaloo
Rice with Green sauce
Salad

KC's Annex Takeout Menu

Fiesta Burger	4.50
Hamburger	3.25
Cheeseburger	3.50
Barbeque Burger	3.75
French Fries	1.75
Onion Rings	2.00
Sausage, Onions, Peppers	4.25

The Bracebridge Dinner

7 courses:

Butternut Soup
Fish
Peacock Pie
The Barren of beef
Salad
Plum Pudding
Whisail

Dante's Inferno

Hot Dogs   15c
   - Relish
   - Lettuce
   - Onion
   - Mustard
   - Tomato
   - Chilli
Devil Dogs   2.50
Sizzling Fries   1.50
Fresh Chips   50c
French Fries   10c
Chicago Dill Pickles   10c
Drinks   5c

Al's Pancake World

Clams (1.5)
Salute to Paraguay (1.15)
Egg Foo Young (2.12)
Garlic Chicken (2.12)
Egg Rolls (2.12, 2.15)
Schezwan Chicken (2.15)
Kung Pao Chicken (2.15)
Garlic Chicken (2.15)
Chicken in Brown Sauce (2.15)
Salute to Jamaica (3.3)
International Grab Bag Night
- Pan-Asian with a hint of English Colonial and a few South African Influences
- Moroccan

Chicken Chow Mein Sandwich (4.20)
Manicotti (5.12)
Shrimp (6.14)

Dragonfly Inn

A Selection of Six Desserts (4.20)
Baked Apple with Cinnamon and Nutmeg (7.5)
Beef carpaccio (6.4)
Beef Tenderlon Chiffonade in Foccaica Rounds (7.14)
Bouillabaisse (7.22)
Braised Lamb Risotto (5.16)
Breads, Cheeses, Chocolates (7.5)
California Roll (7.2)
Carraway Cornbread with Apricots, Bacon and Jalapeno Jam (7.14)
Champagne (4.22)
Chinese Chicken Salad (5.16)
Chocolate Chip Cookies (4.19)
Chocolate Smore's Cake (6.3)
Cold Sandwiches (6.4)
Consommé (4.20)
Continental Breakfast (4.21)
Cranberry Sauce (5.1)
Cream Cheese and Cucumber (7.3)
Dessert Sushi (7.2)
Duck with Bechamel Sauce (5.19)
Fat Free Brownies (7.14)
Fennel Salad with Goat Cheese (5.19)
Fried Chicken (5.12)
Fried Chicken Sushi (7.2)
Garlic Bread (5.12)
Goose with oyster stuffing (6.9)

Gourd Soup (7.4)
Iced Tea (5.6)
Kebabs and pot stickers (6.10)
Lemon Bars, Pecan Squares (7.13)
Lobster Bisque (7.14)
Meatball (7.20)
Meatloaf Sushi (7.2)
Mini Pancakes (5.14)
Muffins (AYITL: Fall)
Onion Soup (4.20)
Pastrami (7.5)
PB&J Sushi (7.2)
Peanut Butter and Jelly Sandwich (7.3)
Pork Chops (5.12)
Pork Tenderloins (5.6)
Pumpernickel, Rye, Mustard, Celery Soda (7.5)
Ratatouille (7.6)
Red Velvet Cake (6.3)
Roast Beef (4.22)
Salad (4.22)
Salads – caprese, endive, arugula (6.4)
Scones (5.16)
Scrambled Eggs (7.20)
Shrimp Salad (7.3)
Smoked Salmon Sandwich (7.3)
Soup and Sammies (AYITL: Spring)
Spinach Quiche (7.3)
Steak Sandwich (5.12)
Stuffed Peppers (5.14)
Sweet Potato Biscuits with Pork Tenderloin and Apple Chutney (7.14)

Tuesday Burger Day (AYITL: Summer)
Thanksgiving Turkey (6.10)
Tuna carpaccio (6.4)
Veal and ham pate (6.10)
Vegetable carpaccio (6.4)
Walnut, Arugula, Gorgonzola Crostini (7.14)
Wednesday is 'Stump the Chef' day (5.6)
Wild Rice (5.1)
Zucchini Soup (4.20)

Luke's Diner

Breakfast

Eggs
Cheese Omelette (Extra Cheddar, No Jack) With Sourdough Toast (AYITL: Winter), 2 Bacons, 2 Sausages, And 1 Pancake (4.9)
Chilli Bean Omelette (4.9)
Denver Omelette (6.21)
Egg White Omelette with a Side of Spinach (2.6)
Egg, Bacon and Hashbrowns (7.22)
Eggs on Toast (2.6, 2.17), Sunny Side Up (7.1)
French Toast (2.17, 2.18, 7.20), with Bacon (1.19, 2.6), With Brown Sugar (7.18)
Jack Omelette with Bacon on The Side (3.15)
Luke's Special Omelette (3 Eggs, Bacon, Cubed Tomatoes, Swiss Cheese and A Dash of Oregano) (2.18)
Omelette (5.16)
Poached Eggs (2.3, 2.5)
Scrambled Eggs (7.1, AYITL: Winter) On Toast "Adam And Eve on A Raft and Wreck 'Em" (2.17) , with Cheddar Cheese, Half Bacon/Half Sausage (5.3)
Two Eggs, Over Easy (5.2, 7.4, AYITL: Winter)
Egg White with Cheese (AYITL: Winter)

Pancakes

Banana Pancakes with a Side Of Bacon (2.12)
Blueberry Pancakes (2.3, 4.18, 5.11), With Juice and Coffee (4.10)
Chocolate Chip Pancakes (1.17), with Whipped Cream (6.7)
Pancakes (2.6, 2.14, 3.7, 5.4, 5.11, 5.16, 6.20, 7.4, 7.22), with a Fried Egg And A Side Of Bacon (3.2), with Two Eggs (1.19, 2.22, 6.16)
Pumpkin Pancakes with Homemade Cinnamon Butter (4.9)

Other

½ A Grapefruit (Available on Request) (2.12, 5.5)
Bagels (4.9, AYITL: Winter) - Onion, Poppy Seed (7.4)
Blackened Cajun Bread, Fishy Bacon with Runny Eggs (5.16)
Shredded Wheat (7.18)
Breakfast Quesadilla (4.16)
Cold Bananas (6.20)
Cream of Wheat (7.17)
Muffins (2.7, 2.9, 4.12, 7.3, 7.21)
Oatmeal (4.15, 4.20, 7.16)
Toast (2.14), Wheat Toast (5.21), with Marmalade (7.4)

Light and Main Meals

Burgers
Burger (5.2, 7.18, 7.22), well done (7.18), with Double Cheese (4.5)
Cheeseburger (1.12, 2.5, 4.6, 5.1, 5.16), Swiss, Double Pickles and Fries (7.13)
Hamburger "Burn One" (2.17, 5.1, 6.9, 7.14), and Fries (1.2, 4.7)
Kale Burger (6.4)
Turkey Burger (2.8, 4.19), with Onions "Wimpy With A Rose Pinned On It" (2.17)

Sandwiches
BLT (1.14, 6.6, 7.17, 7.18, AYITL: Spring), No T (7.18), No B (7.18), No Mayo (2.17)
Club Sandwich (5.7)
Grilled Cheese (2.5, 6.4) With Tomatoes (4.19), Platter with French Fries and Pickles (7.17)
Ham and Cheese Sandwich (7.6), Rye (2.22)
Ham and Swiss (7.18), On Rye (6.18)
Ham Sandwich (5.1), on Rye, Mustard (No Mayo) (3.3)
Monte Cristo Sandwich (3.16)
Pastrami on Rye (7.18), Mustard, No Mayo (7.13)
Patty Melt (3.6, 7.18)
Peanut Butter and Jelly Sandwich (2.22)
Roasted Chicken Sandwich (1.1)
Rye Toast (4.9)

Tuna Fish Sandwiches (7.13), on Rye (7.18), on Wheat, No Mayo (7.18)
Tuna Melt (4.6, 6.9)
Turkey Melt (6.11)
Turkey on Rye (7.18), With Lettuce, Tomato, Cucumber, Coleslaw And 2 Pickles (4.18), with Swiss (6.4)

Other
Caeser's Salad (5.1)
Chicken Fingers (6.20)
Chicken Noodle Soup with A Side of Mashed Potato (3.2)
Chicken Pot Pie (1.14)
Chilli (7.17)
Chilli Dog (7.18)
Chilli Fries (1.1, 6.6), With Extra Cheese and Onions (5.8)
Cobb Salad – No Blue Cheese, No Bacon, No Avocado (6.9)
Cream of Tomato Soup (1.1)
Filet (7.13)
Fish Sticks (7.13)
Fish Tacos (7.13)
French Dip (7.18)
Fried Fish (7.13)
Fries (2.5, 2.9, 2.15, 4.15, 5.1, 5.7, 5.8, 5.16, 6.4, 6.9, 7.18)
Hot Dogs (7.17, 7.22)
Hot Turkey (1.1)
Lobster Roll (7.13)

Mac and Cheese (2.15, 7.18, 7.20)
Meatloaf (4.6)
Mushroom Soup (7.17)
Nachos -Baked Chips, Low Fat Cheese (6.9)
Onion Rings (4.6, 6.9, 7.18)
Roast Beef (7.18)
Salmon Steaks (5.16)
Scooped Bagel with Cream Cheese and Jam (6.6)
Shepherd's Pie (7.17)
Side of Hash Browns (5.16, 7.4)
Steak and Eggs with Onions (6.9)
Wednesday Special - French Dip with Extra Fries and Cherry Pie (3.9)
Wink Winkers/Nudge Nudgies/Know What I Meanies (5.2)

Desserts

Apple Pie (1.1, 5.16)
Assorted Cakes (1.1)
Banana Muffin (7.6)
Blueberry Muffins (3.15, 5.8)
Blueberry Pie (1.1)
Boysenberry Pie (5.17), With Ice Cream (5.5)
Brownie (2.13)
Cake (6.11)
Cherry Danish (2.5, 4.19)
Chocolate Cake (4.5)
Chocolate Chip Cookies (7.13)
Chocolate Donut (2.22)

Cronut (5.9)
Donut (2.14, 3.8, 4.9, 4.11, 5.17, 6.9, 6.20, 7.18, 7.21)
Fruit Salad (2.14)
Hot Fudge Sundae (5.5)
Ice Cream with Hot Fudge (1.19)
Key Lime Pie (1.2, 1.14)
Lemon and Poppyseed Muffins (3.15)
Lemon Meringue Pie (1.1)
Meringue (2.18)
Mud Pie (5.16)
Peach Pie (4.20, 7.17)
Pecan Pie (5.16)
Pie (2.19, 4.15, 7.13)
Pumpkin Pie (4.5, 5.16)
S'mores (6.17)
Sprinkled Donut (2.22, 4.5)
Strawberry Ice Cream with Chocolate Sauce "Pink Stick And Throw Some Mud On It" (2.17)

Beverages

Black and White Shake (6.6)
Chicory Coffee (6.20)
Cocoa (1.9)
Coffee with Cream And Sugar "Hot Blonde With Sand" (2.17), with Nutmeg (1.12)
Cokes (5.2)
Egg Creme (2.19)

Fudgy Banana Milkshake (AYITL: Winter)
Herbal Tea with Lemon (1.9)
Hot Chocolate (1.10, 2.19)
Hot Water (7.18)
Iced Tea (5.18), With Two Lemons (6.9)
Root Beer (5.1)
Tea (AYITL: Winter)

WIFI Passwords

Dinerluke
DINERDANES321
WafflehouseButterbob

Kirk's Diner
(7.2)

Pie
Arbuckles
French Toast
Pancakes
Buttermilk Pancakes
Beer

Weston's Bakery

Raspberry Cake (2.3)
Mocha Crunch Cream Cake (2.3)
Carrot Cake (2.8)
Rum Ball (2.8)
Cupcake (2.8)
Pie (with or without ice cream) (3.6, 5.16):
Cherry (7.18)
Peach
Pumpkin
Chocolate
Custard
Almond Tart(3.6)
Apple Compote(3.6)
Marizpan Fruits(3.6)
Rumballs (5.16)
Mocha chocolate caramel swirlaccino with extra whipped cream (5.17)
12 layer German Chocolate Cake (5.22)
Cake and coffee (6.14)
Candy Cane Coffee (7.11)
Banana Cream Pie (7.18)
Strawberry Rhubarb Pie (7.18)
Chocolate Raspberry cake (7.21)

Friday Night Dinners

Artichoke (1.19)
Beefaroni (2.1)
Beer/Nitwit Juice (5.7)
Bourbon with a twist (4.18)
Braised lamb shanks (3.2)
Brandy (1.18, 4.18)
Bread (2.2)
Broccoli (4.8)
Cheese and cupcakes (1.18)
Chicken Kiev and Raspberry Souffle (4.21)
Chicken, potatoes and asparagus (3.7)
Club Soda (2.1, 5.20)
Coke, Martini (5.6)
Duck (4.22)
Duck pate (6.14)
Eggs (1.20)
English tea service (2.21)
Escargot (4.16)
Fennel and Potato Puree with chilli (5.3)
Frozen Pizza (5.9), with Freshly Grated Parmesan (1.8)
Fruit and Ice Cream (4.22)
Gin (1.16)
Gin Martini (5.20)
Glenfiddich neat (1.16)

Goose (5.17)
Harry and David Fruit (5.17)
Hungarian cheese (5.3)
Ice Cream (2.5)
Johnny Machete, Champagne and Vanilla birthday cake (3.18)
Lamb and Potatoes (1.1, 2.18)
Leftover Lamb Sandwich (1.20)
Lobster Puffs (1.2)
Lobster Thermidor (4.8)
Manhattan with cherries (2.14)
Martini (4.12, 4.18, AYITL: Winter), with a Twist (3.9, 7.3)
Scotch on the Rocks, Gin and Tonic, Club Soda (7.3)
Marzipan (4.10)
Mashed Banana on Toast (1.9)
Mushroom Caps (3.19)
New Zealand Lamb (7.9)
Omelette (5.3)
Paella (6.22)
Pork (3.5), peas (3.15)
Prime Rib with Salad (3.14)
Pudding (1.6)
Puffs (2.1)
Quail Mazatlan with Tequila Cactus Sauce (7.12)
Rabbit (1.18)
Roast (1.16, 2.2, 5.20)
Roast Duck (5.16)
Salad (2.2, 7.20)

Salad and Bread Rolls, White Meat in a Red Wine Reduction Sauce (6.14)
Salad and Passionfruit Sorbet (6.13)
Salad, Lamb, Rhubarb Pie, Sherry, Port (7.5)
Sand Dabs (3.8)
Scotch (5.7, 5.20, AYITL: Spring)
Rum, Whiskey, Red Wine (5.7)
Sebass with Lemon Dill Sauce (7.15)
Shirley Temple, Roy Rogers (7.15)
Sidecar (5.20)
Spaghetti and Meatballs (6.21)
Spiced nuts (1.18)
Squab (1.11)
Steak on a stick, carrots and pickled herring (5.8)
Strudel (1.20)
Sweet bread (2.12)
Turkey and Salads (3.9)
Twinkies (2.1)
Vodka Martini with a Twist (5.7)
White Wine (3.1)
Wine (2.2)

The Independence Catering Co.

Children's Parties

- Colored Popcorn Balls
- Decorate your own cupcakes!
- Themed birthday cake
- Bagel Dogs
- Tater Tots
- Mini Pizzas
- Mac and Cheese with a jalapeno chipotle cream sauce
- Pizza Puffs
- Chips
- Chocolate cake with a rum raising tropical fruit ganache
- Pigs in a blanket

Adult Parties

- Brie with lavender honey and bourbon sugared pecans
- Blanched veggies with lemon garlic aioli
- Broccoli tart
- Faux Gras with cherry compote

- Roasted asparagus with parmesan
- Trio of winter soups - butternut squash, tomato basil, cannelloni and garlic
- Lobster pot pie

Come and Get it!

Taylor's Old-Fashioned Soda Shoppe and Candy Store

Ice Cream Flavors ($1.75)
Black Forest
White Chocolate
Chocolate Chip
Chocolate Chocolate Chocolate
Lemon
Lime
Rocky Road
Strawberry
Vanilla
Peppermint Stick
Butter Brickle Crunch
Sherbert
Chocolate
Coffee
Orange

Taylor's famous banana split $4.50

Soda Drinks
Egg Creme
Black Cow
Fifty/Fifty

Fountain Flavors
Cherry
Chocolate
Cola
Cream Soda
Ginger Ale
Grape
Lime Rickey
Lemon
Orange
Pecan
Root Beer
Sarsaparilla
Strawberry
Vanilla

Candy
Wax lips
Taffy
Penny Candy
Pixy Stix
Sourballs (4.18)

Other
HoCho (4.12)
European Hot Chocolate (6.13)

All sundaes presented with the Taylor Tip!

Once Your Heart is Involved, It All Comes Out in Moron

Love and Relationships

Love and Relationships in Gilmore Girls

One of the major themes throughout the show, is how the two girls navigate themselves through their romantic relationships, and how these relationships often set the scene for a lot of what goes on in the Gilmore world. Grand gestures such as a room full of daisies, building someone a car, or a constructing a home-built ice rink show that the men of the Gilmore-verse are willing to pull out all of the stops for a Gilmore Girl.

But it wasn't all roses (or daisies). Whiteside points out that "For a small, peaceful town in New England, there sure are a lot of complicated relationships in Stars Hollow."[13] Throughout seven seasons and a revival, we sat with the girls as they watched Judy Garland movies, cried when a flame from school kissed them, and screamed at

---

[13] Stephanie Whiteside, "When Paris Met Rory", in *Coffee at Luke's: An Unauthorised Gilmore Girls Gabfest*, ed. Jennifer Cruise, Leah Wilson (Dallas: BenBella Books, 2007), 21.

the television screen when Luke did not respond to Lorelai's ultimatum. We watched relationships like Luke and Lorelai's evolve from pals to lovers, and rooted for Marty and Tristan when things didn't get off the ground.

Manning writes that "many of the romantic relationships divide audience members in terms of support", and this is certainly true for Rory's boyfriends, and perhaps to a lesser extent for Lorelai's.[14] Most fans have an opinion on Lorelai and Rory's main boyfriends, and are either #TeamDean, #TeamJess, or #TeamLogan. In the lead up to the revival, all of us waited in anticipation to see who Rory had wound up with, and whether Lorelai and Luke had gotten married, or had children. And, it isn't just the main girls that we have such a vested interest in. Many fans felt sad to see that Paris' relationship ends in separation, that Dave went off to college without any further explanation, and that Emily had to find a way to live without Richard. But, the same fans celebrated with Sookie when she married her produce guy, and yelled "Huzzah!" when Liz found tied the knot with T.J. Romantic

---

[14] Jimmie Manning, ""But Luke and Lorelai Belong Together!": Relationships, Social Control, and Gilmore Girls" In *Screwball Television: Critical Perspectives on Gilmore Girls*, ed. Diffrient David Scott and Lavery David (Syracuse, NY: Syracuse University Press, 2010), 303.

relationships in *Gilmore Girls* also affects the relationships between others. Caroline Jones writes that Rory's affair with Dean "affects her relationship with him less than it does her relationship with her mother."[15]

This section contains a guide to all of the love interests in the show – documenting when they are first seen, first kisses, first dates, engagements, weddings, and more. This is followed by a catalogue of relationship 'lists', which allow you to follow any one relationship from start to finish, by watching all of the episodes in the order they are listed. So, go forth, and let yourself get swept away by one of the Gilmore romances. But remember, once your heart is involved, it all comes out in moron.

---

[15] Caroline E. Jones, "Unpleasant Consequences: First Sex in Buffy the Vampire Slayer, Veronica Mars, and Gilmore Girls," in *Jeunesse: Young People, Texts, Cultures* 5, no. 1 (2013): 65-83.

Love Interests

First Seen
Dean Forrester (1.1)
Luke Danes (1.1)
Carrie Duncan (1.1)
Christopher Hayden (1.1) (Richard refers to him at dinner)
Rachel 1.13 (Sookie refers to her at the Bangles concert), (1.16)
Jackson Melville (1.2)
Ian Jack (1.2)
Tristan Dugray (1.2)
Max Medina (1.4)
Christopher Hayden (1.14)
Pennilynn Lott (1.8) (referred to as Lynnie Lott), (4.9)
Henry Cho (1.17)
Jess Mariano (2.5)
Sherry Tinsdale 2.6 (Christopher tells Lorelai he is seeing Sherry from Boston)
Paul 2.9 (the pre-transition guy)
Sherry Tinsdale (2.14) (first appearance)
Shane (3.1)
Jamie (3.1)
Peyton Sanders (3.5)
Alex Lesman (3.11)
Joe Mastoni (3.11)

Nicole Lahey (3.12)
Yiung Chui (3.15)
Trix's companion (man in purple velour jogging suit) (3.15)
Lindsay Lister (3.15)
Marty (4.3)
Jason 'Digger' Stiles (4.3)
Trevor (4.5)
Lulu Kuschner (4.6)
Doyle McMaster (4.8)
Asher Fleming (4.9)
Chester Fleet (Tana mentions that she is hoping to attract his attention) (4.12)
T.J./Gary (4.12)
Graham 'Diaper Boy' Sullivan (4.21)
Logan Huntzberger (5.3)
Robert Grimaldi (5.7)
Simon McLain (5.9)
Linny (6.22)
Susan Bennett (7.6)
Tucker Colbertson (7.14)
Paul (AYITL: Winter)
Teddy Weidermeier III (Lorelai refers to him) (AYITL: Winter)
Frederich (Lorelai refers to him) (AYITL: Winter)
Wookie (AYITL: Spring)
Royston Sinclair III (Lorelai refers to him) (AYITL: Fall)
Jack Smith (AYITL: Winter)

Asked Out
Max asks Lorelai out and gets stood up (1.5)
Sookie asks Jackson out (1.11)
Luke asks Lorelai out but gets interrupted, then later tries again but doesn't go through with it (1.12)
Tristan asks Rory out (1.21)
Trevor asks out Rory (4.5)
Rory incites Trevor to ask her out again (4.5)
Rory asks out William in the laundry room (4.5)
Jason asks Lorelai out (4.6, 4.8, 4.9)
Chester asks out Tanna (4.12)
Luke asks Lorelai to Liz and TJ's wedding (4.20)
Jason asks Lorelai to try again (4.22)
Lane tells Zach she likes him as more than a friend (5.4)
Zach tells Lane he is ready to date (5.7)
Graham asks Rory out (4.21)
Robert asks Rory out (5.17)
Christopher asks Lorelai out (7.1)
Susan asks out Luke (7.6)

First Date
Max and Lorelai (1.8)
Lane and Todd (1.12)
Rune and Lorelai (1.12)
Sookie and Jackson (1.12)
Lorelai and Chase Bradford (1.16)
Paris and Tristan (1.18)
Lorelai and Paul (2.9)

Jess and Rory (Bid on a Basket) (2.13)
Luke and Lorelai (Bid on a Basket) (2.13)
Paris and Jamie (3.1)
Lorelai and Peyton (3.5)
Lorelai and Alex (3.12)
Luke and Nicole (3.13)
Lane and Yiung Chui (3.15)
Rory and Trevor (4.5)
Kirk and Lulu (4.6)
Lorelai and Jason (4.9)
Lorelai and Luke (4.21)
Graham and Rory (4.21)
Zach and Lane (5.7)
Simon McLain (5.9)
Paris and Doyle - no actual date though (5.12)
Luke and Lorelai (Liz's Wedding) (4.21)
Rory and Logan (5.14)
Robert and Rory (5.17)
Logan and Whitney (5.17)

First Kiss
Rory and Dean (1.7)
Tristan and Rory (1.17)
Jess and Rory (2.22)
Lane and Dave (3.12)
Paris and Asher (4.9)
Rory and Paris (4.17)
Luke and Lorelai (4.22)
Zach and Lane (5.7)
Rory and Logan (5.13)
Christopher and Lorelai (referred to) (5.13)

Affairs
Paris and Asher (4.9)
Dean and Rory (4.22)

Marriage Proposals
Luke asks Lorelai to marry him (1.6)
Christopher asks Lorelai to marry him (1.15)
Max asks Lorelai...twice! (1.21)
Jackson asks Sookie (2.13)
Luke asks Nicole (4.1)
Lorelai asks Luke (5.22)
Zach asks Lane (6.16)
Christopher asks Lorelai (7.7)
Logan asks Rory (7.21)

Engagements
Max and Lorelai (2.1)
Sookie and Jackson (2.13)
Dean and Lindsay (3.20)
Honor and Josh (5.19)
Lorelai and Luke (6.1)
Lane and Zach (6.16)
Lane and Zach (officially, in the presence of Mrs. Kim) (6.17)

Engagement Parties
Lorelai and Max (2.1)
Honor and Josh (5.21)

Bachelor/Bachelorette Parties
Lorelai (2.3)
TJ (4.20)
Liz (4.21)
Emily (5.13)
Richard (5.13)
Lane (6.19)
Zach (6.19)

Weddings
Jackie/Jessica and James/Julian (1.3)
Sookie and Jackson (2.22)
James (Kim family wedding) (3.12)
Luke and Nicole (4.1)
Dean and Lindsay (4.4)
Liz and TJ (4.21)
Emily and Richard (5.13)
Honor and Josh (6.16)
Lane and Zach #1 (6.19)
Lane and Zach #2 (6.19)
Lorelai and Christopher (7.7)
Wilson Wedding (7.14)
Mia and Howard (7.17)
Lorelai and Luke (AYITL: Fall)

Break Ups
Max and Lorelai (1.11)
Dean and Rory (1.16, 3.7)
Summer and Tristan (1.17)
Rachel and Luke (1.21)

Max and Lorelai (2.3)
Lane and Henry (2.13)
Lorelai and Christopher (2.22)
Rory and Jess (3.20)
Luke and Nicole (4.1)
Paris and Jamie (4.12)
Luke and Nicole (4.17)
Dean tells Rory that he and Lindsay are over (4.22)
Dean and Lindsay (5.1)
Jason and Lorelai (4.19)
Emily and Richard (5.1)
Rory and Dean (5.8)
Simon and Lorelai (5.12)
Luke and Lorelai (5.14)
Logan and Rory (6.8)
Lane and Zach (6.10)
Linda and Bill (6.15)
Logan and Rory (6.16)
Paris and Doyle (6.16)
Liz and T.J. (6.21)
Lorelai and Luke (6.22)
Marty and Lucy (7.12)
Lorelai and Christopher (7.14)
Doyle and Paris (7.19)
Logan and Rory (7.21)
Doyle and Paris (AYITL: Spring)
Logan and Rory (AYITL: Summer)
Logan and Rory (AYITL: Fall)
Rory and Paul (AYITL: Fall)

Divorced
Luke and Nicole (4.19)
Sherry and Christopher (5.6)
Lorelai and Christopher (7.21)

Back Together
Luke and Rachel (1.16)
Lorelai and Max (1.17)
Rory and Dean (1.21)
Lorelai and Christopher (2.22)
Sherry and Christopher (2.22)
Luke and Nicole (4.7)
Rory and Dean (4.22)
Emily and Richard (5.12)
Luke and Lorelai (5.16)
Logan and Rory (6.13)
Paris and Doyle (6.17)
Logan and Rory (6.17)
Liz and T.J. (6.21)
Lorelai and Christopher (7.3)
Doyle and Paris (7.19)
Luke and Lorelai (7.22)
Logan and Rory (AYIT: Winter)

Pregnancies
Christopher and Sherry (2.22)
Sookie and Jackson (3.16)
Sookie and Jackson (5.6)
Liz and T.J. (6.21)
Lane and Zach (7.2)

Sookie and Jackson (7.12)
Rory (AYITL: Fall)

First 'I Love You'
Dean tells Rory he loves her (1.16)
Rory tells Dean she loves him (1.21)
Rory tells Jess she loves him over the phone (3.22)
Jess tells Rory he loves her (4.13)
Rory tells Logan she loves him (6.6)
Logan tells Rory he loves her (6.11)

Other Significant Events
Emily identifies the chemistry between Luke and Lorelai (1.6)
Lane first expresses her interest in Todd (1.7)
Lane touches Rich Blumenfeld's hair (1.8)
Rory and Dean officially become boyfriend and girlfriend (1.9)
Lorelai is jealous of Rachel (1.13)
Christopher and Lorelai sleep together (1.15)
Tristan and Summer kissing in front of the lockers (1.16)
Rory and Dean three month anniversary (1.16)
Rory wallows (1.17)
Tristan asks to kiss Rory again (1.18)
Max and Luke face off (1.21)
Lorelai wants to start things back up with Christopher (2.6)
Rory and Tristan say goodbye (2.9)

Sookie tells Lorelai that Luke is 'so into' her (2.9)
The ice cream maker arrives for Lorelai and Max's wedding (2.9)
Dean admits that Rory likes Jess (2.18)
Episode One of 'Rory and Jess: The Early Years' (3.8)
Lane tells her mother that she likes Dave (3.12)
Lorelai and Alex overnight date (3.14)
Jess meets Emily (3.14)
Max and Lorelai kiss again (3.16)
Paris and Jamie have sex (3.16)
Luke dreams that Lorelai tells him not to get engaged to Nicole (3.22)
Kirk calls Lulu his girlfriend (4.7)
Mrs. Kim wants Lane to send Dave the marriage jug (4.8)
Jason gives Lorelai the talking key (4.17)
Lorelai meets Jason's parents (4.18)
Jason and Lorelai's relationship is exposed (4.18)
Sookie tries to set Lorelai up with Shell (4.20)
Rory calls Dean after her date with Graham doesn't work out (4.21)
Jess asks Rory to run away with him and start over (4.21)
Lulu and Kirk first overnight (4.22)
Lane realizes she is in love with Zach (5.1)
Rory and Dean double date with Luke and Lorelai (5.5)
Luke meets Lorelai's parents 'officially' (5.7)
Marty tells Rory that Logan likes her (5.12)

Paris goes speed dating (5.10)
Lane tells Zach she can't have sex until marriage (5.16)
Rory breaks up with Logan, but he talks her into a relationship (5.18)
Rory meets Logan's family (5.19)
Logan meets Rory's family (5.20)
Luke buys the Twickham house for his future with Lorelai (5.22)
Paris and Doyle move in together (6.1)
Logan buys Rory the Birkin bag (6.6)
Luke postpones the wedding (6.12)
Lorelai admits that her and Luke won't be marrying (6.21)
Logan and Rory enter a long-distance relationship (6.22)
Kirk decides to break up with Lulu, but Luke talks her out of it (7.6)
Rory tells Logan that she has a crush on her economics teacher (7.14)

Relationship Episode Lists

Lorelai

Lorelai and Luke
1.6, 1.12, 1.13, 1.14, 1.21
2.9, 2.13, 2.17
3.1, 3.17, 3.22
4.5, 4.8, 4.11, 4.13, 4.14, 4.15, 4.17, 4.20, 4.22
5.1, 5.2, 5.3, 5.4, 5.7, 5.8, 5.9, 5.12, 5.13, 5.14,
5.15, 5.16, 5.17, 5.22
6.1, 6.2, 6.3, 6.4, 6.5, 6.6, 6.7, 6.8, 6.9, 6.10, 6.11,
6.12, 6.13, 6.14, 6.15, 6.16, 6.19, 6.20, 6.21, 6.22
7.1, 7.2, 7.3, 7.5, 7.8, 7.10, 7.11, 7.12, 7.13, 7.14,
7.15, 7.16, 7.18, 7.19, 7.20, 7.21, 7.22
AYITL: Winter, Spring, Summer, Fall

Lorelai and Christopher
1.14, 1.15
2.3, 2.6, 2.7, 2.22
3.1, 3.6, 3.13
5.6, 5.9, 5.11, 5.12, 5.13
6.9, 6.10, 6.16, 6.19, 6.22

7.1, 7.2, 7.3, 7.4, 7.5, 7.6, 7.7, 7.8, 7.9, 7.10, 7.11,
7.12, 7.13, 7.14, 7.15, 7.18, 7.21
AYITL: Spring, Fall

Lorelai and Kirk
3.2
4.12

Lorelai and Max
1.4, 1.5, 1.8, 1.11, 1.12, 1.17, 1.21
2.1, 2.2, 2.3, 2.9
3.16, 3.19
6.22
AYITL: Fall

Lorelai and Jason
4.3, 4.6, 4.8, 4.9, 4.10, 4.12, 4.14, 4.17, 4.18,
4.19, 4.22
5.1
AYITL: Winter

Lorelai and Alex
3.11, 3.12, 3.14, 3.15, 3.19

Lorelai and Rune
1.12, 1,19, 2,10

Rory

Rory and Wookie
AYITL: Spring

Rory and Paul
AYITL: Winter, Spring, Summer, Fall

Rory and Jess
2.5, 2.13, 2.15, 2.16, 2.17, 2.18, 2.19, 2.20, 2.21, 2.22
3.1, 3.2, 3.5, 3.6, 3.8, 3.10, 3.14, 3.15, 3.17, 3.18, 3.19, 3.20, 3.21, 3.22
4.12, 4.13, 4.20, 4.21, 4.22
6.8, 6.18
AYITL: Summer, Fall

Rory and Logan
5.3, 5.6, 5.7, 5.8, 5.10, 5.12, 5.13, 5.14, 5.15, 5.16, 5.17, 5.18, 5.19, 5.20, 5.21, 5.22
6.1, 6.3, 6.4, 6.6, 6.7, 6.8, 6.10, 6.11, 6.12, 6.13, 6.14, 6.15, 6.16, 6.17, 6.18, 6.19, 6.20, 6.21, 6.22
7.1, 7.3, 7.5, 7.8, 7.9, 7.10, 7.11, 7.13, 7.14, 7.15, 7.16, 7.17, 7.18, 7.19, 7.21
AYITL Winter, Spring, Summer, Fall

Rory and Marty
4.3, 4.5, 4.9
5.3, 5.9, 5.10, 5.12, 5.15
7.8, 7.9, 7.10, 7.12

Rory and Dean
1.1, 1.5, 1.7, 1.9, 1.14, 1.16, 1.17, 1.20, 1.21
3.1, 3.3, 3.10, 3.14, 3.19, 3.20, 3.22
4.4, 4.14, 4.17, 4.18, 4.21, 4.22
5.1, 5.2, 5.3, 5.4, 5.5, 5.6, 5.7, 5.8, 5.18
7.7
AYITL: Fall

Rory and William
4.5, 4.11

Rory and Tristan
1.2, 1.16, 1.17, 1.18, 1.21
2.9
Rory and Trevor
4.5

Rory and Robert
5.17

Rory and Spring Break Guy
4.17

Paris

Paris and Jamie
3.1, 3.7, 3.9, 3.10, 3.16
4.6, 4.9, 4.10, 4.12

Paris and Doyle
5.6, 5.10, 5.12, 5.15, 5.18, 5.19, 5.20
6.1, 6.7, 6.11, 6.16, 6.17, 6.17
7.9, 7.14, 7.18, 7.19, 7.20, 7.21
AYITL: Winter

Paris and Asher
4.9, 4.10, 4.12, 4.14, 4.17, 4.20
5.3, 5.10

Paris and Tristan
1.18
AYITL: Spring

Emily

Richard and Emily
1.8
4.9, 4.15, 4.16, 4.19, 4.22
5.1, 5.3, 5.5, 5.8, 5.9, 5.12, 5.13
AYITL: Winter

Simon and Emily
5.9, 5.12

Emily and Jack Smith
AYITL: Winter, Summer, Fall

Luke

Luke and Nicole
3.12, 3.13, 3.17, 3.18, 3.19
4.1, 4.5, 4.7, 4.8, 4.11, 4.12, 4.14, 4.16, 4.17, 4.19
5.1
7.12

Luke and Carrie Duncan
4.12, 4.21
5.15

Luke and Rachel
1.13, 1.16, 1.17, 1.19, 1.20, 1.21
AYITL: Fall

Luke and Anna Nardini
6.9, 6.10, 6.11

Luke and Susan
7.6

Lane

Lane and Dave
3.3, 3.4, 3.7, 3.9, 3.12, 3.14, 3.15, 3.19, 3.20
4.8
7.22

Lane and Billy Fink
7.22

Lane and Yiung Chui
3.15, 3.17, 3.19

Lane and Zach
5.1, 5.4, 5.5, 5.7, 5.8, 5.12, 5.16, 5.18
6.3, 6.4, 6.7, 6.10, 6.11, 6.12, 6.16, 6.17, 6.19
7.2, 7.3, 7.7, 7.11, 7.16, 7.17, 7.18, 7.20, 7.22
AYITL Winter, Spring, Summer

Other

Logan and Whitney
5.17

Logan and Odette
AYITL: Winter, Spring, Summer

April and Freddy
6.18

Jess and Shane
3.1, 3.4, 3.7

Tanna and Chester
4.12, 4.21

Marty and Lucy
7.7, 7.8, 7.9, 7.10, 7.12

Dean and Lindsay
3.17, 3.19, 3.20, 3.22
4.4, 4.14, 4.15, 4.18, 4.20, 4.21, 4.22
5.1

Richard and Penilyn Lott
4.9, 4.16
5.1, 5.12

Sherry and Christopher

2.6, 2.14, 2.22
3.1, 3.2, 3.6, 3.13
5.9, 5.12
6.16
7.5

Lana and Christopher
AYITL: Fall

Miss Patty and Jesús
3.6

Honor and Josh
5.19, 5.21, 6.16

Liz and T.J.
4.12, 4.20
5.1, 5.2, 5.8
6.2, 6.21
7.2, 7.9, 7.10, 7.16
AYITL: Spring, Summer, Fall

Kirk and Lulu
4.6, 4.7, 4.12, 4.13, 4.15, 4.20, 4.22,
5.1, 5.5, 5.11, 5.16, 5.17
6.1, 6.19, 6.21
7.1, 7.6
AYITL: Spring

Sookie and Jackson
1.11, 1.12, 1.15, 1.16, 1.17, 1.19

2.1, 2.2, 2.5, 2.10, 2.11, 2.13, 2.17, 2.21, 2.22
3.1, 3.3, 3.6, 3.7, 3.9, 3.11, 3.14, 3.16, 3.18, 3.22
4.1, 4.3, 4.7, 4.18, 4.22
5.1, 5.4, 5.12, 5.19
6.4, 6.9, 6.19, 6.20, 6.21
7.12, 7.19

Chris and Linny
6.22

Naomi and George
AYITL: Spring

Naomi and Colin
AYITL: Spring

Guys Who Saw Lorelai Naked
(6.3)

- Joe
- Pete
- Slim
- Billy
- Teddy

I Need Coffee...In An IV

Trivia and Gilmorism's

Season One

1.1

- The girl in class who tells her friends that Rory is working on the assignment, later appears as the character of Summer, a Chilton student who is seeing Tristan.
- The teacher in this class also appears later as "Crazy Carrie", a friend of Liz's (4.13, 4.21, 5.15)
- Lane talks about her parents as if she has two, but we do not see her father until *A Year in the Life*
- The pilot was shot in and around Toronto, Canada
- The hardware store on the main street was turned into Luke's diner for the show, which prompted the storyline of Luke converting his father's hardware store into a diner
- Friday night dinners are established in this episode
- Alexis Bledel dislikes coffee, and had Coca-Cola in her cup for scenes that required her to drink coffee.
- Luke's character was originally written to be played by a woman, but was cast with a man after producers decided there wasn't enough male characters

- Scott Patterson was originally hired only for the pilot, but was signed for more episodes after the chemistry between Lauren Graham and himself became so apparent on set, and on screen.
- Alexis Bledel was 19 when she began playing 15-year-old Rory. Keiko Agena was 26 years old in the first season, when her character Lane was 15
- The town of Stars Hollow is based on Washington Depot, Connecticut. The show's creator, Amy Sherman-Palladino was inspired when she visited the town with her husband
- This is the only episode where the girl's kitchen has steps into it
- Rory's line, "with the Principal?" is a reference to Forrest Gump
- Because of the amount of fast-paced dialogue, actors were unable to improvise or ad-lib any of their lines. Due to the fast pace of the dialogue in the show, the average script for each episode was nearly twice as many pages as a standard hour-long television episode.
- The character of Lane is based on the co-producer of the show, Helen Pai
- Lorelai and Rory are the only characters to appear in every episode of the series

- Lorelai's line, "What's with the muumuu?" is a reference to a loose Hawaiian dress
- The characters of Dean (originally Nathan Wetherington) and Sookie (originally played by Alex Borstein who played Drella/Miss Celine) were recast. An alternate pilot can be found online that includes these characters in their original roles
- Lauren Graham and Lorelai Gilmore have the same initials
- Lorelai's line that Rory can "pull a Menendez" is a reference to the Menendez brothers' murder
- Sookie was originally to be played by Alex Borstein, but a scheduling conflict meant the role was re-cast. Similarly, Nathan Wetherington was cast as Dean, but later re-cast, and the pilot re-shot
- Emily Kuroda who plays Mrs. Kim has the same middle name as the first name of the actress who plays her on screen daughter: Keiko
- The shot at 27:07 of the girls in Luke's, is the same as the ending shot
- Lorelai's line, "best laid plans" is a reference to the poem "To a Mouse, on Turning Her Up in Her Nest with the Plough" by Robert Burns

- Lorelai drives a different Jeep in the first couple of episodes than the rest of the series. This original Jeep can be seen in 7.19
- Rory is said to be 16 in this episode, though she turns 16 in 1.6
- The working title for the series was, "The Gilmore Way"
- After Luke tells the girls that red meat can kill them, Lorelai's hand moves from touching the coffee cup, to not touching it, between shots

1.2

- Liza Weil originally auditioned for the part of Rory but was unsuccessful. However, she made such an impression on the producers that the role of Paris Geller was written for her.
- Sean Gunn appears twice as Mick and a DSL installer, before he appears in 1.3 as Kirk and becomes a recurring character
- The set of Stars Hollow doubles as the backdrop for many other television show towns, including Rosewood on Pretty Little Liars
- Sally Struthers was cast as Babette after Liz Torres was cast. The producers felt that their onscreen relationship in *All in*

the Family would make a great addition to *Gilmore Girls*
- 'playing quarters' is a drinking game
- Exterior, foyer and hallway shots of Lorelai's house are filmed on the outdoor set, while most of the interior scenes were built on a soundstage. This is because the back of Lorelai's house is actually the front of Sookie's house. They are one house with two different frontages
- According to the town sign in 1.2, the population of Stars Hollow is 9,973
- Rory's conversation with Headmaster Charleston discusses several journalists: Christiane Amanpour is a journalist and foreign correspondent for CNN, 'Cokie' Roberts is an American journalist, Oprah Winfrey, and Rosie O'Donnell are American TV show hosts. The View is an American talk show
- Luke's screwdriver moves, in the scene where he is fixing the toaster
- Lorelai throws Rory's bag into the car twice when she picks her up
- Lorelai turns down a Chilton dad in this episode because she feels it would be a conflict of interest for Rory. But she later dates, and becomes engaged to, a teacher from Chilton

1.3

- This episode is the first mention of the backpacking trip that takes place between seasons 3 and 4
- Sean Gunn appears as the swan delivery man in this episode
- This is the second mention of Rory being 16, episodes before she actually turns 16 in 1.6
- Lorelai's food keeps changing on the plate, between shots
- Richard talks about his mother as if she was dead, although she later appears in 1.18
- Lorelai's comment about that "lunatic rich lady with the lion head" is a reference to Jocelyn Wildenstein

1.4

- "What's up Quimby?" is a reference to mayor Quimby from *The Simpsons*
- At the end of the episode when the girls arrive home, someone's elbow is visible to the left of the shot
- Third reference to Rory being 16, before she is. If Rory is, in fact, only 15, the driving herself to school alone would have been breaking the law

1.5

- Sean Gunn appears for the first time as Kirk
- Dolly Madison is an American bakery brand
- In 3.18 we learn that Lorelai was born in 1968. This would make her around 15 months old when she met Claudia, and it seems unreasonable that Emily should expect her to remember it
- First episode written by Daniel Palladino
- Kirk and Miss Patty act like they have never met, yet in 6.5, Miss Patty says Kirk performed on her stage 20 years ago
- First episode that uses the new permanent credit music
- Cinnamon is referred to as a 'she', but was referred to as a 'he' in the previous episode

1.6

- Rory's birthday is October 8th
- Lorelai can be seen eating an apple in this episode. In 5.21, Lorelai states that she hasn't wanted an apple since she was pregnant
- During her phone call with Emily, the apple moves between shots
- Miss Patty's full name is revealed to be Patricia LaCosta

- Rory is wearing a new dress that Emily bought her, but Lorelai wore it in 1.3
- Henny Youngman was a comedian

1.7

- Dean says he has "sisters", but we only meet one as the series goes on, Clara.
- The comment about the dancing prince seems odd, since Cinderella's prince danced as well
- This is the only episode where the downstairs closet is a bathroom
- After Lorelai serves herself, Luke picks up the money twice
- Lorelai discusses Hubbell leaving his child for Katie in *The Way We Were*, but in the film it's with Katie that he has a child

1.8

- Rory tells her mother that their conversation will end up in a book she writes. In the revival, Rory does write an autobiographical book about their lives
- First time Lorelai brings a guy to her house
- Harry, the town mayor, appears in this episode, but is not mentioned again once Taylor steps into the role of Town

Selectman, and the role of mayor is never mentioned again
- When Rory takes off her bag to put the chemistry book in, the bag is in the front then the back, then the book is in the bag, then out of it
- First and only mention of Emily's sister Hope
- The bookstore appears for the first time in this episode as "Once Upon a Bookstore", but appears to have the same signage and placement as Stars Hollow Books, which appears for the first time in 1.15

1.9

- Rory talks of her plans to backpack around Europe after graduation and her grandparents do not express any disapproval, yet in 3.13 they are very explicit about their disdain for the idea
- Rory is seen reading Dorothy Parker. The production company for *Gilmore Girls* is named after Dorothy Parker

- Only episode where Lorelai calls Emily 'mommy'
- This is the longest episode in the original series seasons
- Caesar appears in the background of the confrontation taking place at the dance

1.10

- When Lorelai gets Rory's message, Luke's order pad goes from in his pocket to gone, between shots
- Lorelai's purse also moves in the hospital scene
- Lorelai eats salad out of a bag, even though it is repeatedly said later in the series that she doesn't eat vegetables or green food

1.11

- The waiter at the restaurant appears in 3.11 as Joe Mastoni from the Deerhill Lodge
- Sookie keeps confusing the order of the words, in her conversation about the stuffed fried squash blossoms
- During Max's class, a boom mic can be seen at the top off the scree

1.12

- Lorelai states that she would not have lied to Mrs. Kim if she knew that Lane was not supposed to be at the movies. This 'code' doesn't appear to matter later on when Lorelai encourages Lane to attend The Bangles show with them
- Lorelai jokes to Sookie that she will wear a blue dress to her wedding with Jackson.

In 3.22, Sookie does wear a blue dress to marry Jackson

1.14

- The information that Rory found on her research about Donna Reed, is from IMDB.com
- This episode marks the first appearance of the town troubadour
- During 'Donna Reed night', the song "Johnny Angel" can be heard playing. This was recorded by Shelley Fabares who played the daughter on *The Donna Reed Show*

1.15

- Dean tells Christopher he has an 86 Suzuki, yet in 1.7 he tells Lorelai he doesn't have a motorbike.

1.16

- Chase Bradford says his dobermans are named Leopold and Loeb. These are the names of the convicted murderers of Bobby Frank, and are later used as names for Luke and Lorelai's twins in 3.1

1.19
- The house exterior used for The Dragonfly is the same as the house on *The Waltons*
- The title of the episode is a reference to *Alice in Wonderland*

1.20
- Rory says that she loves Spanish class. This may be a reference to Alex Bledel, as her first language was Spanish

1.21
- First appearance of the second troubadour

Season Two

2.1

- Lorelai refers to the TV show *All in the Family*, which Sally Struthers who plays Babette was in

2.2

- This marks the first episode where Paris is a main character

2.3

- Lorelai tells the bouncer at the bar that Rory is an international model. Alexis Bledel was a model, and traveled to Tokyo, Milan, New York and Los Angeles for modeling

2.4

- Lorelai tells Rory that Fred Gwynee who played Herman on *The Munsters* attended Harvard. Edward Hermann who plays Richard played Herman in *Here Come the Munsters*

- On the wall of Harvard valedictorians, comedian Anthony Jeselnik's picture can be seen

2.5

- Milo Ventimiglia's character, Jess, was originally only to make a few appearances as Luke's nephew. The producer's liked him so much that he was signed as a series regular

2.6

- Debutante Libby, who is played by Samantha Shelton, also appears as Walker in 6.16

2.7

- Lance Barber, who played the man building the fashion show runway, also appears as Hugo in 7.8

2.12

- Richard says that Lorelai has never invited him to her home before, even though he was invited in 1.6

2.15

- Rory and Lorelai's discussion about Like being called Duke is a reference to Luke's original character name being Duke

2.16

- Paris talks to her Portuguese nanny on the phone in Spanish
- Emilly says at the bar that she doesn't dance. Kelly Bishop is a broadway dancer, and was in the film *Dirty Dancing*

2.20

- The music store owner, Sophie, is played by Carole King who wrote and sings the theme tune, "Where You Lead"
- Richard refers the TV show M*A*S*H. Edward Hermann was in an episode of M*A*S*H

2.21

- The record store owner is played by blues musician Chuck E. Weiss

- Lorelai's name is revealed to be Lorelai Victoria GIlmore in this episode
- Seth McFarlane who created *Family Guy* features in this episode

2.22

- Sookie and Jackson are using the Chuppah that Luke made for Lorelai and Max at their wedding. The Chuppah can be seen back in Lorelai's front yard in 4.12
- This episode is named after the Ella Fitzgerald song that plays at the wedding
- The Gilmore maid in this episode is Alexis Bledel's stand-in

Season Three

3.1

- This episode marks the first appearance of Sean Gunn in the opening credits
- The return address on Rory's mail says ""Dean Forester, 106 Don Ridge Dr. Chicago, IL 60620". Rory's address reads, "Rory Gilmore, 1765 Harring, Washington DC, 2005". Neither of these addresses exist.

3.3

- Dave Ryglaski is the name of Helen Pai's husband, who the character of Lane is based on. He actually appears as a character on the show in 6.22, as part of a trio singing "A Beaver Ate My Thumb"

3.4

- Lorelai accused Luke of being a "Buffethead". The actual terms for fans of Jimmy Buffett is "Parrothead"

- The blonde girl in class who asks Lorelai about her pregnancy appears later in the series as Juliet (5.15, 6.1, 6.8, 6.19)

3.5

- During Lorelai's phone call with Peyton, Lorelai says that his jet got back "from Maui", although this is clearly a voiceover, as her lips appear to say "from Bali". This may be a last minute change due to a terrorist attack in Bali which occurred days before the episode aired
- Richard's phone conversation with Lorelai was actually with Patty Malcolm, Lauren Graham's stand-in

3.6

- First episode with the new Caesar
- After the town meeting, Lorelai sings the opening theme to *The Patty Duke Show*

3.7

- Alexis Bledel and Milo Ventimiglia dated outside of the show, for several years.

3.10

- The title for this episode is a reference to a line in the film *Babe*

3.11

- Seth McFarlane is the voice of Bob Merriam, the lawyer on the phone with Lorelai

3.12

- Jess calls himself a carnivore. Milo Ventimiglia is actually a vegetarian

3.13

- The actress who played a teen Lorelai had to wear blue contacts, as her natural eye colour is brown

3.15

- Brad Langford is re-introduced to the class, after having been in the Broadway production of *Into the Woods*. Adam Wylie who plays Brad actually was a cast member in *Into the Woods*

3.19

- Max tells Lorelai that she is like a mythological creature who casts a spell on him. According to German folklore, "Die Lorelai" were sirens who lured sailors to their deaths using song
- Kyle's house in this episode is the same as Mia's house in 7.17

3.20

- This is the first episode where Caesar is credited. Aris Alvarado is the third actor to play Caesar, but the first to have lines
- Melissa' McCarthy's husband plays the role of Mr. Brink and a pallbearer in 3.22

3.21

- Jess was supposed to star in a spin-off called *Windward Circle*, following on from the storyline in this episode. The high cost of filming the series in Venice prohibited the series from going ahead
- Alex Borstein appears as Miss Celine, after appearing in season 1 as Drella. Alex

was married to Jackson Douglas, who plays Jackson Belleville on the show

- Sasha is played by Sherilynn Fenn, who later goes on to play Anna Nardini. The show's creator, Amy Sherman-Palladino originally had Sherilyn Fenn (who plays Anna Nardini/Sasha) in mind for the character of Lorelai

3.22

- There is an alternative ending where a flashback of a young Lorelai and Rory are at the Independence Inn
- This episode reveals that Rory's middle name is Leigh, and Pari's is Eustace

Season Four

4.1

- This marks the first episode in HDTV

4.2

- Both Lady Bird Johnson and Pat Summerall were alive when this episode aired
- "Dewey, Cheatem and Howe" was invented by the Car Talk brothers
- This was the first episode to feature a 'previously on' segment at the start

4.4

- Dave's absence was said to have been due to his attendance at a university in California. The actor Adam Brody left the show to pursue a role on The O.C. which is set in California. Similarly, Tristan states that his father is sending him to military school in North Carolina, where Chad Michael Murray's role in One Tree Hill was set.

4.5

- Lorelai tells Luke she has a problem with his baseball cap, even though she gave it to him in 1.10
- Rory accuses Lorelai of not ever having dated either, even though there is a significant discussion about her casual date with Paul in 2.9

4.7

- Gil is introduced in this episode, played by Sebastian Bach - the original singer of Skid Row
- Lane's band, Hep Alien, is an anagram of Helen Pai's name

4.8

- Seth and Rachael MacFarlane are the folk singers that Rory reviews at the end of the episode

4.9

- Lisa Weil who plays Paris, sleeps with another character named Asher on the TV show *How to Get Away with Murder*

4.11

- Lane is wearing Lorelai's sweater from 1.17
- CBGB stands for "Country, Blue Grass, and Blues"
- Rory says she hates mushrooms, even though she said in 3.19 that she loved the Mushroom Caps served at the Gilmore's

4.12

- The Tolstoy quote is "All happy families resemble one another, each unhappy family is unhappy in its own way"
- First appearance of Liz Danes
- Jason refers to Luke as Duke, which connects to a conversation between Rory and Lorelai in 2.15

4.13

- The title is an explanation of the "Nag Hammadi" reference that everyone laughs at but doesn't understand

4.15

- The mall they visit is the Burbank Mall

4.16

- Several people play more than one character in the show, including Marion Ross who plays Trix and Marilyn
- Gran is said to have met Kennedy, Johnson, and Nixon. These are the presidents that Forrest Gump met

4.17

- The band playing the club is The Shins. Rory borrows their album from Lane in season 3

4.18

- Bob calls golf "a good walk spoiled", which is what Richard calls golf in 1.3
- Kirk's easter egg pep talk is a reference to Howard Dean's yell speech in 2004

4.19

- Zach and Brian are playing Soulcalibur II
- The café where Jason and Lorelai break up is the same one where her and Max decide to date, and later take a break

4.20

- This episode features three actors from the same family: Michael DeLuise as TJ, Dom Deluise is visible in the movie that Rory and Lorelai are watching, and David DeLuise plays TJ's brother.
- The hospital is filmed on the set of ER

4.21

- The roommate collage has pictures duplicated

- Graham Sullivan was supposed to be Rory's new love interest in season 5 but was instead picked up by Veronica Mars. Logan was written into the show as the new love interest.
- Liz says she had three husbands, plus a boyfriend, which makes TJ her 4th husband. In a later episode, TJ also says she had an ex named "Art" (5.9)

Season Five

5.1

- Luke leaves Lorelai voice messages with his phone number: (860) 294 – 1986. This number was used to take donations for a new children's and maternal hospital, that Scott Patterson's brother was the director of.

- Rory and Dean's song is from the movie *Willy Wonka and the Chocolate Factory* which they watched on their first date

- The episode title is a reference to the Henry James book 'Daisy Miller'

- Rory says that she slept with Dean on an "Al Gilbert" record. Al Gilbert is a tap dancing instructor who had a line of records to teach graded tap dancing

5.2

- Lorelai saying "is our town, it is so glamorous" is a reference to the Go-Go's song "This Town"

- Emily says "gracias" (Spanish) when she is supposed to be speaking Italian

5.3

- The maid in this episode is named after Madonna (Madonna Louise Ciccone)
- Lorelai talks about the plot from "Some Kind of Wonderful" when planning her and Luke's first date
- Paris references Dick Shawn who died in the middle of a comic routine, leaving the audience to think it was a part of the act

5.4

- Taylor's statement that Stars Hollow "would have him to kick around again' is a reference to President Nixon's farewell speech

5.5

- The maid in this episode is the same maid from 3.2, 'Sarah'.

5.6

- The Life and Death Brigade is based on the Skull and Bones society - a secret society at Yale that was founded in the early 1800s. The movie The Skulls was loosely based on this also.

5.7

- The title of this episode is a reference to *Titanic* (1997)
- Margie can be seen working as Richard's secretary again, now that he is back at the company. In 2.20, he was upset that she wouldn't be working with her anymore.

5.10

- The 'nose touching' between Richard and Rory is a reference to the film *The Sting* (1973)
- Rory references characters from *Buffy the Vampire Slayer*, which Danny Strong who plays Doyle starred in
- Kirk is reading *Yoga for Dummies* at Miss Patty's celebration

- Paris' hair is up when she leaves for speed dating, but down when she arrives

5.13

- This marks the 100th episode of the series!
- Second appearance of cousin Marilyn
- Lorelai and Rory plan a *Cop Rock* marathon. Kathleen Wilhoite who plays Liz can be seen in three episodes of the show
- Richard and Emily's wedding takes place at the same venue as Rory's debutante ball in 2.6
- Marilyn's interest in gardeners is a reference to *Desperate Housewives*

5.15

- Rikki Lindhome who was in 3.4 now returns as Juliet
- The piano player in this episode was the piano player on *Glee*. He returns in AYITL: Summer to reprise his role

5.17

- Alexis Bledel starred herself in a Quentin Tarantino movie, *Sin City*
- Luke breaks his own "NO cell phones" rule
- Rory wears her Chilton uniform to Finn's party

5.18

- Jared Padalecki was written out of the show after he was picked up for *Supernatural.* This is the last episode with Dean until *AYITL*
- When Lane and Sophie are talking about the old record, you can hear "Pleasant Valley Sunday" in the background, which was written by Carole King who plays Sophie
- Jackson Douglas who plays Jackson, directed this episode
- Sophie calls Lane "Garrison Keeler". Garrison Keeler is an author and storyteller
- Dean is not wearing a wedding ring in this episode, so we can assume that he did not get back together with Lindsay

5.19

- Logan's family business is loosely based on the Sulzberger family who own the New York Times. Emily refers to the family in 7.20

5.20

- The idea of a 'kropog' is based on an MIT fraternity prank from 1958 when Oliver R. Smoot lay down on the Harvard Bridge. His fraternity brothers then measured the bridge in "Smoots". These markings can still be seen on the bridge.

5.22

- Lorelai references an episode of *NYPD Blue (1993)* where Sipowicz's son was arrested. This was played my Michael Deluise, who plays T.J. on *Gilmore Girls*
- Lorelai's dollhouse from 6.6 can be seen on the clearance table at Kim's Antiques
- Lorelai claims that Rory has never stolen anything, despite her shoplifting in 1.7

- Rory's court date is set for June 3rd, which will become Luke and Lorelai's wedding date in season 6

Season Six

6.2

- Rory tells Esperanza that she speaks a little Spanish. Alexis Bledel's first language was Spanish and she speaks it fluently
- Lorelai suggests turning her house into a recording studio so she can rent it to Korn. Korn were tenants of Trix's house in Connecticut in 3.10

6.3

- Michel says that Paris mocked her and called her "Canadian". Yanic Truesdale who plays Michel is originally from Quebec, Canada
- Emily calls Rory "Valeria Plame". Plame was the CIA operative who was outed as a spy in the Washington Post in 2003
- The Gloucestershire Cheese Rolling event that Logan references is a real event which takes place in Brockworth, Gloucester every year on the May Bank Holiday

- When Rory visits Yale, the freshman counsellor is the same one that did Rory's orientation in 4.1
- Paris jokes with Lorelai about building an ark. In 2007, Lauren Graham starred in *Evan Almighty* about a man who builds an ark

6.4

- The title of this episode is a reference to the phrase "Always a bridesmaid, never a bride"

6.5

- The Hermes Birkin bag from Logan costs approximately $38,900.00
- The title of this episode is the same as *Pretty Little Liars* 2.5

6.7

- Rory's dream is a replay of the conversation that Lorelai had with Rory in 1.6

- The Rory is the same recipe as a flirtini - champagne, vodka, pineapple juice and grenadine

6.8

- The title for this episode is a reference to The Beatles song "Back in the USSR"

6.11

- Rory's debutante dress can be spotted in the wedding shop
- Sherilynn Fenn returns as Anna, after appearing as Sasha in 3.21
- When Paris hands out the assignments at the Yale Daily News, she says that the sport beat goes to Russ Tamblyn. Russ is an actor, and father of actress Amber Tamblyn who acted in *The Sisterhood of the Traveling Pants* (2005) with Alexis Bledel
- We find out this episode that Luke is a Boston Red Sox fan
- Lorelai says "blah" about the idea of a town wedding that includes the gazebo, even though this is the kind of wedding she ends up having in AYITL

- When Rory drives away, it is clear that she is not actually the driver

6.12

- Zach says "Welcome to the S.H. bitch!" This is a reference to *The O.C.* (2003)
- The episode title is a reference to Gwen Stefani and Gavin Rossdale who married in 2002
- The contents of the letter in this episode was a mystery until it was spotted by a fan on a tour of the Warner Bros. Studio in Burbank

6.13

- The episode title is a reference to Elton John's son "Saturday Night's Alright for Fighting"

6.15

- Rory says that her 'zen place' is Greece. In *The Sisterhood of the Traveling Pants* (2005) this is where Alexis Bledel's character spends her summer

6.16

- The editor of the Daily Princetonian is played by Leslie Odom Jr. who is a Broadway star. He played Aaron Burr in *Hamilton.* Burr graduation from Princeton (originally called The College of New Jersey) in 1772.
- Samantha Shelton appears in this episode as a bridesmaid, after appearing as a debutante in 2.6
- Rory says that her and Logan were not broken up, despite telling Paris in 6.11 that they are

6.18

- The kids are singing "The Elements" by Tom Lehrer. The melody for this song is eseentially the same as "The Major General Song" from *The Pirates of Penzance"*. It can also be heard in *Animaniacs* (1993)
- Richard and Emily tell Lorelai that they plan to visit Washington Depot to shop for

antiques. This is the town that Stars Hollow was based on

6.19

- Lane and Zach's pose on the wedding cake is a reference to the White Stripes album cover "Get Behind Me Satan"
- Lane's Korean name is Hyun-jung
- This is the second time that a groom becomes obsessed with the wedding attire that he has one. Zach loves the silk of his Korean dress, and T.J. liked his 'air pants' in 4.21.

6.20

- Lorelai tells the girls that Molly Ringwald is "someone very special" to her. Lauren Graham actually starred with Molly Ringwald in *Townies* (1996)
- Lorelai's comment about stealing the Declaration of Independence is a reference to *National Treasure* (2004)
- Finn refers to Mitchum as "The Dark Lord", which is probably a reference to Voldemort from The Harry Potter series

6.22

- This is the last episode where Amy Sherman-Palladino is the writer and executive producer, until AYITL
- This is also the last episode of the original series to be broadcast on the WB Television Network
- The trio singing "A Beaver Ate My Thumb" includes Daniel Palladino, and the real-life Dave Rygalski
- Sam Phillips, the writer and performer of the show's famous "la-la's" also performs as a troubadour in this episode, singing "Taking Pictures"

Season Seven

7.1

- This is the only season to not be overseen by the Palladino's
- When Lorelai says "The Prodigal Daughter Returns!" she is referencing 6.9

7.2

- The Buddha statue that can be seen when Rory walks into the house is the same one from Lane's wedding

7.3

- Lane is reading "What to Expect When You're Expecting, Third Edition" by Heidi Murkoff, Arlene Eisenberg, and Sandee Hathaway
- Rory is reading "Sexus: The Rosy Crucifixion I" by Henry Miller

7.4

- The episode title is a reference to *Funny Face* (1957)

7.5

- When Lorelai complains about the music Christopher is playing in the car, it is "Eighteen and Life" by the band Skid Row (the lead singer Sebastian Bach plays Gil in *Gilmore Girls)*.

7.6

- The Yale scenes were filmed at the University for Southern California. The parents weekend banner is actually covering the sign for Bovard Auditorium
- The room that Christopher and Lorelai are in for the astrophysics lecture is the same room where the boys play the classroom prank in 5.10

7.7

- The bedding in Paris is Lorelai's bedding from 7.1, and can be seen again in 7.10

7.9

- The basketball game that Christopher and Jackson watch at the bar is University of Kentucky vs. the University of Alabama, played at Freedom Hall in Louisville, KY on January 21, 1998.

7.10

- During Luke and Christopher's fight, the leg of a cameraman can be spotted

7.12

- The vasectomy issue was written in to get around Melissa McCarthy's pregnancy, after Sookie had finished having children

7.13

- The title of this episode is a reference to a W.C. Fields quote, "I'd rather be in Philadelphia." Ronald Reagan later said it after an assassination attempt against him

7.14

- Lane and Luke have no lines in this episode

7.15

- Lorelai compares her parents house to a "Skinner box" - a reference to psychologist BF Skinner who raised his daughter in a specially designed room

7.16

- Sebastian Bach appears for the final time in the original series

7.17

- Zach says it's obvious that Luke used to play ball. Scott Patterson who plays Luke used to be a minor league baseball player before *Gilmore Girls*
- Mia in this episode is different from the actress who played Mia in 2.8
- Mia's house is the same on as Kyle's house in 3.19\

7.18

- Although it's referred to as a hay bale maze, it appears more like straw
- April's discussion on the Apache tribe suggests she lives in northern New Mexico near the Colorado state border

7.19

- Rory's address is 544 Howe Street, Apartment #8, New Haven, Connecticut 06511. This street exists, and is within blocks of the Old Campus at Yale, however the street numbers don't go that high

7.20

- One of the signs in the karaoke bar says "Boozoo Barns". Boozoo was in the Zydeco band in 6.15
- First appearance of Lane and Zach's twins
- Lorelai's dollhouse appears in the dream sequence unbroken, despite Jackson breaking it in 7.19
- This is the first episode where Luke wears Lorelai's hat again, since the breakup

- Zach says he will be touring with the Tokyo Police Club, a real band formed in Canada
- Logan's family business is loosely based on the Sulzberger family who own the New York Times. Emily refers to them in this episode

7.21

- The title of this episode is a reference to Shakespeare's *Henry V* (Act III)
- Kirk in a box is a reference to David Blaine's "Above the Below" where he was sealed inside Plexiglas for 44 days

A Year in the Life

Winter

- Richard Gilmore's death was written into A Year in the Life, after Edward Hermann sadly passed away in 2014. The credits for this episode are in memory to Edward Hermann.
- The sister of the Troubadour is played by Louise Gofiin who performs in the show's theme song with her mother Carole King
- The new sign in Luke's says "NO Texting while ordering"
- Luke mentions "Restless Virgins" when going through Lorelai's DVR. Vanessa Marano who plays April starred in this film
- The actress in Luke's requesting the WIFI password is the casting director for the original series
- Luke gives the following passwords to his customers : Dinerluke, DINERDANES321, wafflehouseButterbob

- Paris mentions the TV show *Buffy the Vampire Slayer*. Danny Strong who plays Doyle played Jonathon on the show
- Lorelai and Rory make several mentions of how long it has been since they have seen each other, a nod to the long gap between the original series and the revival
- Alex Kingston's character stealing food from a doctor is a reference to *Doctor Who* (2005) where she plays a thief who causes trouble for The Doctor
- Paul says "I will follow", as a reference to the theme song
- Doyle is said to have become a successful Hollywood screenwriter. Danny Strong who plays Doyle is a Hollywood screenwriter, and worked on the screenplay for films such as *The Hunger Games: Mockingjay Part 1* (2014) and *Part 2* (2015)

Spring

- Mr. Kim appears for the first time in this episode
- Marcy is played by Mae Whitman, who starred opposite Lauren Graham in *Parenthood*

- Monique Aswell bakery is a reference to Dominique Ansel Bakery who is famously credited with creating the cronut
- Sandee, played by Julia Goldani Telles, starred in *Bunheads* (2012), which was created by Amy Sherman-Palladino
- A body double was used for Tristan
- Kirk gets upset when he sees a pig being roasted at the festival. This is the first time we find out that Kirk is vegetarian. Sean Gunn, who plays Kirk, is also vegetarian

Summer

- Sutton Foster and Christian Borle who play the couple in the Stars Hollow Musical, are both Tony award winners, and used to be married. Sutton also had the lead role in *Bunheads*
- The Stars Hollow musical was written by Jeanine Tesori, who has written several Broadway musicals
- Carole King who plays Sophie, plays one of her hit songs "I Feel the Earth Move"
- The piano player in this episode was the piano player on *Glee*.

Fall

- The park ranger is played by Peter Krause, who is in a relationship off-screen with Lauren Graham
- Dean's wife "jenny" may be a reference to Jared Padalecki's wife Genevieve
- Lorelai's suggestion that Rory should drop the "the" from the book title is a reference to *The Social Network* (2010)
- The Halfway House Coffee shop that Lorelai goes into can be seen in 1.13 of *Parenthood*
- Emily changing her shoes is a reference to *Dirty Dancing* (1987)
- In the original script, the famous four words read "the final four words are said"
- "Reflecting Light", the wedding song, is a nod to Luke and Lorelai's first dance in 4.21
- The cornstarch joke at Doose's is a reference to 1.7
- Lorelai says she watched *An Unmarried Woman* (1978) with Richard. Kelly Bishop who plays Emily was in that film

- The goodbyes with the Life and Death Brigade members is a reference to *The Wizard of Oz* (1939)
- The conversation between Emily and Lorelai about the loan mirrors the one between Lorelai, Emily and Richard in the pilot, when Lorelai asks for a loan for Chilton
- Lorelai and Luke get married on November 5th

I'M WRITING A LETTER. I CAN'T WRITE A LETTER. WHY CAN'T I WRITE A LETTER?

DOCUMENTS

Documents in Gilmore Girls

Those this section is not long, and does not comprise cultural references made in the show, it is an important addition, and more importantly, a fun one.

Inspiration for this section came from the early years of Gilmore fandom when speculation over what Lorelai said in her letter to Rory, was at its peak. This mystery had remained unsolved when I visited the Warner Bros. studio in California in 2013, and was one of the first fans to see the famous letter on display in a glass case. Since then, photos have been taken of it which can be found circulating on Pinterest, fan groups, and undoubtedly Google images.

The letter, handwritten, has been transcribed into this section of the book, as well as many other letters and documents which feature in the show, starting with the document that started it all – Rory's acceptance letter from Chilton, which Lorelai reads out in the pilot. Other important documents, such as Lorelai's character reference for Luke, become central to the narrative arc, and have significant impact on the characters in the show. It is my hope that reading through these documents, and seeing them written down, will somehow help you to connect, or re-connect with the meaning of them for the characters, and the storylines.

Chilton Acceptance Letter
(1.1)

Dear Ms. Gilmore,

We are happy to inform you that we have a vacancy at Chilton Preparatory starting immediately. Due to your daughter's excellent credentials and your enthusiastic pursuit of her enrolment, we would be happy to accept her as soon as the first semester's tuition has been received.

Yours Sincerely,

Headmaster Charleston

Note - Lorelai to her Parents
(3.13)

Dear Mom and Dad,

I'm in Labor.

See you later,

Lorelai

Letter from Trix to Richard
(4.16)

My Dearest Richard,

It is with heavy heart that I write you this letter tonight, but I cannot stand by and let you make a terrible mistake. Until now, I had thought, hoped, prayed that you would come to the same conclusion that I have. But you have not, and therefore, I feel it is my duty as your mother to beg you to reconsider your impending marriage. I'm sure that Emily is a very suitable woman for someone, but not for you. She will not be able to make you happy. She does not have the Gilmore stamina or spark. She is simply not a Gilmore.

I don't know the circumstances surrounding your breakup with Pennilyn Lott, but it is still my belief that she is much better suited for you than Emily.
I know that the timing of this is particularly awkward, since you are to be married tomorrow, but your happiness is too important to me, so timing be damned.

Lorelai's Character Reference for Luke
(7.12)

Jan 9, 2007

To Whom It May Concern,

In the nearly 10 years that I have known Luke Danes, I have come to know him as an honest and decent man. He is also one of the most kind and caring people I have ever met.
I am a single mother and I raised my daughter by myself, but once Luke Danes became my friend in this town, I never really felt alone. Luke and I have had our ups and downs over the years, but through it all, his relationship with my daughter Rory has never changed.

He's always been there for her no matter what. He was there to celebrate her birthdays, he was there cheering her on at her high school graduation. Luke has been a sort of father figure in my daughter's life. With his own daughter, Luke wasn't given the opportunity to be there for her first 12 years, but he should be given that opportunity now. Once Luke Danes is in your life, he's in your life forever.

I know from personal experience what an amazing gift that is and not to allow him access to his daughter would be to seriously deprive her of all this man has to offer and he offers so much.

Thank you for your time.

Sincerely,

Lorelai Gilmore

Letter to Rory from Lorelai
(6.12)

Dear Rory,

So, right now you are reading my sealed words of wisdom as the tormented, foolish (but persistent) cad hangs off every nuance of your reactions, his heart and mind in a dizzying flurry of questions as to how the outcome will play out… As you read this, delight in the knowledge that this love-sick pup before you does not have a clue…

Now, ordinarily, after a fool has taken my daughter's love for granted, if I did not kill him through a slow and excruciatingly painful death, I would instruct my daughter, much like Miss Havisham did to Estella in 'Great Expectations', to be cold blooded and calculating, to dash his hopes, and to crush him. However, the decision is all yours to make. Love is elusive and all-encompassing; when you fall under its intoxicating spell, you have little recourse but to live out its devices. If you love this boy, maybe you want to give it another chance…?

Good luck, love you,

Mom

Ideas for Inn Names
(2.8)

~~The Rachel Property~~
~~The Crap Shack~~
~~The Paul Revere~~
~~The Country Rose~~
~~The Inn by the Hollow~~
~~The Money Pit~~
~~The Outhouse~~
~~The Inn Heading for Bankruptcy~~
~~Fran's Old Place~~
~~The In Inn~~

<u>The Dragonfly</u>

Band Name Ideas

(3.19)

~~The Harry Potters~~
~~Devil's Advocate~~
~~Follow Me to the Edge of the Desert~~
~~The We~~
~~The Chops~~

<u>Hep Alien</u>

Cease and Desist Order - Dragonfly Inn
(4.4)

Dear Lorelai Gilmore,

It has come to the attention of the Stars Hollow Historical Preservation Society that you and Ms. Sookie St. James intend to commence construction on The Dragonfly Inn.

Any proposed renovations must be submitted, discussed, and approved by the Stars Hollow Historical Preservation Society. We must therefore ask that all work halt until such time that this procedure has been followed.

Thank you, and have a historical day.

Taylor Doose
Stars Hollow Historical Preservation Society

Lane's Letter to Rory
(6.19)

Dear Rory,

How was your lunch? Mine was bad. Did you have ham again? If you did, I am sorry, but mine was worse. I thought you should know that today at recess I decided that I'm going to marry Alex Backus. He has a very nice head, and his ears don't stick out like Ronnie Winston's do. I will love him forever, no matter what. See you at brownies.

Love, Lane

Teen Mom Loralai Gilmore Arrives in Stars Hollow Takes Job at Independence Inn

(AYITL: Summer)

By JOSEPH MASON
Gazette Staff Writer

When Star's Hollow's newest resident, Loralai Gilmore, first showed up on the steps of the Independence Inn, she had a baby in her arms. "I haven't a clue where she came from," say Independence Inn owner, Mia Bass. "But once I saw that beautiful little baby, I couldn't turn her away." That little baby is Loralai Gilmore's daughter, Rory, whom Loralai is raising as a single mother. Since their unexpected arrival at the Independence Inn, Loralai has

READ MORE ON *Page 2*

Lorelai's Deposition for Emily
(3.11)

Why has your mother dismissed maids in the past?
Different reasons.

Can you expand on that?
Gee, how much time do you have?

I mean, if you guys have a lunch or an afternoon squash game or something. . .you look like the kind of guys who play squash. And hey, why's it called squash? Is it something to do with the fruit? Or vegetable, right? A squash is a vegetable, though if you ask me, it's gross no matter what you call it. Well, anyway, what I'm saying is you might want to clear your afternoon.

Would you say your mother sets impossible goals which people cannot help but fail to reach, thereby reinforcing her already formed opinion of their deficiencies?
Only for her daughter.

Would you call your mother an extremely critical woman?
Long pause.

On a scale from one to ten, what would you rate your mother in terms of compassion for others' feelings?

6.6

THE GOOD NEWS DAILY

Nothing But Good News Everyday

THIS ISSUE'S FEATURED ARTICLES:

No Civil War in Canada!

Cars Drive down road without incident!

PUPPIES

How cute are they? In-depth expose

Subscription is free!

You Jump, I Jump, Jack

The Rest of the Gilmore World

The Rest of the Gilmore World

This section is the messiest, but in some ways the most interesting. When I was compiling this book, and researching for it (watching the show over and OVER again), it very quickly became clear that there was a lot to be included, that did not naturally fit into any of the pre-ordained sections that came together so nicely (music, books, movies, etc.) The choice left was to either not include this material, or to try and make it fit into a book that was, up until this point, very systematized. Had I not been a fan myself, I may have chosen the former, but I knew that if I were buying this book, I would want these important features of the show included in it. Thus, my choice was clear.

The material in this section contains lists and guides to some of the key features of the show, without which, *Gilmore Girls* would not be the same. This section opens with a list of places that *Gilmore Girls* has been referenced, providing a catalogue of every other TV show, film, and video game that has ever referred to the show. This list is a reversal of the other lists in this book because it starts outside of the show, and references back to it, rather than being something from within *Gilmore Girls.* This list also reflects the impact that the show has had on many other television shows which followed.

Every illness ever mentioned, pet or animal, and geographical location can be found in this section, as well as a comprehensive list which catalogues Emily's revolving door of maids. This is followed by a guide which traces Rory's study habits throughout high school, and college, and offers a compelling path to 'Studying like a Gilmore'. Briefer, and potentially more fun lists like 'Things Paul Anka is scared of' offer light entertainment, and provide further insight into some of the smaller storylines in the show that are overshadowed by the major themes. I hope you will find the material in here as interesting as I did, and prove my decision right – that it had to be included.

Gilmore Girls: Referenced In

While *Gilmore Girls* is packed full of references, it has also been the subject of much referencing within the T.V. world. The following list provides you with every television episode which has discussed the beloved *Gilmore Girls*.

T.V. Series

- 2 Broke Girls: And the Attack of the Killer Apartment (2016)
- American Dad!: Finances with Wolves (2006)
- Brooklyn Nine-Nine: Johnny and Dora (2015)
- Chasing Life: Wild Thing (2015)
- Chuck: Chuck Versus the Alma Mater (2007)
- Degrassi: Next Class: #NotAllMen (2016)
- Diamond (2016)
- Difficult People: Patches (2016)
- EW Reunites: The Cast of Gilmore Girls (2016)
- Family Guy: A Lot Going on Upstairs (2016)

- Family Guy: From Method to Madness (2002)
- Family Guy: The Perfect Castaway (2005)
- Finding Carter: Pilot (2014)
- Girls: Gummies (2017)
- Glee: The Role You Were Born to Play (2012)
- Gossip Girl: You've Got Yale! (2009)
- Great TV Mistakes (2010)
- Greek: Hazed and Confused (2007)
- Happy Endings: Yesandwitch (2011)
- I Be Geniusen Stuff: Gilmore Girls Part 1 (2015)
- I Be Geniusen Stuff: Gilmore Girls Part 2 (2015)
- I Be Geniusen Stuff: Gilmore Girls Part 3 (2015)
- I Be Geniusen Stuff: Gilmore Girls: A Year in the Life (2017)
- Jeopardy!: Episode #33.63 (2016)
- Joey: Joey and the ESL (2005)
- Kathy Griffin: Everybody Can Suck It (2007)
- Late Night with Seth Meyers: Jeff Daniels/Sutton Foster/Cynthia D'Aprix Sweeney (2016)
- Late Night with Seth Meyers: Lauren Graham/Rainn Wilson/Brian Michael Bendis (2015)
- Mad: Ko-Bee Movie/Law & Ogre (2011)
- Men at Work: Long Distance Tyler (2013)

- Midnight Screenings: Gilmore Girls: A Year in the Life/Moonlight (2016)
- Midnight Screenings: Gilmore Girls: A Year in the Life/Sing (2016)
- Mike and Mike in the Morning: Episode dated 27 June 2016 (2016)
- Mixxxer Show: Kovy (2016)
- Party Down: Nick DiCintio's Orgy Night (2010)
- Playing House: Drumline (2014)
- Richard Roeper & the Movies: The Good Guy (2010)
- Robson Arms: Mean Girls (2008)
- Saturday Night Live: Alec Baldwin/Missy Elliott (2003)
- Saturday Night Live: Emma Stone/Shawn Mendes (2016)
- Saturday Night Live: Kirsten Dunst/Eminem (2002)
- Saturday Night Live: Paul Giamatti/Ludacris featuring Sum-41 (2005)
- Scrubs: My Chopped Liver (2006)
- Scrubs: My Lips Are Sealed (2005)
- Smash: The Parents (2013)
- Still Standing: Still Graduating (2006)
- Studio C: Episode #6.8 (2015)
- Suburgatory: Dalia Nicole Smith (2014)
- Super Fun Night: ...Till the Fat Lady Sings (2014)

- Tante Soesa & Sassefras: Een Jaar Vol Gedoe (2020)
- Talk Show the Game Show: She Ready, Boo! (2017)
- The 100 Scariest Movie Moments (2004)
- The Cinema Snob: Friday the 13th: A Nude Beginning (2015)
- The Cinema Snob: The Oogieloves in the Big Balloon Adventure (2016)
- The Cleveland Show: Who Done Did It? (2013)
- The Nostalgia Critic: Free Willy (2010)
- The Rotten Tomatoes Show: Inglourious Basterds/Post Grad/World's Greatest Dad (2009)
- The Rotten Tomatoes Show: Shutter Island/The Ghost Writer/Happy Tears (2010)
- The Tonight Show Starring Jimmy Fallon: Bill Maher/Chicago Cubs/Daveed Diggs/MUNA (2016)
- The Tonight Show Starring Jimmy Fallon: Emily Blunt/Mario Batali/Chance the Rapper (2016)
- The Tonight Show Starring Jimmy Fallon: Billy Bob Thornton/Andy Cohen/Little Big Town (2016)
- The Tonight Show Starring Jimmy Fallon: Gwyneth Paltrow/Tyler Oakley/The Who (2016)

- The Tonight Show Starring Jimmy Fallon: Jennifer Aniston/Bill Gates/Mario Batali (2015)
  Red Band Society: Waiting for Superman (2015)
- The Tonight Show Starring Jimmy Fallon: John Goodman/Alexis Bledel/David Gray (2016)
- The Tonight Show Starring Jimmy Fallon: Jude Law/Sterling K. Brown/Macklemore feat. Ariana DeBoo (2016)
- The Tonight Show Starring Jimmy Fallon: Justin Timberlake/Tracey Ullman/Stanaj (2016)
- The Tonight Show Starring Jimmy Fallon: Benedict Cumberbatch/Rachel Maddow/Jim James (2016)
- The Tonight Show Starring Jimmy Fallon: Natalie Portman/J.J. Abrams/Neil
- The Tonight Show Starring Jimmy Fallon: Warren Beatty/Naomie Harris/Robbie Robertson/Aminé (2016)
- EW Reunites: The Cast of Gilmore Girls (2016)
- The Tonight Show Starring Jimmy Fallon: Jude Law/Sterling K. Brown/Macklemore feat. Ariana DeBoo (2016)
- The Tonight Show Starring Jimmy Fallon: Jason Sudeikis/Kristin Chenoweth/DNCE (2016)

- The Tonight Show Starring Jimmy Fallon: Sarah Jessica Parker/Scott Patterson - Liza Weil - Sean Gunn/Frank Pellegrino Jr. (2016)
- The Tonight Show Starring Jimmy Fallon: John Goodman/Alexis Bledel/David Gray (2016)
- The Tonight Show Starring Jimmy Fallon: Katie Holmes/David Wain & Michael Showalter/Sage the Gemini feat. Nick Jonas (2015)
- The Tonight Show Starring Jimmy Fallon: Melissa McCarthy/Christian Slater/Jennifer Lopez & Lin-Manuel Miranda (2016)
- The Tonight Show Starring Jimmy Fallon: Sarah Jessica Parker/Scott Patterson - Liza Weil - Sean Gunn/Frank Pellegrino Jr. (2016)
- The Tonight Show Starring Jimmy Fallon: Seth MacFarlane/Amber Heard/Leon Bridges (2015)
- The Tonight Show Starring Jimmy Fallon: Warren Beatty/Naomie Harris/Robbie Robertson/Aminé (2016)
- The Tonight Show Starring Jimmy Fallon: Will Forte/Milo Ventimiglia/Future (2017)
- Powerless: Emily Dates a Henchman (2017)
- The Tonight Show with Jay Leno: Episode #18.21 (2010)

- The Tonight Show with Jay Leno: Episode #18.71 (2010)
- The Tonight Show with Jay Leno: Episode #20.7 (2011)
- The Venture Bros.: Return to Malice (2009)
- This Is Us: The Big Three (2016)
- United Travel Getaway: Getaway Goes to Hollywood (2004)
- WatchMojo: Top 10 Worst Girlfriends in TV (2018)
- Will & Grace: 5.23 (2003)
- Wheel of Fortune: Girlfriend Getaways 1 (2016)
- Whitney: The Ex Box (2012)
- Who Wants to Be a Millionaire: Episode #8.71 (2009)
- Younger: The Exes (2015)

Movies:
- 12 Stories About Eileen (2003)
- Office Christmas Party (2016)
- Robot Chicken DC Comics Special 3: Magical Friendship (2015)
- Saturday Night Live: The Best of Commercial Parodies (2005)
- The TV Set (2006)
- Sideline Secrets 1 (2006)
- Studio 60 on the Sunset Strip: The Wrap Party (2006)

- Robot Chicken: Drippy Pony (2006)
- My Boys: Released (2006)
- The Nines (2007)
- Veronica Mars: Papa's Cabin (2007)
- TMNT (2007)
- Supernatural: Hollywood Babylon (2007)
- Killer Pad (2008)
- Old Dogs (2009)
- Living Will... (2010)
- Lake Placid: The Final Chapter (2012)
- Super Size Me (2004)
- Supernatural (2005)

Illnesses

Allergies (3.16, 7.18)
Aneurysm (2.3, 5.5)
Angina (4.20)
Arachnophobia (6.22)
Asthma (3.19)
Back Spasm (1.9)
Bipolar (1.16)
Bird Flu/Asian Bird Flu/Avian Flu (5.8, 6.9, 6.12, 6.14)
Black Eye (7.1)
Blood Sugar Issues (2.20)
Boils (6.6)
Broken Ankle (6.20)
Broken Crown, Teeth (4.15)
Broken Leg (1.6, 7.4)
Broken Hip (AYITL: Winter)
Broken Ribs (6.20)
Bubonic Plague (7.19)
Bunions (3.6, 6.6, 7.21)
Chicken Pox (4.11, 7.19)
Cold (1.14, 3.2, 5.16)
Collapsed Lung (6.20)
Concussion (6.20)
Consumption (AYITL: Winter), With A Touch Of The Vapors (2.11)
Coronary Artery Disease (7.13)
Depression (5.14)
Detached Retina (6.12)

Diabetes (1.1, 6.7)
Dinging/Pinging Brain (1.14)
Diphtheria (1.16, AYITL: Winter)
Ear Infection (5.13)
Eroding Gums (5.5)
Exterminatoritis (2.11)
Fever (6.20)
Flu (1.9, 1.10)
Frostbite (1.8)
Gangrene (2.15)
Glaucoma (2.4)
Hand-To-Moth-To-Mouth Disease (5.6)
Hangover (5.18)
Haunted Leg (3.2)
Headache (1.18)
Heart Attack (2.15, 7.13, 7.22, AYITL: Spring)
Heartburn (3.19)
Hummus Dip (AYITL: Winter)
Hyperventilation (6.11)
Hypochondria (1.14)
Hypoglycemia (3.15)
Ingrown Toenail (7.4)
Internal Bleeding (6.20, 7.3)
Lactose Intolerance (7.18)
Lactose Resistance (7.18)
Laryngitis (1.11)
Leprosy (6.6)
Locked Elbow (6.18)
Low Blood Sugar (7.19)
Mad Cow Disease (3.7)
Malaria (6.3)

Melancholia (6.6)
Mexican Parasite (7.2)
Mood Swings (7.18)
Mumps (1.11)
Myocardial Infarction (7.13, 7.14)
Narcolepsy (1.11)
Nausea (5.7)
Osteoporosis (1.11)
Panic Attack (4.16, 6.5)
Popped Ear Drum (7.22)
Romantic Nausea (5.17)
Rotavirus (AYITL: Spring)
Salmonella (6.18)
Scabies (AYITL: Winter)
Scurvy (1.14, 6.21, AYITL: Summer)
Sleepwalking (6.1)
Sores (6.6)
Splinter (4.4)
Stomach Ache (4.20, 7.10)
Stress Fractures (7.4)
Stroke (2.10, 2.12)
Swollen Ankles (7.22)
Tension Headache (2.11)
Tinnitus (4.11)
Torn Cartilage (6.20)
Tourette's (5.7)
Vertigo (2.15)

Sports and Games

1, 2, 3, He's Yours! (1.20)
Aggravation (3.5)
Backgammon (7.9)
Bagel Hockey (2.13, 2.14)
Ballet (1.1, 1.6, 1.7, 4.8, 5.21, 6.5, 7.4)
Ballroom Dancing (2.6)
Base Jumping (6.18)
Baseball (5.7, 7.17)
Bash (4.21)
Basketball (1.3, 2.8)
Baton Twirling (1.1, 1.2, 3.14, 6.5)
Battleship (4.21)
Battleship (6.16)
Bike Riding (1.4, 5.22, 7.19)
Bingo (3.6)
Birdwatching (7.9, 7.18)
Bop it (5.5, 6.10)
Bowling (7.17)
Boxing (5.7)
Bridge (1.1, 2.11, 6.8)
Bull Fighting (4.1)
Camping (2.2)
Candyland (3.5, 6.16)
Cha Cha (1.11)
Charades (3.5)
Chase the Rainbow (4.15)
Cheerleading (1.1)
Chess (3.5)

Chinese Checkers (3.5)
Climbing (1.13)
Clue (3.5)
Clue (4.21)
Cotton Ball Scoop (3.6)
Craps (4.8)
Cross Country Running (7.1)
Curling (5.11)
Dirty Diapers (3.6)
Dance Extreme (5.14)
Darts (7.9)
Dog Sledding (7.19)
Don't Say Baby (3.6)
Duck Hunting (6.1)
Dungeons and Dragons (2.13)
Easter Egg Hunt (4.18)
Easy Money (3.5)
Equestrian (1.3, 4.14, 4.22)
Fishing (1.12, 2.20, 2.21, 3.12, 3.13)
Food Fight (1.6)
Football (1.17, 2.11, 4.9, 5.7, 6.8)
Galaga (4.15)
Game of the year (3.5)
Go For It (3.5)
Golf (1.2, 1.3, 1.4, 1.10, 3.13, , 4.13, 4.18, 4.19, 5.7, 7.3, 7.15, 7.17)
Gymnastics (1.1, 3.14)
Hangman (3.5)
Hay bale maze (7.18)
Hiking (1.8)
Hungry Hungry Hippos (3.5)

Hurdling (7.1)
Ice Hockey (3.15. 5.7, 7.6)
Ice Skating (1.1, 1.11, 5.11)
Jogging (1.19, 3.15)
Juggling (4.21)
Karaoke (3.6)
Krav Maga (5.15)
Krumping 6.5
Lacrosse (1.3, 4.8, 6.11, 7.6)
Little League (7.9)
Marco Polo (1.4)
Mastermind (3.5)
Maypole (4.21)
Miniature Golf (6.6)
Modelling (1.1)
Monopoly (3.5, 6.16)
Mousetrap (4.21)
Mud Wrestling (1.6)
Night Rider (4.15)
Operation (3.5)
Pilates (7.1)
Poker (1.12, 5.18)
Pool (6.21)
Pyramid (3.5)
Racquetball (7.1)
Revenge From Mars (4.15)
Risk (3.5)
Riverdance (3.7)
Rodeo (1.2)
Roulette (4.8)
Roulette (5.18)

Rubik's Cube (6.12, 7.9)
Running (1.10, 2.14, 5.20, 7.1)
Scattergories (3.5)
Scavenger Hunt (6.20)
Scrabble (6.16)
Scuba Diving (6.2)
Shuffleboard (6.21)
Skeet Shooting (2.21)
Skiing (1.12, 3.5)
Skiing (7.12)
Sledding (1.8)
Sleigh Rides (5.11)
Slot Machines (4.8)
Snorkelling (7.2)
Snowball Fights (5.11)
Soccer (5.7, 6.8)
Softball (1.15. 5.5)
Sorry! (3.5)
Spirograph (4.21)
Surfing (6.1)
Swimming (1.3, 2.5, 6.2)
Tae Bo (1.10)
Tai Chi (6.10)
Tap Dancing (2.2)
Tarot (6.12)
Tennis (5.20)
Thumb Wrestling (1.11)
Times to Remember (3.5)
Track (1.3)
Trivial Pursuit (3.5)
Twister (3.5)

Video Trivia (3.19)
Volleyball (1.1)
Walking (1.5, 1.19, 2.7, 2.16, 3.14, 6.18, 7.15)
Whac-A-Mole (1.16)
White Water Rafting (6.18)
Wrestling (2.11)
Yahtzee (3.5, 4.21)
Yoga (1.6)
'Tossing a ball' (1.1)

Animals and Pets

Unnamed dog - in Gloria's lap at the club (1.2)
Cinnamon - Babette's Cat (1.3)
Unnamed Deer (1.4)
Buttercup - Dog for adoption in the town square (1.11)
Skippy - Lorelai's Hamster (1.11)
Leopold and Lobe - Chase Bradford's Dobermans (1.16)
Apricot - Babette and Maury's new kitten (1.14)
Stella/Case Study #12 - baby chick Rory brings home from school (1.14)
Sammy - cat at The Cheshire Cat B&B (2.4)
Petey - parrot of Luke's cousin Frannie (2.17)
Cat Kirk (3.9)
Jayne Mansfield – fish Lorelai caught (3.12)
Papaya - stray cat at the inn (3.17)
Satchimo - spider that Jackson killed (3.17)
Murray - rabbit that is discussed at Lorelai's birthday dinner (3.18)
Chin Chin and Paw Paw - Michel adopts them from Frank (3.19)

Sasha's dogs (3.21) :
- Angus
- Chowder
- Rufus
- Legolas
- Caligula

- General Lee
- Terry Lewis
- Spot
- Mudball
- Jimmy Jam

Dan – Yale mascot (4.9)
Cyrus - Jason 'Digger' Stiles' dog (4.10)
Desdemona and Cletus - horses at the Dragonfly Inn (4.14)
Snuggles - dog whose owner Kirk is trying to locate (4.15)
Buster - Lulu's dog (4.15)
Unnamed cat #1 (4.20)
Unnamed cat #2 (4.20)
Princess - Emily finds this in the yard (5.11)
Coco/Co-kie/Kookie/Tookie/Paul Anka (6.2)
Stan – the raccoon that lives in the Huntzberger house at Martha's Vineyard (6.15)
Davey's Goldfish (7.19)
Petal – Kirk's pig (AYITL: Winter)
Sherlock – Donald's Dog (AYITL: Spring)

Why Luke Doesn't Like Dogs
(6.2)

- They're dirty
- They're a pain to train
- They're a pain to wash
- They bark when they shouldn't
- They jump on you when you don't want them to
- They chew things
- They shed
- They lick themselves
- They make your house smell
- They make your car smell
- They make you smell
- They have fleas and malaria on them

Things Paul Anka Doesn't Like

- Toys
- Rawhide bones
- Popcorn
- Watches
- Tissue holders
- Paperbacks
- CD's
- Framed pictures
- Lint
- Drinking
- Bottle openers
- Peas
- People watching him eat
- Stairs
- His leash

Emily's Staff

- Unnamed Maid (1.1)
- Unnamed Maid (1.2)
- Mira/Sarah (1.3)
- Heidi (1.3)
- Trina (1.3)
- Sophia (1.3)
- Anton (1.3)
- Anna (1.8)
- Florence (1.8)
- Rosa (1.8)
- Unnamed Maid (1.10)
- Leigh (1.16)
- Siri (1.18)
- Unnamed Maid (1.18)
- Stella (1.18)
- Antonia (2.1)
- Marina (2.2)
- Liesl (2.6, 3.16)
- Marisela (2.8)
- Graziella (2.12)
- Unnamed Maid (2.12)
- Heloise (2.12)
- Unnamed Maid (2.18)
- Beatrice (2.21)
- Inger (2.22)
- Lilliana (3.8)
- Gerta (3.11, 4.1, 6.22)
- Brooke (3.11)

- Theresa (3.18)
- Lupe (3.21)
- Unnamed Maid (4.5)
- Unnamed Maid (4.6)
- Unnamed Maid (4.8)
- Sandy (4.9)
- Chersey (4.14)
- Tilda (4.16)
- Elsa (4.18)
- Unnamed Maid (4.19)
- Kiki (4.21)
- Shriva (4.22)
- Unnamed Maid (5.1)
- Robert (5.3)
- Madonna Louise (5.3)
- Sarah (5.5)
- Jeeves (5.5)
- Unnamed Maid (5.6)
- Unnamed Maid (5.7)
- Olga (5.8)
- Unnamed Maid (5.8)
- Gretchen (5.12)
- Eliza (5.16)
- Olympia (5.17)
- Beatrice (5.20)
- Devita (5.22)
- Hosanna (6.1)
- Unnamed Maid (6.2)
- Esperanza (6.2)
- Dracuda (6.2)
- Unnamed Maid (6.3)

- Unnamed Maid (6.4)
- Unnamed Maids x 2 (6.7)
- Consuela (6.6)
- Simatra (6.9)
- Unnamed Maid (6.13)
- Letitia (6.14)
- Musepa (6.21)
- Unnamed Maid (6.21)
- Unnamed Maid (7.3)
- Unnamed Maid (7.5)
- Bridget (7.12)
- Aurora (7.15)
- Unnamed Maid (7.15)
- Unnamed Maids x2 (7.17)
- Alexandra (7.20)
- Berta (AYITL: Winter, Spring, Summer, Fall)
- Alejandro (AYITL: Winter)
- Unnamed Gardener (AYITL: Winter)
- Unnamed Pool Man (AYITL: Winter)
- Unnamed Car Cleaners x3 (AYITL: Summer)

Places

North America

Pacific Crest Trail
- Lorelai is going to 'do Wild' (AYITL: Summer)

Maryland
- Where Lorelai wants Luke to elope to (6.22)
- Where Luke wants to take Lorelai (7.1)
- Where Back-Fat-Pat is from (AYITL: Summer)

Iowa
- Rory has to be here on Monday (7.22)

Vermont
- Where Luke wants to take Lorelai (7.1)
- Where Emily could also die (AYITL: Winter)

Illinois
- **Chicago**
    - Windy, Oprah (1.1)
    - Where Dean moved from (1.1)

- ○ Where Rachel decided to come back to Luke (1.16)
- ○ Where the Bracebridge's are snowed in (2.10)
- ○ Where Dean is visiting his grandmother (2.19)
- ○ Where Trevor is from (4.5)
- ○ Where Richard and Dicky will be in the Chicago office (5.5)
- **Springfield**
  - ○ Lorelai and Rory are going here on their roller coast trip (7.22)

Nevada
- **Reno**
  - ○ Where Emily wants to be driven to because she is open for business (5.1)
  - ○ Where Rory shot a man (6.3)
- **Las Vegas**
  - ○ Where Richard has a stopover
  - ○ Where Luke wants to take Lorelai (7.1)
  - ○ Where Logan is going with Colin and Finn (7.16)
  - ○ Where Colin, Finn and Logan went (7.17)
  - ○ Where Logan was gambling (7.18)
  - ○ Rory says what happens in Vegas stays in Vegas (AYITL: Winter)

Mexico

- Emily's maid is from one of the small countries near here (2.8)
- Where Lane and Zach went on their honeymoon (7.1)
- Where Lane got pregnant (7.3)
- **Baja**
    - Where Emily should go for a night out (5.3)
    - Where Miss Patty will be for the first two weeks of April (6.11)
- Where Pedro's Paradise is (7.2)

Virginia
- **Woodbridge**
    - Where April and Anna live (6.10)
    - Where Anna's store is (6.17)
    - Where Richard and Emily are antiquing (6.18)
- Where Janey Freidman moved to at the end of last year (7.9)

New Hampshire
- Where the LBD stay (AYITL: Fall)

Connecticut
- Where it is illegal to talk on your phone whilst driving a car (7.4)
- **Bristol**

- o Lorelai and Rory are going to hit Lake Compounce on their roller coast trip (7.22)
- **Hartford**
    - o Rory was born (1.1)
    - o Where the Gilmore's live (1.1)
    - o Where Chilton is (1.1)
    - o Where Taylor's father took him to see Pat Boone (6.22)
    - o Where Christopher has a meeting at 2 (7.10)
    - o Where Kirk broke down (AYITL: Winter)
- **Bridgeport**
    - o Where the mayor's wife went to bingo (1.16)
    - o Where the Gilmore cousins live (6.7)
- **Groton**
    - o Cousin Claudia lives there. Emily and Lorelai went to her house to watch the moon landing (1.5)
- **Wadsworth Mansion, Middletown**
    - o Where the Chilton senior prom will take place (3.10)
- **New Haven**
    - o Yale (3.8)
    - o Where Rory is catching the train back to (7.17)
- **Preston**

- ○ Where Richard and Emily are (6.17)
- **New London**
  - ○ Where Richard and Emily are supposed to be (6.17)
- **Litchfield**
  - ○ Where Luke and Nicole have a townhouse (4.11)
  - ○ Where Luke is going to have to go to get good lobster (6.15)
  - ○ Where Richard and Emily are antiquing (6.18)
- **Beacon Falls**
  - ○ Where Zach's bachelorette party are considering going (6.19)
- **Woodbury**
  - ○ Where Mrs. Lanahan bought her lettuce (2.8)
  - ○ Where the inn doors are (4.22)
  - ○ Where Kirk was born (7.7)
  - ○ Luke doesn't want to go here to get a lightbulb
  - ○ Where the A-list actors are staying (AYITL: Spring)
- Where Luke should focus his franchise initially (5.7)
- **Washington Depot**
  - ○ Where Richard and Emily are antiquing (6.18)
- **Naugatuck**

- Lorelai hopes it's within walking distance (7.15)

Texas
- Michel tells the French group at the inn that he's from there (1.5)
- **Houston**
  - Where the financial wash ups wash up (4.19)
- Sookie wants to know if anyone is coming from here to stay at the inn (5.16)

Philadelphia
- Lane wants to move there to hang out with M. Night Shyamalan (1.5)
- Where Luke thought Rachel was (1.16)
- Where Richard is (4.21)
- Where Jess is living (6.8)
- Where Truncheon Books is (6.18)
- Where Richard would rather be (7.13)
- Liberty Bell, Cream cheese, Philly cheese steaks (7.13)
- Lane will come to Zach's show here (7.20)

Seattle
- Where Christopher came back from (5.6)
- Where Richard was (6.9)

Massachusetts
- **Martha's Vineyard**

- The Gilmore's usual holiday spot (1.14, 3.1)
- Where there can be no more gorgeous a spot for a wedding (5.20)
- Where Rory and Logan are heading soon (6.6)
- Where Rory and Logan, Luke and Lorelai go for Valentine's (6.15)
- Gayhead – where there is no connection to spermaceti (6.15)

- **Nantucket**
  - Where Emily is going to live (AYITL: Fall)
- **Boston**
  - Where the girls go on their road trip (2.4)
  - Baked Beans, cream pie, tea party, strangler (2.6)
  - Where Sherry is from (2.6)
  - Lane will come to Zach's show here (7.20)
- **Concord**
  - Rory reads this off the map (2.4)
- **Manchester**
  - Rory reads this off the map (2.4)
- **Salem**
  - Rory reads this off the map (2.4)
- **Newton**
  - Rory reads this off the map (2.4)
- **Needham**

- Rory reads this off the map (2.4)
- **Cape Cod**
  - Kids love this place (5.20)
  - Where Rory and Logan would look very cute (5.20)

South Dakota
- The most boring state in the nation (6.21)

Guam
- The most boring state in the nation (6.21)

New York
- Maury's band is playing at a club there (1.14)
- **Pennsylvania**
  - Where the Pennsylvania Gilmore's live (2.9)
  - Where Logan is moving to (7.8)
- **Washington Square Park**
  - Where Jess hangs out (2.21)
  - Where Lorelai should have been a monkey (6.22)
- Where Alex takes Lorelai to a show, on a double date with Sookie and Jackson (3.14)
- Where Lorelai needs stuff picked up (4.20)

- Where Luke should focus his franchise initially (5.7)
- Where Logan is heading for his father's party (5.12)
- Where Logan wants him and Rory to go (5.17)
- Where Sophie Bloom has lived (5.18)
- Where Rory and Logan are going for the weekend (6.4)
- Where Logan is meeting his father (6.7)
- Where Lorelai is not going on her date (7.4)
- Where you can get a good cup of coffee (7.17)
- Lane will come to Zach's show here (7.20)
- Rory can stay at Paris' place (AYITL: Winter)
- Where Michel is on vacation (AYITL: Spring)
- Rory does her 'lines' article about New Yorker's who wait in lines (AYITL: Spring)
- The couple from table 6 are from here (AYITL: Summer)
- **Manhattan**
    - Where Luke and Lorelai go to the party (5.21)
    - Providence is not this (7.18)
    - Where Lucy and Olivia just signed a lease (7.19)

- - Where Emily and Richard want to buy an apartment (7.20)
    - Where Doyle has rented an apartment
  - **Soho**
    - A beer in Stars Hollow tastes just as god as one here (7.9)
  - **Brooklyn**
    - Lorelai and Rory are going to hit Coney Island on their roller coast trip (7.22)
    - Where Rory's apartment was (AYITL: Winter)

Rhode Island
- **Providence**
  - It's no Manhattan (7.18)
  - Where Rory can't show her face anymore (7.20)

Tortola
- Where Trip is building a house

The Bahamas
- Strobe and Francine have retired there (1.15)
- Where Emily and Richard vacationed last year (2.10)
- **Bimini**

- Where Finn and Logan had a sultry night (6.18)

California
- Where Christopher's business is based (1.15)
- Gold Country - where Fran toured ten years ago (2.8)
- Where Max has been teaching (3.16)
- Where Jess goes to visit his Dad (3.21)
- Michel has just come back from there (5.17)
- Where Logan wants Rory to live with him (7.20)
- The nuns have a new place at Pebble Beach (AYITL: Fall)
- Serena worked in Brentwood (AYITL: Fall)
- **San Francisco**
  - George Lucas owns this (6.2)
  - Where Lorelai is not going (7.4)
  - Logan's job will take him here (7.20)

Maine
- Where Emily got her dinings chairs (1.19)
- Where TJ and Liz had their accident (5.1)
- Where Dean is going for his parents wedding anniversary (5.6)
- Where Linny just moved from (6.22)
- Where Luke wants to take Lorelai (7.1)

- Logan gives Rory a key to his family house here (AYITL: Fall)

Ohio
- Lorelai and Rory are going to go here on their roller coast trip (7.22)
- **Akron**
  - Where Richard is (2.8)
- **Cleveland**
  - Where Miss Patty's first off-Broadway production took place (5.10)

North Carolina
- Where Tristan is going to military school (2.9)
- Where the Waffle Ranch is (7.17)
- **Charlotte**
  - Where Mia is getting married (7.17)

Montana
- Where Bootsy spent a summer training horses (2.10)

Hawaii
- Where the twins are going on vacation (4.3)
- Where Lorelai has always wanted to go (7.20)

- A waterfall in Lorelai's living room would be just like living here (7.8)

Washington
- Where Rory spent the summer as an intern (3.1)
- **Seattle**
  - Where the bad coffee is (7.17)
- Where a guy from Rory's class just got signed for a think tank (7.19)
- Where Emily will die (AYITL: Winter)

New Jersey
- **Princeton**
  - Where Jamie goes (3.21)
- **Atlantic City**
  - Where Richard and Jason had their launch party (4.8)
  - Where Rory and Lorelai were going for her 21st (6.7)
  - Where Rory and Lorelai did go for a belated 21st (6.11)
- Where people love Sookie's Chinese Chicken Salad (5.16)

Michigan
- Lorelai wants to run around Michigan (7.1)

Florida
- **Miami**

- - Where the 'Hippo' ballerina performed (4.8)
  - Where Rory and Paris go on spring break (4.17)
  - Where Mrs. Thompson is going (5.10)
  - Where Lulu will be between May 15th and June 1st (6.11)
  - Emily asks if a friend is there now (AYITL: Winter)

Brazil
- Rory has a poster of Brazil on her wall (1.17)
- This country is represented at the Spring International Food Festival (AYITL: Spring)

El Salvador
- Where a flash flood was last night (6.18)

Virgin Islands
- This country is represented at the Spring International Food Festival (AYITL: Spring)

Panama
- Where the Life and Death Brigade don't want to land (6.18)

Nicaragua

- Where the Life and Death Brigade don't want to land (6.18)

Costa Rica
- Where the Life and Death Brigade are base driving of a cliff
- Where the LBD girls are going to meet Logan, Colin, Finn and Robert (6.19)

Peru
- Rory has a poster of Peru on her wall (1.17)
- Where Rory and Logan are not moving (6.6)
- Paul's flowers are indigenous to Peru

Argentina
- Where Richard may be eating his weird food (2.8)
- Lucy will be hiding out here because of her lost Yale library books (7.21)

Idaho
- **Boise**
  - Where Lorelai hopes Richard has moved on to, for Akron's sake (2.8)

Nebraska
- **Omaha**

- Where Logan goes with his Dad (6.8)

Kansas
- Where people talk funny (6.9)

Alaska
- Were the Sudberry's cruised (7.4)

New Mexico
- Where April and Anna are moving (7.9)
- Where Luke can visit April every other month (7.10)
- Where Anna wants to move (7.10)

Mexico
- Where Emily and Richard were served Quail Mazatlan (7.12)

Arizona
- Tuscan – somewhere Richard would rather be (7.13)

Asia

- Where Rory did not go (7.1)

China
- Ian Jack is going there on business (1.2)
- Where Bruce spent two years (4.7)
- That's how long Lorelai's list is (4.20)
- Rory is planning this place as part of her and Logan's Asia trip (6.15)
- Logan has been on the phone for an hour to a rep here (AYITL: Summer)
- **Xi'an**
  - Where Logan and Rory were going to see the Terracotta Soldiers (7.2)
- **Peking, Bejiing**
  - Where Rory and Logan were going to go to the opera and have duck (7.2)
- **Tibet**
  - Rory wants to see this (7.2)
  - This country is represented at the Spring International Food Festival (AYITL: Spring)

Kazakhstan
- This country is represented at the Spring International Food Festival (AYITL: Spring)

Bangladesh
- Luke doesn't want to go here to get a baby (AYITL: Winter)
- This country is represented at the Spring International Food Festival (AYITL: Spring)

Nepal
- Kathmandu – Where Richard did not take Lorelai (AYITL: Winter)

Siberia
- Where Mrs. Kim threatened to send Lane to a convent (1.12)

Cambodia
- Small village - Where Trix went and didn't eat dessert (1.18)

Korea
- Lane is supposed to be pondering the reunification of the two Korea's (1.5)
- Where Lane is spending the summer (1.18)
- Lane says she escaped from here (2.4)

India
- **Calcutta**

- What Richard's pool house looks like (5.5)
- **Bangalore**
    - Where April's internet friend is from (6.12)
    - Rory uses this to deflect conversation from Lorelai and Luke's breakup (7.3)
- Where Paris is going to travel aggressively (7.21)
- Paris and Doyle went to Star Bombay in preparation for their trip here (7.21)
- Where Naomi Shropshire will come back from (AYITL: Winter)

Vietnam
- Where Rory is not shipping off to (2.13)
- Where Parker did not save Michel's life (6.14)
- Rory is planning this place as part of her and Logan's Asia trip (6.15)
- **An Thoi Islands**
    - Where Rory wants to snorkel (7.2)

Israel
- Where the "long haired freak" is travelling to now that his produce has sold out (2.17)

- This country is represented at the Spring International Food Festival (AYITL: Spring)

Hong Kong
- Where Sookie has to call to cancel wedding bookings (2.17)

Burma (Myanmar)
- Where it's warm (4.17)
- Where Rory would be married (4.17)

Tokyo
- Seoul - where the Kim's exchange student is from (4.19)
- **Harajuku District**
    o Where Rory wants to see the fashions (7.2)

Thailand
- Rory is planning this place as part of her and Logan's Asia trip (6.15)

Japan
- Land of the rising sun (7.2)

United Arab Emirates
    o Dubai – the journalist who had Rory's job had a fiancé who got a job here (7.22)

Singapore
- This country is represented at the Spring International Food Festival (AYITL: Spring)

Europe

Europe
- "a different place" (2.8)
- Where they eat salad last and the main course first (3.8)
- Rory should do it properly at least once in her life (4.22)
- Where Logan, Colin and Finn came back from (6.3)
- Where Richard and Emily are going for two months (6.22)

France
- Where Michel is from
- Where Lorelai and Christopher came back from (7.8)
- Paris
    - Where Rory wants to go (1.3)
    - Where Hopey lives (1.8)
    - Where Emily found the best papier mache maker (2.17)
    - Where Sherry is (5.6)
    - Consulate that Lorelai has to call (4.1)
    - The most romantic city in the world (7.1)
    - Where Rory is going for Christmas (7.1)
    - Where Sherry is living (7.5)

        - Where Christopher and Lorelai are going in two weeks (7.6)
        - Christopher and Lorelai take Gigi here to see Sherry (7.7)
        - Lorelai flew over oceans and oceans from there to see Rory (7.8)
        - Were Lorelai and Christopher eloped (7.9)
        - Where Odette lives (AYITL: Spring)
    - **Marseille**
        - Where Lorelai is an orphan (7.6)
    - **Giverny**
        - Where Lorelai and Christopher got married (7.8)
    - Where Claude and Monique are from (3.9)
    - Where you can have the table as long as you want (5.19)
    - Where Rory and Lorelai went backpacking (4.1)
    - Were Luke's fancy jam came from, according to legend (4.1)
    - Where Emily is going (5.1)
    - Sookie wants to know if anyone is coming from here to stay at the inn (5.16)

Italy
- **Rome**
    - Where Rory wants to go (1.3)

- - - Where Rory and Emily have their last stop (5.2)
    - Romans live there (5.9)
    - Where Rory thinks Lorelai should get married (1.18)
    - Where Lorelai is going to send Rory to get away from
    - Where Rory is going for Christmas (7.1)
    - This country is represented at the Spring International Food Festival (AYITL: Spring)
  - **Vatican**
    - Where Rory and Lorelai went backpacking (4.1)
  - **Florence**
    - Where the Rizosco's live (4.1)
    - Where the concierge stuck Emily and Rory with a Belgium couple (5.2)

Czech Republic
- **Prague**
  - Where Rory wants to go (1.3)
  - Richard is there on business (1.9)
  - Where Lorelai and Rory took a train ride from Paris (4.1)
- Where Sookie downloaded her color samples from (2.17)
- Where Christopher wants to buy Lorelai a castle (6.10)

- Milan Kundera is the Robin Williams of the Czech Republic (7.21)

United Kingdom
- **London**
    - Where Rory wants to go (1.3)
    - Where Lorelai's dress came from (1.8)
    - Where Trix lives (1.18)
    - Where the Talbud's live (4.1)
    - Where Logan is going (6.15)
    - Where Logan is going to work for his dad (6.22)
    - The most sex obsessed city in the world (7.1)
    - Where Rory is going for Christmas (7.1)
    - When you are tired of London, you are tired of life (7.4)
    - Where Rory was at the end of December (7.11)
    - Rory has to be back on the red eye here (AYITL: Winter)
    - Rory will call from here (AYITL: Winter)
- **Bermuda**
    - Where the ice hotel is (7.5)
- **Bath**
    - Where Rory and Lorelai went backpacking (4.1)
- **Oxford**

- - Where Asher asked Paris to go (4.20)
  - **Cambridge**
    - Where Paris sent Asher's body (5.3)
  - **Gloucestershire**
    - Where Logan, Colin and Finn rolled cheese down the hill (6.3)

Spain
- Where Emily should be (2.6)
- **Lerma**
  - Richard uses this village in Spain to avoid Lorelai's breakup with Luke (73)

Belgium
- Where the not best papier mache maker was (2.17)
- Where Sookie got her salad bowl (3.8)
- Consulate that Lorelai has to call (4.1)
- Where the chocolates are from (4.19)
- Where Lorelai thought Richard went while Lorelai was playing hide and seek (AYITL: Winter)

Norway
- **Oslo**
  - Where Sookie has to call to cancel wedding bookings (2.17)

Denmark
- **Copenhagen**
  - Where Sookie has to call to cancel wedding bookings (2.17)
  - Where Rory dreamt of her clothes (4.1)
- Where the Eggerholme's live (4.1)
- Where Emily's earrings are from

The Netherlands
- Where Colin fell in love with a milk maid (6.3)
- Where Lorelai thought Richard went while Lorelai was playing hide and seek (AYITL: Winter)
- **Amsterdam**
  - Where everything looks good, after stumbling out of a coffee shop (6.4)
  - Consulate that Lorelai has to call (4.1)
  - Rory is at Yale, not here (4.5)

Portugal
- **Lisbon**
  - Consulate that Lorelai has to call (4.1)

Greece
- **Attica**

- Where Jess is probably going (2.15)
- Where Richard and Emily are (5.16)
- Where Rory goes during a massage (6.15)
- **Santorini**
  - Where Logan is not whisking Rory off to (6.7)
- **Athens**
  - Where Emily thought of Rory (5.16)

Croatia
- Where Richard actually went while Lorelai was playing hide and seek (AYITL: Winter)

Germany
- Where Richard is, on business (1.5)
- Where Christopher wants to buy Lorelai a castle (6.10)
- April is going on an exchange here (AYITL: Summer)
- **Berlin**
  - Consulate that Lorelai has to call (4.1)
  - Where Clara is living (AYITL: Fall)
- **Hamburg**

- - Logan says Rory was wearing her lucky outfit when he saw her there (AYITL: Winter)

Ireland
- **Dublin**
    - Where Lorelai and Rory staked out The Clarence Hotel (4.1)
    - Where Christopher wants to buy Lorelai a castle (6.10)

Switzerland
- **Zurich**
    - Where the Gunderson's live (4.1)

Spain
- **Barcelona**
    - Where Trevor is going next year (4.5)

Poland
- Rory has a poster of Poland on her wall (1.17)
    - Naomi's face is Poland (AYITL: Spring)
    - This country is represented at the Spring International Food Festival (AYITL: Spring)

Finland

- **Helsinki**
    - Where Lorelai claims she is (5.19)

Romania
- Where the maid is from (6.2)

Austria
- **Vienna**
    - Where the wedding planner met Franco Zefirelli (7.10)

Bulgaria
- This country is represented at the Spring International Food Festival (AYITL: Spring)

Turks and Caicos Islands
- This country is represented at the Spring International Food Festival (AYITL: Spring)

Slovenia
- This country is represented at the Spring International Food Festival (AYITL: Spring)

Africa

Burundi
- This country is represented at the Spring International Food Festival (AYITL: Spring)

Chad
- This country is represented at the Spring International Food Festival (AYITL: Spring)

Fez, Morocco
- Where Rory wants to go (1.3)
- Where Richard may be eating his weird food (2.8)

Turkey
- Where Rory wants to go (1.3)
- Lorelai wants to stay at the place from Midnight Express (1.9)

Congo
- Where Luke thought Rachel was (1.16)

Middle East
- Where Rachel actually was (1.16)
- **Kuwaiti**
  - Chris said Straub was like this (5.11)
- **Qatar**

- This country is represented at the Spring International Food Festival (AYITL: Spring)

Oceania

French Polynesia
- **Bora Bora**
  - Where Sookie has to call to cancel wedding bookings (2.17)

Australia
- Where Jason drank and thought a lot about Lorelai (4.10)
- Where they use too much salt (5.7)

Fiji
- Where Logan sank his father's yacht (5.6)
- Where the ultimate gift ship has sailed (6.7)

New Zealand
- Where Emily's had the lamb flown in from (7.9)
- Robert said Finn was from here (AYITL: Fall)

Papua New Guinea
- This country is represented at the Spring International Food Festival (AYITL: Spring)

Islands of Kuribati

- This country is represented at the Spring International Food Festival (AYITL: Spring)

Actors Who Play Multiple Characters

Sherilynn Fenn - Sasha/Anna
Alex Borstein - Drella/Ms. Celine/Doris/Unaired Pilot Sookie
Sean Gunn - Mick/DSL Installer/Kirk
Marion Ross - Trix/Marilynn
Riki Lindhome - Stars Hollow High Student/Juliet
Samantha Shelton - Libby/Walker
Seth McFarlane - Zac/Bob Merriam
Lance Barber - Hugo/Builder at the Independence Inn
Mary Lynn Rajskub - Actor in Kirk's film/Troubadour
Rose Abdoo - Gypsy/Berta
Jacqui Maxwell - Stars Hollow High Student/Summer
Floyd Van Buskirk - Jed/Henry
Jill Brennan - Mrs. Traister/Carrie Duncan
Eileen Barnett - Nanette/Mrs/ Leahy
George Bell - Professor Bell/Stanley
Luciano Giancarlo - Chic guy/Italian Waiter
Brandon Novitsky - AV Geek/Howard
Tiffany Fraser - Shannon/The Hostess
Patty Malcolm - Woman #1, Customer #4, Mrs Harris
Charles C. Stevenson - Reverend Wilder/Julian Johnson

Chase Penny - Rich Bloomenfeld/Kyle's cousin
Rich DiDonato - Cliff/Eddie the Mailman
Mary Linda Phillips - Dede/Linda
Karl T Wright - Yale Professor/Harvard Professor
Richard Topol - Independence Inn waiter/Doctor
Devon Cromwell - Chip/Jonah
Paul Messenger - Sid/Earl

Sookie's Slumber Party 'To Do List'

(2.11)

- Raid the fridge
- Make an avocado mango face mask
- Read Tarot cards
- Tell fortunes
- Play Twister
- Make a Häagen-Dazs chocolate chocolate chip ice cream milkshake
- Watch Purple Rain

Hep Alien
Set List

Fell in Love with a Girl - The White Stripes cover (3.19)
White Riot - The Clash cover (3.19)
Head On - The Jesus and Mary Chain cover (4.7)
Crazy Beat - Blur cover (4.11)
Time Bomb - Rancid cover (4.19)
Believe It or Not - Joey Scarbury cover (5.4)
The Star Spangled Banner - Jimi Hendrix cover (5.4)
Brian's Tune (5.5)
Can't Stand Me Now - The Libertines cover (5.12)
Hanging On The Telephone- Blondie Cover (6.3)
Lorraine (6.10)
Stella (6.10)
Melissa (6.10)
Calling Francine (6.10)
Rebecca in the Morning (6.10)
Lane (6.10)
Dear Maureen (6.10)
Linda Marie (6.10)
Hollaback Girl – Gwen Stefani Cover (6.16)
My Humps – Black Eyed Peas Cover (6.16)
Hava Nagila (6.16)

I'm a Believer – The Monkees Cover (6.19)
I'm The Man - Joe Jackson Cover (AYITL: Winter)

Town Troubadour Set List

Raise the Spirit by Grant Lee Phillips
Me and Julio Down by the Schoolyard by Paul Simon
Lily-A-Passion by Grant Lee Phillips
Mona Lisa by Grant Lee Phillips
Peace Train – Cat Stevens Cover
Smile by Grant Lee Phillips
Wake Me Up Before You Go-Go – Wham Cover
Be True to Your School by Grant Lee Phillips
Spring Released by Grant Lee Phillips
Nothing Is for Sure by Grant Lee Phillips
Sadness Soot by Grant Lee Phillips
Everybody Needs A Little Sanctuary by Grant Lee Phillips
It's the Life by Grant Lee Buffalo
Heavenly by Grant Lee Phillips
Honey Don't Think by Grant Lee Phillips
Winterglow by Grant-Lee Phillips
Valley Winter Song by Grant-Lee Phillips

Themed Episode Lists

Valentine's Day
6.15

Births
Georgia Hayden (3.13)
Rory Gilmore (3.13)
Davy Belleville (4.7)
Martha Belleville (5.21)
Doula (7.9)
Kwan and Steve Van Gerbig (7.17)

Deaths
Cousin Claudia (1.5)
Cinnamon (1.5)
Louis Danes (2.17)
Fran Weston (3.20)
Stan Green (4.11)
Melinda 'Sweetie' Nelson (4.16)
Lorelai 'Trix' Gilmore (4.16)
Asher Fleming (5.3)
Straub Hayden (5.11)
Joshua 'Old Man' Twickham (5.18)
Christopher's Grandfather (6.10)
Chin-Chin (7.14)

Richard Gilmore (AYITL: Winter)

Birthdays
1.6
3.18
6.7
6.20
7.15

Graduations
2.21
3.22
6.22
7.22

Baptism
6.4

Christmas/Holiday
1.10
2.10
3.10
4.11
5.11
6.12
7.11
AYITL: Winter

Thanksgiving
1.7
3.9

6.10

LBD (Life and Death Brigade)
5.6
5.7
5.10
5.20
5.22
6.1
6.4
6.8
6.19
6.20
AYITL: Fall

DAR (Daughters of the American Revolution)
1.16
2.12, 2.16, 2.17
3.05, 3.13, 3.14, 3.16, 3.20
4.3, 4.12
6.2, 6.3, 6.4, 6.5, 6.6, 6.7, 6.8, 6.13, 6.15, 6.21
7.15
AYITL: Summer
AYITL: Fall

Friday Night Dinners

1.1, 1.2, 1.6, 1.8, 1.9, 1.10, 1.11 (x2), 1.14 (x2),
1.15, 1.16, 1.18 (x3), 1.19 (x2), 1.20

2.1 (x2), 2.2, 2.5, 2.7, 2.8, 2.10, 2.11 (x2), 2.12, 2.13, 2.14, 2.18 (x2), 2.20, 2.21, 2.22
3.1, 3.2 (x2), 3.3, 3.5 (x2), 3.7, 3.8, 3.9, 3.10, 3.11 (x2), 3.13, 3.14 (x2), 3.15 (x2), 3.16, 3.18, 3.19
4.1, 4.3, 4.5, 4.6, 4.8 (x2), 4.9, 4.10 (x2), 4.12, 4.14, 4.15, 4.16, 4.18 (x2), 4.19, 4.21, 4.22
5.3, 5.6, 5.7, 5.8, 5.9, 5.11, 5.12, 5.16, 5.17, 5.20 (x2), 5.21 (x2), 5.22
6.13, 6.14, 6.21, 6.22
7.3, 7.5, 7.9, 7.15, 7.20, 7.12, 7.22
AYITL: Winter, Spring

Gilmore's by the Numbers

Movies: 522

TV Shows: 235

Songs: 488

Books: 431

Coffees: 503

Friday Night Dinners: 100

Emily's Staff: 82

Pets: 38

Businesses: 160

Stars Hollow Events: 37

Kirk jobs: 67

Births: 7

Deaths: 13

Graduations: 4

Weddings: 11

Honorary Gilmore Girls

The Fan Community

The Fans

While this book up until this point has focused on the elements of the show—and Stars Hollow—that make it what it is, it would not be complete without a brief section which pays homage to the illuminating community of fans that have kept the spirit of *Gilmore Girls* alive, 20 years after it first aired on TV. The ongoing fan presence online, and in life, undoubtedly contributed to the reboot which gave us *A Year in the Life*, and has ensured that the show will go down in history, having achieved a 'cult' status. According to Diffrient, the show "built up a strong cult following and became an object of intense devotion among fans who flocked to their TV sets weekly, seeking comfort in the fictional Hamlet of Stars Hollow."[16] Whilst others books may have focused on the actors, the script, and the behind-the-scenes activities of the show, this book has presented a Gilmore way of life, and in some ways, this chapter reveals what is really at the heart of the *Gilmore Girls* culture—the fans.

According to Smith-Rowsey, the fans "extend and illuminate the glory of *Gilmore* Girls, and the ongoing presence of the fan community has led to

---

[16] Diffrient, "Introduction," xvii.

the creation of several fan-oriented initiatives.[17] These include, but are not limited to, an enormous catalogue of fan fiction, a weekend long fan festival which takes place annually (and often sells out), merchandising businesses which create products and subscription boxes for Gilmore lovers, and hundreds of Facebook groups which are rooted in a shared love for all things Gilmore, and the fictional town of Stars Hollow. Many of these online communities are focused around finding the small details of the show, and having lively discussions during subsequent 're-watches'. By their own admission, many fans engage in re-watching frequently, and in some cases, continually. I have spoken with many fans who claim to watch the show year round, as the show provides comfort, entertainment and a sense of familiarity in the background of their busy lives. According to Petersen, "Watching the Gilmore Girls intensely offers an opportunity to constantly balance the experiences of the characters against your own experiences, even though the characters in this show are, in a sense, 'stuck in time', while fans are watching the events in the seven seasons over and over again".

---

[17] Daniel Smith-Rowsey, "Still More Gilmore How Online Fan Communities Remediate Gilmore Girls," in *Gilmore Girls: The Politics of Identity*, ed. Ritch Calvin, (Jefferson, NC: McFarland & Company Inc., 2008), 202.

[18] In a 2019 "Cameo" video by David Sutcliffe (who plays Christopher Hayden on the show), Sutcliffe states that watching the show over and over again, has become somewhat of an "epidemic" among fans, and questions whether it is an "obsession".[19] Petersen argues that "constantly re-watching Gilmore Girls offers fans a way to combine their past with their future in constantly new and unexpected ways through the series' narrative."[20] It may be an epidemic, and an obsession, but it is one that fans warmly welcome.

It has even been argued that *Gilmore Girls* can only be properly understood after multiple rewatches, because of the dense population of cultural references that are embedded within it. David Scott Diffrient suggests that the cultural references in *Gilmore Girls* "continuously tests the audience's knowledge", much like Darren does at the lunch table in 3.3.[21] He goes onto argue that in order to really understand the show, "one must have more than passing familiarity

---

[18] Line Nybro Petersen, "Gilmore Girls Generations: Disrupting Generational Belonging in Long-Term Fandom", in *Celebrity Studies* 9:2 (Taylor & Francis: Routledge, 2018), 219.
[19] David Sutcliffe, "For Madeline," *Cameo*, https://www.cameo.com/v/5e45fe5746fc9901a55dbcbd
[20] Ibid., 228.
[21] Diffrient, "Introduction," xvi.

641

with pop culture history; with the movies, TV shows, songs and other artifacts".[22] In this sense, Rory may very well be correct in encouraging Logan to re-watch *The Office* at least four times. Perhaps like *Gilmore Girls,* it is only after these multiple re-watches that it can truly be appreciated.

One might even argue that no true fan has watched it only once. Lizardi argues that the revival could only be truly understood, if fans have a good understanding of the original show, and points out that "considering the nine-year gap in Gilmore content, the references to the original series are so obscure and brief that even familiar fans might not catch them all unless they recently binged the series in anticipation of the revival."[23]

Because *Gilmore Girls* hits at so many issues, the resonation of it with fans goes much deeper than surface level chit chat about the story lines, or the quoting of lines from the script. I am in a group on Facebook which has laughed and cried with each other, and which celebrates the ups and downs of the lives of its members. In a way, the entire fan community replicates the world of Stars

---

[22] Ibid.
[23] Ryan Lizardi, "Mourning and Melancholia: Conflicting Approaches to Reviving Gilmore Girls One Season at a Time," in *Television & New Media 19:4* (2018), 385-6.

Hollow, as fans seek to reproduce, and integrate parts of the Gilmore world into their own lives, and share their experiences with others. For many fans, *Gilmore Girls* becomes part of the landscape of life, and fans feel that as much as the show belongs to them, we too, belong to it. We are Gilmore girls, by proxy.

Some scholars have even argued that the fandom surrounding the show, has actually become in itself, a part of the show. Rather than fans being passive viewers of the show, the fans themselves contribute to *Gilmore Girls,* and function as an "actual interpretative community...who watch episodes together and frequently comment to one another about such things as the plotline, the themes, the characters, and the qualitative worth (the "goodness" or "badness") of particular episodes."[24] Fans become a part of the "*Gilmore*verse", since "the act of viewing...is itself a text-making event as well as a communication process through which members of a real community share a common language" and "continually replenish the text, keeping it fresh for subsequent viewings".[25] This

---

[24] Diffrient, "The Gift of Gilmore Girls' Gab: Fan Podcasts and the Task of "Talking Back" to TV," In *Screwball Television: Critical Perspectives on Gilmore Girls*, ed. Diffrient David Scott and Lavery David (Syracuse, NY: Syracuse University Press, 2010), 105.
[25] Ibid.

engagement, and contribution to the show increased after *Gilmore Girls* was added to Netflix, and after the release of the long-awaited revival. Stache and Davidson point out that AYITL had "five million viewers in the first three days of the launch, a number that speaks to the appeal of the original series and the desperate desire to reconnect with Stars Hollow and the gang."[26]

I mentioned in the introduction to this book, that every fan of the show has a story. I would like to leave this introduction to the fan section with the words, and story, of another fan who emailed me during a Covid19 lockdown. She describes how the show helped her through these unprecedented times, which, at the time of print, are still ongoing. Her experience will undoubtedly resonate with all who read them:

> *There are hundreds of new television shows and films being aired every month but for some reason I find myself drawn back to Gilmore Girls. I have watched the show all the way through numerous times and two specific episodes a lot more. Why do I keep watching them?*

---

[26] Lara C. Stache and Rachel Davidson, *Gilmore Girls: A Cultural History*, (Lanham, Maryland: Rowman and Littlefield, 2019), xii.

The answer is comfort. I find Gilmore Girls beyond comforting during these incredibly difficult times.

I miss my family and for the time being Lorelai, Rory and Luke have become my family. Sookie, Jackson, Lane and all of the characters have become my friends just like they did the first time I ever watched Gilmore Girls.

Rory said, "I live in two worlds" and at times like this, I feel like I do also.

Whilst I am sure there are hundreds of wonderful new TV shows to watch, I'm happy to spend my time at home self-isolating with my real family and my family in my other world – Stars Hollow.

- Naomi Beddoes

Gilmore Girls Bucket List

With all of the enthusiasm from fans to mirror our lives wih those of The *Gilmore Girls*, it is necessary to think about what that might look like. To help you on this journey, here is the ultimate *Gilmore Girls* bucket list. Any true *Gilmore Girl* would strive to accomplish some of these, and I would love to hear if anyone has crossed them all off!

Go on a hayride (1.1)
Name your child after yourself (1.1)
Play volleyball (1.1)
Take a business class at college (1.1)
Join the German Club (1.2)
Play golf at the Country Club (1.3)
Take a steam (1.3)
Date a teacher (1.5)
Get your face printed on a birthday cake (1.6)
Kiss the boy in the grocery store and shoplift cornstarch (1.7)
Watch Willy Wonka and the Chocolate Factory and eat junk food (1.7)
Take a walk in the first snow of the season (1.8)

Go to a black and white movie on a first date (1.8)
Go to a dance with your gentleman caller (1.9)
Kiss said gentleman caller on the dance floor (1.9)
Exchange a gift for a semi-pornographic leering monkey lamp (1.9)
Take part in the community Christmas production (1.10)
Go on a double date (1.12)
Go to a Bangles concert (1.13)
Buy some clothes from a rummage sale (1.13)
Watch the Donna Reed Show and eat pizza (1.14)
Hold a Donna Reed night (1.14)
Go watch a community softball game (1.15)
Re-arrange your lounge furniture (1.17)
Wallow (1.17)
Make a list of all the things you intend on doing on weekends, but never get around to. Then fulfill the list (1.17)
Go to a party, stay till at least 10.30pm and catch up on your reading (1.17)
Explore an old abandoned Inn (1.19)
See an old movie at the local cinema (1.19)
Play 1, 2, 3, He's Yours! (1.20)
Volunteer at a charity building project (2.2)
Have a wedding shower (2.2)
Sample wedding cakes (2.3)
Have a bachelorette party (2.3)
Go on an impromptu road trip (2.3)
Stop at a roadside nut stall (2.4)

Stay at a B&B and sign the guestbook (2.4)
Visit Harvard University and buy merchandise (2.4)
Use 'existentialist' in a sentence (2.4)
'Come out' at a debutante ball (2.6)
Learn the Viennese Waltz (2.8)
Join a secret society (2.7)
Join the booster club (2.7)
Take part in a fashion show (2.7)
Act in a Shakespeare play (2.9)
Hold an authentic 'Bracebridge' dinner (2.10)
Enter a snowman competition (2.10)
Dress up and go see the Rocky Horror Picture Show (2.11)
Get photo printed pyjamas (2.11)
Join the cheerleading team (2.11)
Plan the family burial spaces (2.12)
Go on a romantic picnic date (2.13)
Get pizza and hit the bookstore (2.13)
Jump into a pile of dirty laundry (2.14)
Play bagel hockey (2.14)
Take part in a formal debate (2.14)
Hire a local teenager to clean your rain gutters (2.14)
Buy a clock radio that makes barnyard animal noises (2.15)
Go on a spa weekend with your mother (2.16)
Go to a 60/40 bar for a steak (2.16)
Graduate from community college (2.21)
Shoot clay pigeons (2.21)
Have an after finals margherita (2.21)

Buy a hot dog from a street cart (2.21)
Go on the subway (2.21)
Be in your best friend's wedding (2.22)
Go to Martha's Vineyard for the summer (3.1)
Visit the Smithsonian Museum (3.1)
Dye your hair bright purple (3.3)
Attend a vintage auction (3.5)
Attend a baby shower (3.6)
Participate in a dance-a-thon (3.7)
Take a class at the local learning center (3.11)
Take a fencing class (3.11)
Attend a family wedding of your best friend (3.12)
Clean out your garage (3.12)
Go on a fishing date (3.12)
Be accepted into Ivy League colleges (3.16)
Have a birthday party with the world's biggest pizza (almost) (3.18)
Wind up as the grad night treasurer for the Booster club (3.19)
Go backpacking around Europe before college (3.22)
Try out all the takeaway outlets in your area and rate them according to a system (4.1)
Plant bulbs from your neighbor because cultivating new life which will help distract from your current emptiness and sense of loss (4.5)
Go to a food court for a smorgasbord lunch (4.15)
Go window shopping, walking arm in arm like movie ladies (4.15)
Have a pizza and The Power of Myth night (4.17)

Attend a live public book reading (4.19)
Open an Inn (4.22)
Join a Barbershop Quartet (5.5)
Do a 'bumper sticker test' (5.7)
Don't use the letter "E" for an entire evening (5.7)
Go glamping with a safari theme (5.7)
Have an ice rink built in your front yard (5.11)
Renew your wedding vows (5.13)
Have your business feature in a magazine (5.18)
Take a newspaper internship (5.19)
Sponsor a dancer (5.21)
Throw your best friend a baby shower (5.21, 7.16)
Steal a yacht (5.21)
Drop out of college (5.22)
Move in with your grandparents (5.22)
Get engaged (6.1)
Join the DAR (6.3)
Go on a tour with your band (6.3)
Be a godmother to your best friend's baby (6.4)
Run a 1940s, Hollywood canteen themed fundraiser (6.4)
Have a 21st birthday party (6.7)
Get a part-time job writing for a newspaper (6.9)
Go back to college after a semester long break (6.10)
Go to Atlantic city for your 21st birthday, play 21, buy 21 things and get 21 guys' phone numbers (6.11)
Be evaluated by a psychologist (6.11)

Become the editor of your college newspaper (6.14)
Give your father a tour of your college campus (6.14)
Go on a Valentine's weekend getaway to Martha's Vineyard (6.15)
Go to the gym to drink cucumber water and get a massage (6.15)
Ruin your friend's wedding dress (6.18)
Have a college building named after you (6.22)
Throw a bon voyage party (6.22)
Take a job teaching SAT Prep (7.3)
Attend an art show (7.4)
Go on a private drive-in movie date (7.4)
Pick your mother up from jail (7.4)
Go to Paris and elope (7.7)
Plan a wedding party (7.10)
Go out with friends to an Indian restaurant (7.10)
Go spend Christmas overseas with a boyfriend (7.11)
Make cookies from scratching (7.11)
Make popcorn and cranberry strings (7.11)
Go out for candy cane coffee (7.11)
Write a character reference for a friend (7.11)
Babysit so a friend can go skiing (7.12)
Have a flat-screen T.V. installed at home (7.12)
Write an apology to a friend (7.12)
Go tray sliding (7.12)
Attend a dog funeral (7.14)
Go through a haybale maze (7.18)
Get your ears pierced like (7.18)

Attend a Spring Fling festival (7.18)
Bring your boyfriend home for the weekend (7.18)
Read the newspaper while you take a train ride (7.18)
Write a pro/con list (7.18)
Get a job writing for a local newspaper (7.18)
Be accepted into Yale Law school (7.19)
Be accepted into Harvard Medical School (7.19)
Be accepted into the University of Pennsylvania School of Medicine (7.19)
Be accepted into Columbia University (7.19)
Be accepted into Stanford University (7.19)
Ride your bike to work (7.19)
Plan a six-week cruise down the coast of Maine (7.20)
Visit the Mark Twain Museum (7.20)
Go to a karaoke night (7.20)
Spackle the walls (7.21)
Visit a piece of street performance art (7.21)
Have a graduation party (7.21)
Graduate from Yale University (7.21)
Meet Christiane Amanpour (7.22)
Plan a roller coaster trip around the U.S. (7.22)
Get a job writing for an online magazine (7.22)
Throw a surprise party (7.22)
Learn tap dancing for relaxation (AYITL: Winter)
Move back home (AYITL: Winter)
Start things up with an old lover (AYITL: Winter)
Use a local ride share company (AYITL: Winter)

Clear your house according to Marie Kondo's method (AYITL: Winter)
Go to therapy with a family member (AYITL: Spring)
Go to an international food festival (AYITL: Spring)
Go to the pool (AYITL: Summer)
Go to a tango club (AYITL: Fall)
Organise a flash mob for your wedding (AYITL: Fall)
Get married (AYITL: Fall)
Drink wine in a gazebo (AYITL: Fall)
Get pregnant (AYITL: Fall)

Other:

Read all of the books in this book
Watch all of the movies in this book
Watch all of the television shows in this book
Make all of the food in the 'Eat like a Gilmore' Cookbooks
Attend a town meeting
Live in a small town, and take part in community events
Go to the annual fan festival
Listen to the Gilmore Guys podcasts

What She Tackles, She Conquers

How to Study Like a Gilmore

Study like a Gilmore

According to Armstrong, "Colleges are now brimming with overachieving little Rory Gilmores".[27] As I outlined in my introduction, watching Rory's academic journey from Stars Hollow High through to her Yale graduation, impacted significantly on my own study journey, and I cannot help but credit a large portion of my college success to *Gilmore Girls.* You might think that spending time watching a television show would derail study efforts, but I found the opposite to be true. Watching Rory go from 'zero to studying' in two minutes motivated me to smash through my own college work, and I found myself resonating with Dean and Jess when they thanked Rory for the part she played in their success.

Sborgi points out that "Rory is fascinated with prestigious universities such as Yale and Harvard because of her love of knowledge and because

---

[27] Jennifer Armstrong, "Boys Not Alllowed" in Coffee at Luke's: An Unauthorized Gilmore Girls Gabfest, ed. Jennifer Crusie, Leah Wilson (Dallas: BenBella Books, 2007), 17.

she hopes to pursue her dream of becoming a journalist through further acquisition of said knowledge".[28] Fans of the show have also become interested in prestigious education institutions, Yale, in particular. I myself, went and listened in on a public lecture here in New Zealand, just because a lecturer from Yale was delivering it, a direct result of Gilmore fandom.

If there is one academic role model who can help you through a study rut, then it is Rory Gilmore (and potentially Lorelai during her community college years). Seeing Rory's stacks of books and wearing college merchandise always sends me into a studying binge and inspires me to achieve. No matter what is going on in the background of Rory's life, she is faithfully devoted to her academic life. Like Rory, I recognise that these kinds of achievements are not accomplished alone. Rory's parents, grandparents, and the town of Stars Hollow supported her, and guided her through her achievements – celebrating with her, and even financing her tuition. However, this support would not have brought about Rory's valedictorian results without her

---

[28] Anna Viola Sborgi, ""The Thing That Reads a Lot": Bibliophilia, College Life, and Literary Culture in Gilmore Girls." In *Screwball Television: Critical Perspectives on Gilmore Girls*, ed. Diffrient David Scott and Lavery David (Syracuse, NY: Syracuse University Press, 2010), 192.

hyper-organisation and relentless determination to succeed.

Though Rory stumbles in season six, allowing one person's opinion to crush her lofty academic goals, she rises from the ashes and comes back better than before. Where she has previously balanced her college life with romantic relationships and social events, she now pushes her way into a position as a writer for a newspaper, and accelerates her course load to ensure that she completes her degree at the same time as she would have before her hiatus from Yale. This shift in motivation is interesting, particularly after she struggled with her heavy course load in her earlier years at Yale, without the burden of a writing job at that time. Rory 2.0 seems to take every opportunity and makes it her mission to get things done.

While many online discussions have debated the motivation of adult Rory, who appears to have little direction, there is no doubting that when Rory wants to achieve something, she does. Sborgi even argues that Rory's "passion for studying seems almost excessive".[29] While her heart may not have been in the autobiography which seemed to move at a snail's pace in AYITL, her own story, *Gilmore Girls*, was

---

[29] Sborgi, ""The Thing That Reads a Lot," 189.

churned out in a little over an episode once she decided that this was going to be her *Magnum Opus*.

Of course, we know that Rory is not the only character on the show who studies. Lorelai attends a community college in the early seasons to learn business, Lane studies after school with Rory and Dean and is later admitted to Seventh Day Adventist school. The academic rigour of the show is of course supplemented by Paris who, according to Nelson is "obsessed (to put it mildly) with academic and professional success".[30] This section contains a list of Rory's (and sometimes Lorelai's) study habits through two high schools, and college, detailing the tools for success that anyone can use, to achieve academic success like Rory. Though Rory is smart, it is not her smarts that achieve great things – it is her drive. As Richard reminds Emily, "What she tackles, she conquers" (6.5).

---

[30] Matthew C. Nelson, "Stars Hollow, Chilton, and the Politics of Education in Gilmore Girls." In *Screwball Television: Critical Perspectives on Gilmore Girls*, ed. Diffrient David Scott and Lavery David (Syracuse, NY: Syracuse University Press, 2010), 207.

High School

Utilize class time to work on assignments (1.1)
Take a business class at your local community college (1.1)
Maintain a 4.0 (1.2)
Study alone, and decline invitations to study with others (1.2)
Turn down ice cream during study sessions (1.4)
Pull an all-nighter when you are cramming for a test (1.4)
Have your mum speak with the headmaster when you miss your test (1.4)
Attend class, even on your birthday (1.6)
Attend the college fair every year (1.6)
Take notes during class (1.13)
Host group projects at your house (1.13)
Take time off from studying to help out a friend (1.18)
Fall asleep with your study materials (1.19)
Listen to gloomy music during study sessions (1.19)
Enrol in summer school (2.2)
Do volunteer work to boost your college applications (2.2)
Take a night to plan your extracurriculars (2.2)
Join the high school newspaper (2.5)
Catch up on your reading while you are waiting for meetings to start (2.5)
Buy folders to keep your notes neat (2.5)

Get good scores on the PSAT's (2.11)
Attend school every single day (2.12)
Have study session/sleepovers (2.16)
Run for student body president (2.22)
Spend a summer as an intern in Washington (3.1)
Make sure nobody knows that you were watching the Brady bunch Variety Hour when your college applications arrive (3.3)
Learn to go from 'zero to studying' in less than 60 seconds (3.6)
Take an alumni tour of a university campus (3.8)
Apply to other colleges as 'back-ups' (3.9)
Apply for the school speech competition (3.16)
Stay a virgin so that you will get into Harvard (3.16)
Make a pro/con list to decide which college you will attend (3.17)
Attend school even once you have matriculated (3.17)
Request extra graduation tickets (3.19)
Make a list of "things to do before graduation" (3.21)
Switch subjects back and forth when studying for finals to maximize productivity (3.21)
Stay up and study even when you are excited (3;.21)
Graduate high school (3.22)
Borrow your college tuition from your grandparents (3.22)
Give the valedictorian speech at your graduation (3.22)

Have an after-grad party at your house (3.22)

College

Freshman

Attend college orientation and memorize the schedule (4.1)
Take your own mattress to your dorm room (4.1)
Make notes at orientation (4.1)
Have your Mom come and stay the night on your first night at college (4.1)
Hold a take-out party in your dorm room to try all the takeaways in the area (4.1)
Howl back to the guys in the dorm (4.1)
Go to "shopping week" - pick 50 classses, plus another 10 to squeeze in if you have time (4.3)
Rush to your first class like an hour early (4.3)
Leave your door open for the dorm floor party to get to know the other students (4.3)
Take a course in 'Japanese fiction' (4.3)
Get a haircut to celebrate your newfound independence (4.4)
Go home in the weekend for the perfect Stars Hollow day - hang out in town, read, veg, drink coffee and hit Luke's for a late lunch (4.4)
Take your reading, homework, and laundry home for the weekend (4.5)

Take five courses at a time, because you like to be busy (4.6)
Find a quiet place to study, even if it means paying someone $20 to sit under your study tree (4.6)
Write articles for the college newspaper (4.8)
Write theatre reviews that eviscerate people (4.8)
Use the internet for research (4.8)
Go into finals induced hibernation (4.9)
Take a course in 'Contemporary Political Fiction' (4.10)
Contribute to group discussions in class (4.11)
Join the International Relations Club (4.12)
Take game theory (4.14)
Pad a paper from one course with research from another (4.14)
Drop a course after receiving a D paper (4.14)
Nap between classes (4.14)
Take Major English Poets (4.14)
Borrow notes from a classmate so you can skip a class (4.14)
Play hooky to go window shipping (4.15)
Pick up a part-time job as a food hall card swiper (4.14)
Use the newsroom resources to research a family obituary (4.16)
Sign up to man a petition table (4.17)
Go on Spring Break in Florida (4.17)
Go home during weekends to concentrate on upcoming assignments (4.18)
Question your grade with your professor (4.19)

Take 'Philosophy' (4.21)
Think about Kafka and Chaucer even when your finals are finished (4.21)
Get a summer job so that you can save and avoid a semester time job (4.22)

Sophomore

Move into Branford College (5.3)
Secure the position of Feature Writer at the college newspaper (5.6)
Stay in the newspaper office late to work on a scoop (5.6)
Take 'Comparative Religions' (5.8)
Attend a Yale alumni party (5.8)
Study with a friend (5.9)
Host a student from your old high school, and show them college life (5.10)
Take 'Morals and Principles' (5.11)
Take 'Modern Poetry' (5.12)
Accept an internship at a local newspaper (5.19)
Sit through your final in a haze, and do not complete it (5.22)
Drop out of Yale, after deflating comments from a mentor upset you (5.22)
Take 'Poetry' (7.12

Junior

Go back to Yale (6.9)
Be pushy until you are offered a writing position at a newspaper (6.9)
Add to courses to your study load so that you graduate at the time that you would have (6.11)
Make notes while you walk (6.13)
Buy and wear college merchandise (6.14)
Become the editor of your college newspaper (6.14)
Take 'Micro Economics' (6.14)
Take part in a journalism panel (6.16)

Senior

Take a job teaching SAT Prep (7.3)
Review an art exhibition for the college newspaper (7.4)
Take "Economics" (7.5)
Major in English (7.5)
Host your parents at "Parents Weekend" (7.6)
Get to class on time (7.6)
Take 'Major English Poets' (7.8)
Network at parties (7.8)
Submit articles for an online magazine (7.8)
Submit a piece for an online publication (7.8)
Draw up on 'Operation Finish line" (7.12)

Use your academic connections to get letters of recommendation (7.12)
Boost your resume with volunteer work (7.12)
Work on your resume (7.14)
Meet with a top journalist to make connections (7.16)
Apply for the Reston fellowship (7.16)
Set up interviews at newspapers (7.17)
Take '20th Century Poets' (7.19)

Post-College

Write an article about people waiting in lines (AYITL: Spring)
Look for your lucky outfit (AYITL: Spring)
Go to Alumni Day and speak at your old high school (AYITL: Spring)
Take an interview with an online publication which headhunted you (AYITL: Spring)
Take a job as editor of a local newspaper (AYITL: Summer)
Outline an autobiographical book (AYITL: Summer)
Stay in a house by yourself to work on your book (AYITL: Fall)

Operation Finish Line
(7.12)

Typical College Experiences
☐ Drama School
☐ Up and Coming Stars at Yale
☐ Post Drama Production
☐ Art Show at Puke Hall
☐ Pizza at Wooster Square
☐ Climb East Rock
☐ Exotica Erotica
☐ Poposaurus Project at the Peabody
☐ Cafeteria Trays
☐ Ultimate Frisbee
☐ Frat Party

Tests
☐ MCATs
☐ GREs
☐ LSAT's

Final Exams May 8-15
☐ MCAT
☐ GRE

☐ LSAT

☐ Job Testing
☐ Boston Consultation
☐ Merrill Lynch

Faculty Recommendations
☐ Prof. Carrigan
☐ Prof. Gleeson
☐ Richard Gilmore
☐ Prof. Robinson
☐ Prof. Donaldson
☐ Prof. Edwards
☐ Prof. Flash
☐ Prof. Franks
☐ Prof. Jacquith
☐ Prof. Gonsalvez
☐ Prof. Masterston

Job Fairs

January
19th New England Health Professions Career Expo
21st Corporate Career Fair
24 JP Morgan 3.30p
26th Citibank 7pm
27th Mercer Cons 10am-2pm
27th Towers Perrin 3pm

28th Merill Lynch

February
2 Boston Consulting Group 6pm-10pm
3 HSBC 9am-3pm
8 McKinsey 6pm-11 Woolsey Hall
9 Citigroup 5pm-10pm Cross Campus
11 Yale New Haven Hospital 3pm-6pm
16 Yale Law School 1pm-6pm
17 Career Toolbox 10am-7pm
22 Fedore! Career Day Fair 3:30p
24 Leiman Bros 5:30p

March
2 HSBC 2pm-6pm
3 Credit Sense
5 New England Health Professions Career Expo
6 International Opportunities
17 Corporate Career Day
18 Wall Street
31

May
3rd Goldman Sachs 6pm <u>Must attend!</u>
4 Merrill Lynch 3pm
5 Yale New Haven Hospital 5.30
16 Credit Suisse 2:30
17 Towers Perrin 10-4.30p
19 Boston Consulting Day 7:30pm <u>Attend if needed</u>

20 Citibank 5:30 <u>keep informed reattend if needed!</u>

Volunteer
- St. Thomas More Soup Kitchen
- Westchester Children's Hospital
- Yale New Haven Hospital
- Peabody Museum
- Tutoring
- Respect Line Project
- Yale University Library

Grants and Scholarships
- Fullbright
- Yale Medical
- Yale Law
- Wharton
- Oxford
- Marshall
- Rhodes
- Gates Cambridge
- Winston Churchill Foundation

Seminars
- Careers that Span the Business/Social Divide
- Role of the IMF and the World Back in an age of

☐ Calhoun College Seminar, The Language of Music and Poetry Workshop
☐ Davenport College seminar
    The Press, Business and the Economy
☐ Military Leadership and the Social Class
    Jonathon Edwards College
☐ Trumbull College Seminar
    Twentieth Century Financial Booms & Busts
    Youth Cultures in the United States

Chilton Academy Events

Bake Sale (1.5)
Inter-Collegiate Recruiting Fair (1.6)
The Chilton Formal (1.9)
Parent's Day (1.11)
Summer School (2.2)
Booster Club Fashion Show (2.7)
The Puffs Initiation Ceremony (2.8)
Interpretive Shakespeare Production (2.9)
Interscholastic Debate Tournament (2.14)
Annual Business Fair (2.18)
Student Body President Forum (2.22)
Student Body Government (3.2)
'The Business of Getting In' Seminar (3.3)
Senior Prom (3.11)
Health Week (3.11)
Annual Blood Drive (3.11)
Bicentennial Celebration (3.16)
Bicentennial Speech Contest (3.16)
Booster Grad Night (3.19)
Graduation (3.21, 3.22)
Chilton Alumni, hosting a Chilton student (5.10)
Alumni Day (AYITL: Spring)

The Puffs Pledge

I pledge myself to the Puff's: loyal I'll always be.
A 'P' to start, two 'F's at the end, and a 'U'
sitting in between

Rory's Valedictorian Speech
(3.22)

Headmaster Charleston, faculty members, fellow students, family and friends, welcome. We never thought this day would come. We prayed for its quick delivery, crossed days off our calendars, counted hours, minutes, and seconds, and now that it's here, I'm sorry it is because it means leaving friends who inspire me and teachers who have been my mentors - so many people who have shaped my life and my fellow students' lives impermeably and forever.
I live in two worlds. One is a world of books. I've been a resident of Faulkner's Yoknapatawpha County, hunted the white whale aboard the Pequod, fought alongside Napoleon, sailed a raft with Huck and Jim, committed absurdities with Ignatius J. Reilly, rode a sad train with Anna Karenina, and strolled down Swann's Way. It's a rewarding world, but my second one is by far superior.
My second one is populated with characters slightly less eccentric but supremely real, made of flesh and bone, full of love, who are my ultimate inspiration for everything.

Richard and Emily Gilmore are kind, decent,

unfailingly generous people. They are my twin pillars without whom I could not stand. I am proud to be their grandchild.
But my ultimate inspiration comes from my best friend, the dazzling woman from whom I received my name and my life's blood, Lorelai Gilmore. My mother never gave me any idea that I couldn't do whatever I wanted to do or be whomever I wanted to be. She filled our house with love and fun and books and music, unflagging in her efforts to give me role models from Jane Austen to Eudora Welty to Patti Smith. As she guided me through these incredible eighteen years, I don't know if she ever realized that the person I most wanted to be was her.

Thank you, Mom. You are my guidepost for everything.

Quickfire Lists

As explained in the introduction of this book, the lists in this section are not as detailed as the ones found throughout this book, but rather are included for quick access—they are intended to be a resource that allows for a quick check on what books, or movies are included in the show, for example. So, if you want to know where the movie *Hard Bodies* is referenced in the show, then you won't find it here, but if you want to just check 'if' *Hard Bodies* is referenced in the show, then you have come to the right section.

It is my hope that this section will be helpful for those wanting to work their way through every book or movie mentioned on the show, and will serve as a handy reference guide.

Character List

A
A.K., Aaron, Alejandro, Alex Lesman, Alexandra, Alice, Alise, Allen Prescott, Allie, Allison, Althea, Amir, Andre, Andrew, Andy, Ann, Anna Fairchild, Anna Nardini, Anson, Antonia, April Nardini, Arletta, Arthur Gordon, Asher Fleming, Audrey Moreno, Aunt June, Aurora

B
Babette Dell, Banyon Boy, Barbara Boxer, Barbara Campbell, Barbara Epstein, Beatrice, Beau Belleville, Ben, Bennie, Bernadette, Bernice, Bertram Linds, Beth, Bette Davis, Beverly, Bill, Bill Borden, Billy, Bob Merriam, Bob Sutton, Bobby, Bonnie, Bootsy, Bowman, Brad Langford, Bradley, Brandon, Brenda, Brent, Brian Fuller, Brooke, Bruce, Buff Otis, Burt, Buzu Barnes

C
Caddy Steve, Caesar, Carl, Carla, Carol Springsteen, Carol Stiles, Caroline, Carolyn Bates,
Carrie Duncan, Cassie, Catarina, Chad, Charlie Davenport, Charlie Eichner, Charlotte

Courtwright, Chase Bradford, Cherry, Cheryl, Chester Fleet, Chip, Chris, Chrissy, Christine Christopher Hayden, Christy, Chuck, Cissy, Claire, Clara Forester, Claude, Claude Clemenceau
Claudia, Clementina, Cliff, Colin McCrae, Connor, Coop, Cousin David, Craig

D
Daisy Morton, Damon, Daniel, Darcy, Darren Springsteen, Darryl, Dave Rygalski, Davey, Davida, Dean Forester, Debbie Fincher, DeDe, Delia, Denise, Dennis, Dereck, Derek, Dewey Diane McLane, Docent, Donald, Donna, Donnen, Doris, Dorrie the Docent, Doug Doose, Douglas Swope, Doyle McMaster, Dr. Goldstein, Dr. Joshua Reynolds, Dr. Schultz, Dr. Shapiro, Dr. Sue, Draguta, Drella, Dwight

E
Earl, East Side Tillie, Ed, Edgar Pullings, Edwin, Eliza, Ellen, Ellory, Elzira Emily Gilmore, Enrique, Eric, Esperanza, Esther, Ethan Krumholtz, Eva

F
Finn, Floyd Stiles, Fran Weston, Francette, Francie Jarvis, Francine Hayden, Francis, Francoise,

677

Frank, Frankie, Franklin, Fred Larson, Fred Larson Jr., Freddy

G
Gabriela, Gail, Gary, George, Georgia 'GG' Hayden, Gerta, Gil, Ginger, Gisele Gerard, Glenda, Glenn Babble, Gloria, Graham Sullivan, Grandpa Huntzberger, Gypsy

H
Hal, Hanlin Charleston, Hannah, Harris Fellows, Harry, Harvey Tunnell, Heather, Heidi, Helen Thompson, Helmut, Henry Cho, Ho Kyung, Hollan Prescott, Honor Huntzberger, Howard, Hugo

I
Ian Jack, Ida, Irate Mother, Iris Medlock, Ivy

J
Jack Smith, Jack Springsteen, Jackie Shales, Jackson Belleville, Jacob, Jacqueline, Jake Huber, James Edwards, Jamie Jan, Janet Billings, Jason Stiles, Jeannie, Jennifer Springsteen, Jenson, Jess Mariano, Jessica Shales, Jim Hatlestad, Jim Nelson, Jim Romaine, Jimmy, Joan, Joanna Krumholtz, Joe Mastoni, Joel, Joey, John Mattern, Jonesy, Joni, Jordan Chase, Josh Davies, Josie, Judy, Julian Edwards, Juliet, Justin

K

Kaitlin, Karen, Kate, Katie, Katrinka, Kelly, Kid Sinclair, Kimberly Wells, Kip, Kirk Gleason, Kleebold, Kwan, Kyle, Kyon

L

Lacey, LaDawn, Lana, Lance, Lane Kim, Lanny, Laura, Laurie, LeAnne Harris, Leisal, Lemon, Len, Lenny, Leon, Leslie, Lev, Liam Drayson, Libby Doty, Lily, Linda, Lindsay Forester, Lisa, Liz Danes, Liza, Lloyd, Logan Huntzberger, Lois, Loreen, Lorelai Gilmore, Lorelai 'Trix' Gilmore, Lou Morton, Louise Grant, Lowell, Lucas, Luciano, Lucille, Lucy, Luis, Luke Danes, Lulu

M

Malcolm, Madeline Lynn, Madonna Louise, Maggie, Maisy Fortner, Manny, Marcia, Marcie, Marcy, Margaret, Marie Springsteen, Marjorie Rogers, Mark, Marla, Marshall, Martha, Martin, Marty, Mary, Matt, Matthew, Maureen Rollins, Maurice Chevalier Lipsyncer, Max Medina, May, May Forester, Maybelle, Mayor Harry Porter, Meena, Megan, Melanie, Mia, Michel Gerard, Mick, Mickey, Mike Krumholtz, Mikey, Mikhail, Miles Hahn, Millicent, Mira, Miriam, Miss Celine, Miss James, Miss Patty, Mitchum Huntzberger, Mitzi, Molly, Monique Clemenceau,

Morey Dell, Morgan, Mr. Blodgett, Mr. Brink, Mr. Cannold, Mr. Covitt, Mr. Fink, Mr. Hollister, Mr. Hunter, Mr. Kim, Mr. Leahy, Mr. Munster, Mr. Radis, Mr. Remmy, Mr. Smalls, Mr. Stein, Mrs. Burdiness, Mrs. Caldicott, Mrs. Cannold, Mrs. Cunningham, Mrs. Fielding, Mrs. Geller, Mrs. Kim, Mrs. Lanahan, Mrs. Leahy, Mrs. Moore, Mrs. Ness , Mrs. O'Malley, Mrs. Savitt, Mrs. Shales, Mrs. Sinclair, Mrs. Slutsky, Mrs. Thompson, Mrs. Traiger, Mrs. Van Wyck, Ms. Lomet

N
Nancy, Nancy Krumholtz, Nancy Waterford, Naomi Shropshire, Nat Compton, Natalie Swope, Natalie Zimmermann, Nick, Nicole Leahy, Nikki, Nora, Norman Mailer, Nurse Russell,

O
Officer Scanlon, Olivia, Olympia

P
Paris Geller, Pastor Tim, Pat, Patel Chandrasekhar, Paul, Paul Anka, Peg, Pennilyn Lott, Peter, Peyton Sanders, Phan, Phil, Philip, Pola, Polly, Principal Merton, Professor Anderson, Professor Bell, Professor Coppedge, Professor Freedman, Professor Geline, Professor Gilbert, Professor Quincy

Q
Quentin Walsh

R
Rabbi David Barans, Rachael Ray, Rachel, Raj, Randall Farber, Ranger Bill, Raul, Rebecca Redmond, Reverend Archie Skinner, Reverend Boteright, Reverend Hackett, Rich Bloomenfeld, Richard Gilmore, Riley, Rob, Robert Castellanos, Robert Grimaldi, Robert the Valet, Robin, Roger, Ronald, Ronnie, Rory Gilmore, Rose Samuels, Rosemary, Roy Choi, Rune, Russell Bynes, Ruthie

S
Salvador, Sam Duncan, Sandee, Sandra, Sandy, Sarah, Saul, Sean, Serena Ainsworth, Seth, Shane, Shannon, Sheila, Shel Sauceman, Shelby, Shelly, Sherry Tinsdale, Shira Huntzberger, Simon Mclaine, Sofia, Sookie St. James, Sophie Bloom, Stanley, Stefan, Steve the Bartender, Straub Hayden, Stu, Stuart Wultz, Sue, Sugarman, Summer, Sunny, Supervisor Phil, Susan Bennett, Susie, Sy

T
T.J., T.J.'s Brother, Tana Schrick, Tara, Taylor Doose, Ted, Terrence, Terry, Tess, Town Troubadour, Theresa Lister, Thumbless Freddie,

Tiffany, Tim, Timoteo, Tobey, Tobin, Todd, Tom, Toni, Tracey, Trevor, Trina, Trip, Tristin Dugray, Tucker Culbertson, Turner, Tweenie Halpern

V
Violet, Vivian Lewis

W
Wallace, Whitney, William

Y
Young Chui

Z
Zack Van Gerbig

Music

(Take Me) Riding In My Car by Woody Guthrie
18 And Life by Skid Row
20th Century Girl by Pizzicato Five
40 Years by House of Freaks
52 Girls by B-52's
99 Luftballons by Nena
A Beaver Ate My Thumb by Daniel Palladino
A Cockeyed Optimist by Rogers and Hammerstein
A Foggy Day in London Town by Frank Sinatra
A Kiss to Build a Dream On by Louis Armstrong
A Mighty Fortress is Our God written by Martin Luthor
A String of Pearls by Glenn Miller
A Whiter Shade Of Pale by Procol Harum
ABC by Jackson 5
Act of Love by Neil Young
Agrophobia by Incubus
All Fired Up by Tralala
All My Life by The Point
Amazing Glow by Joe Pernice
Amazing Grace by John Newton
Amazing Grace in Korean
Angels We Have Heard on High
Angst in My Pants by Sparks
Aquarius by The Fifth Dimension

Archives by Louise Goffin
Around the World by Daft Punk
As time goes by Made famous by Sinatra
Ave Maria by Franz Schubert
B-A-B-Y by Rachel Sweet
Baby Face by Bennie Davise and Harry Akst
Baby One More Time by Britney Spears
Bad Moon Rising by Creedence Clearwater Revival
Ballet Waltz #3 by Herman Beeftink
Ballo, e canto de' villanelli by Antonio Vivaldi

Be True To Your School by Grant Lee Phillips
Beanbag Chair by Yo La Tengo
Beautiful Dreamers by Grant Lee Phillips
Begin the Beguine by Cole Porter
Bei Mir Bist du Schon by The Andrew Sisters
Bette Davis Eyes by Kim Carnes
Big Blue Buzz by Ric Menck
Big in Japan by Tom Waits
Blankest Year by Nada Surf
Bluebird by The Rosebuds
Botch-A-Me (Ba-Ba-Baciami Piccina) by Rosemary Clooney
Boys Don't Cry by The Cure
Bright Future In Sales by Fountains Of Wayne
Bubbles: by The Free Design
Buff Right
Burning Down the House by Talking Heads
By the Beautiful Sea performed by the Swingin Deacons

Bye Bye Blackbird by Peggy Lee
Calling All Enthusiasts by Radio 4
Can't Stand Me Now by the Libertines
Candy Man by Sammy Davis, Jr
Car Song by Elastica
Castle Of Spirits by Parvaneh Butterfly & Jonny Franco
Catch a Wave by the Beach Boys
Cat's in The Cradle by Harry Chapin
Ce petit coeur [This Small Heart] by Francoise Hardy
Celebration by Kool and the Gang
Chain Gang by Sam Cooke
Chain Gang by Sam Cooke
Charma Chameleon by Boy George
Cherish by The Association
Child Psychology by Black Box Recorder
Chimacum Rain by Linda Perhacs
Christmas Wrapping by The Waitresses
Church of the Poison Mind by Culture Club
Cities in Dust by Siouxsie and the Banshees
Come a Little Bit Closer by Jay and the Americans
Come Fly With Me by Frank Sinatra
Come on Feel The Noize by Slade
Come On-A My house by Rosemary Clooney

Conscience Clean (I Went to Spain) by Pernice Brothers
Crazy Beat by Blur
Crazy by Patsy Cline

Crosseyed And Painless by Talking Heads
Crystal Lake by Grandaddy
Dance This Mess Around by B-52's
Dance To The Underground by Radio 4
Deck the Halls
Deora AR Mo Chroi by Enya
Diamond Dogs by David Bowie
Do That There by Lyrics Born
Do You Love Me from Fiddler on the Roof
Do You Really Want to Hurt Me? by Culture Club
Don't Know Why (You Stay) by The Essex Green
Don't Go Sit Under The Apple Tree by The Andrew Sisters
Don't Mug Yourself by The Streets
I Do The Rock by Time Curry
Don't Sleep on the Subway by Petula Clark
Down by Pidgeon
Drunk by North Green
Du Hast by Rammstein
Dust That Dreams of Brooms by Aveo
Early in the Morning by Buckwheat Zydeco
Earn Enough for Us by XTC
Easter Parade by Judy Garland
Eleanor Put Your Boots on by Franz Ferdinand
Endless Love by Lionel Ritchie and Diana Ross
Eternal Flame by the Bangles
Everlong by The Foo Fighters
Everybody Have Fun Tonight by Wang Chung

Everybody Needs a Little Sanctuary by Grant Lee Phillips
Everyday I Write the Book by Elvis Costello
Fade Into You by Mazzy Star
Fell in Love with a Girl by The White Stripes
Fever by Peggy Lee
Fillmore Blues by Chuck Berry
Fingersnap by Chucho Merchan
Flower Girl in Bordeaux by Esquivel
Fly Away by Lenny Kravitz
Fly Me to the Moon by Frank Sinatra
Folsom Prison Blues by Johnny Cash
Freaking Out by Graham Coxon
Ant Music by Adam and the Ants
Friendship by Judy Garland and Johnny Mercer
From Red to Blue by Billy Bragg
Fuckin' Up by Neil Young
Funky Days are Back Again by Cornershop
Funkytown by Lipps Inc.
Funny Face by Fred Astaire
Genius of Love by Tom Tom Club
Get Happy by Judy Garland
Get The Party Started by Pink
Get Yourself Together by Tahiti 80
Girl From Mars by Ash
Girls Just Wanna Have Fun by Cyndi Lauper
God Only Knows by Claudine Longet
Gonna Fly Now Theme from Rocky by Bill Conti
Gotango by Olof Roter
Greatest American Hero - (Believe it or Not) by Joey Scarbury

Gypsies, Tramps, and Thieves by Cher
Hang Down Your Head Tom Dooley by Kingston Trio
Hanging On The Telephone by Blondie
Happy Birthday by Mildred J. Hill and Dr. Patty Smith Hill
Happy Days Are Here Again by Guy Lombardo

Happy Kid by Nada Surf
Happy Song by Milkshake
Happy X-Mas by John Lennon and Yoko Ono
Hava Nagila a Jewish folk song
Head On by Jesus And Mary Jane
Heart of Glass by Blondie
Heartland by George Strait
Heavenly by Grant Lee Phillips
Heavy Metal Drummer by Wilco
Hello Dolly by Louis Armstrong
Here They Go by Sam Phillips
Here You Come Again by Dolly Parton
Hero Takes a Fall by The Bangles
Hiding in The Trees by Mindcleaner
Holding on to the Earth by Sam Phillips
Hollaback Girl by Gwen Stefani
Honey Don't Think by Grant Lee Buffalo
Hong Kong Garden by Siouxsie and the Banshees

Hot Blooded by Foreigner
How to Dream by Sam Phillips
Human Behavior by Bjork
Hurt So Good by John Mellencamp

Hush, Little Baby (Mockingbird song)
I Can't Get Started by Ella Fitzgerald
I Can't Give You Anything But Love, Baby by Jimmy McHugh
I Don't Know How to Say Goodbye to You by Sam Phillips
I Don't Mind by Slumber Party   I Dreamed a Dream by Anne Hathaway
I Feel The Earth Move by Carole King
I Found Love by the Free Design
I Get Around by The Beach Boys
I Think It's Gonna Rain Today by Claudine Longet
I Thought About You by Johnny Mercer and James Van Heusen
I Try by Macy Gray
I Wanna Be Sedated by the Ramones
I Will Always Love You by Dolly Parton
I Will Always Love You by Dolly Parton
I Will Always Love You by Whitney Houston
I Won't Grow Up by Rickie Lee Jones
Tropical Ice-Land by The Fiery Furnaces
Pretty In Pink by The Psychedelic Furs
I Would Go by Smoosh
I'll Dance At Your Wedding by Vic Damone
Ice Ice Baby by Vanilla Ice
If I Could Write by Sam Phillips
I'll Be Home For Christmas by Bing Crosby
I'll Be With You In Apple Blossom Time by The Andrew Sisters
I'll Be Your Mirror by The Velvet Underground

I'm a Believer by The Monkees
I'm Gonna Make You Love Me by the Jayhawks

I'm the Man Who Murdered Love by XTC
I'm The Man by Joe Jackson
In a Big Country by Big Country
In a Gadda Da Vida by Iron Butterfly
In a Young Man's Mind by the Mooney Suzuki
In My Honey's Lovin' Arms by Robert Mitchum
In the Cool Cool Cool of the evening by Rosemary Clooney
In The Mood by Glenn Miller
Inside Out by Mighty Lemon Drops
Iron Man by Black Sabbath
Ironic by Alanis Morisette
It's a Small World by Robert and Richard Sherman
It's De-lovely by Cole Porter
It's a Good Day by Peggy Lee
It's Alright, Baby by Komeda
It's Getting Hot In Herre by Nelly
It's the Life by Grant Lee Buffalo
Ja Glory by Toots Bombarde
Jacqueline by Franz Ferdinand
Jagged Little Pill by Alanis Morrissette
Jailhouse Rock by Elvis Presley
Jeannie Theme from I Dream of Jeannie by Buddy Kaye and Hugo Montenegro
Johnny Angel by Shelley Fabares
Jolene by Dolly Parton
Jubilee by Grant Lee Buffalo

Kiss Me by Vic Damone
Know Your Onion by The Shins
Kool Thing by Sonic Youth
La Casa by Graham Preskett/Mauricio Venegas
La La by Shark Quest
L'anamour [The Anamour] by Jane Birkin
Last Train to Clarksville by The Monkees
Legal Man by Belle and Sebastian
Let Your Ya Be Ya by Ranking Roy
Like a Virgin by Madonna
Lily is a Passion by Grant Lee Phillips
Lily-A-Passion by Grant-Lee Phillips
Lively Up Yourself by The Family Zigag
Livin' La Vida Loca by Ricky Martin
Living On A Prayer by Bon Jovi
London Calling by The Clash
Lonesome Street by Blur
Looks Like We Made It by Barry Manilow
Los Angeles by X
Lost Volvo by Mary Lynn Rajskub
Louie Louie by Richard Berry
Love Burns by BRMC
L-O-V-E by Irving
Love Is Everywhere I Go by Sam Phillips
Love Revolution by Daniel Palladino, Jeanine Tesori
Love Will Keep Us Together by Captain and Tennille
Lucy in the Sky with Diamonds by William Shatner
Lullaby by Johannes Brahm

Maggie Blues by Bing and Gary Crosby
Maggie's Farm by Bob Dylan
Magic Moments by Perry Como
Making Noises by The SqueeGees
Mama Tried by Merle Haggard
Mambo Italiano by Dean Martin
Man! I Feel Like a Woman! by Shania Twain
Man, I Feel Like a Woman! by Shania Twain
Manic Monday by the Bangles
Margaritaville Jimmy Buffett
Me and Julio Down By The School Yard by Paul Simon
Mein kleiner grüner Kaktus by the Comedian Harmonists
Mexican Shuffle by Herb Alpert and the Tijuana Brass
Midnight at the Oasis by Maria Muldaur
Mixed Business by Beck
Mockingbirds by Grant Lee Buffalo
Mona Lisa by Grant Phillips
Monkey Gone to Heaven by the Pixies
Moon River by Audrey Hepburn
Ms. Jackson by Outkast
My Darling by Wilco
My Favourite Letter by Stephen Lang
My Happy Ending by Avril Lavigne
My Heart Belongs to Daddy by Marilyn Monroe
My Heart Belongs to Me by Barbra Streisand
My Heart Belongs to You by Jim Brickman
My Heart Stood Still by Ray Conniff
My Heart Will Go On by Celine Dion

My Little Corner of the World by Yo La Tengo
My Melancholy Baby By Dorsey Brothers & Their Orchestra
Man Who Sold the World by David Bowie
My Sharona by The Knack
Naima by John Coltrane
Nookie by Limp Bizkit
Nothin' is For Sure by Grant Lee Phillips
Oblivious by Aztec Camera
Oh My Love by John Lennon
Oh, What A Beautiful Morning by Rogers & Hammerstein
On the Road Again by Willie Nelson
One Fine Day by The Chiffons
One For My Baby by Frank Sinatra
One Line by PJ Harvey
One Step Beyond by Madness
One Way or Another by Blondie
O'Oh by Yoko Ono
Our Lips Are Sealed by The Go-Go's
Peace Train by Cat Stevens
Pennies from Heaven by Louis Armstrong
Perfect Situation for a Fool by Jai Josefs
Perfume by Sparks
Piano Sonata No. 2 in B Minor, Op. 35: III. Marche funèbre: Lento by Vitalij Margulis
Pick Yourself Up by Fred Astaire & Ginger Rogers
Pictures of You by The Cure
Pink Steam by Sonic Youth
Pipeline by The Chantays

Pippi Longstocking by Astrid Lindgren
Pleasant Vally Sunday by The Monkees
Pomp and Circumstance
Pomp and Circumstance written by Edward Elgar
Pre-owned heart by Grant Lee Phillips
Price Yeah! by Pavement
Prologue Into the Woods from the musical Into the Woods
Purple Rain by Prince
Raise the Spirit by Grant Lee Phillips
Reflecting Light by Sam Phillips
Reflecting Light by Sam Phillips
Relax by Frankie Goes to Hollywood
Relax by Frankie Goes To Hollywood
Ring of Fire by Johnny Cash
Roam by The B52s
Robots by the Futureheads
Rockin with the Rhythm of the Rain by The Judds
Roxanne by The Police
Rusholme Ruffians by The Smiths
Russian Rhapsody by The Ossipov Balalaika orchestra, Nikolai Kalinin
'S Wonderful by Audrey Hepburn & Fred Astaire
Saccharine by Sunday's Best
Saddest Quo by Pernice Brothers
Sadie, Sadie by Barbra Streisand
Sadness Soot by Grant Lee Phillips
Santa Claus is Coming to Town by Tony Bennett

Satellite of Love by Lou Reed

Saturday Night's Alright by Elton John
Science vs. Romance by Rilo Kiley
Selling Yourself Short by What Made Milwaukee Famous
Semper Fidelis by John Phillip Sousa
Seventh Son by Mose Allison
Shadow Dancing by Andy Gibb
Shy Boy by Bananarama
Side Streets by Saint Etienne
Sing Sing Sing (With a Swing) by James Horner Prima
Six Months In A Leaky Boat by Split Enz
Slow Hands by Interpol
Slung-Lo by Erin McKeown
Smile by Grant-Lee Phillips
So Long, Farewell by Rogers & Hammerstein
So Long, Farewell by Rogers and Hammerstein
So Says I by The Shins
Some People by Bernadette Peters and William Parry
Someone to Watch Over Me by Frank Sinatra
Something Good from The Sound of Music
Sometimes Always by Jesus and Mary Chain
Songbird by Kenny G
Space Odity by David Bowie
Spring Released by Grant Lee Phillips
Stand By Your Man by Tammy Wynette
Star Spangled Banner by Francis Scott Key, John Stafford Smith, and Springfield Digital Orchestra
Starcrossed by Ash

Stars and Stripes Forever by John Phillip Sousa

Stayin' Alive by The Bee Gees
Step Into My Office Baby by Belle and Sebastian
String of Pearls by Glenn Miller
Stuck In The Middle With You by Stealer's Wheel
Suburban Homeboy by Sparks
Suffragette City by David Bowie
Summer by Charlotte Hatherley
Sunday Best by Grant Lee Phillips
Superfreak by Rick James
Suppertime by Clark Genser
Suspended from Class by Camera Obscura
Swan Lake -- Ballet -- Ste Op. 20a: Sea in the Moonlight by Tchaikovsky
Symphony No. 7 in E minor (Song of the Night) by New York Philharmonic with Henry Grossman
Symphony No.1 in D Major, Titan, Movement IV by Gustav Mahler
Everything I've Got (Belongs to You) by Blossom Dearie
Take My Breath Away by Berlin
Takin' Care of Business by Bachman-Turner Overdrive
Taking Pictures by Sam Phillips
Tambourine Man by William Shatner
Teach Me Tonight by Sammy Cahn and Gene De Paul
Tears in Heaven by Eric Clapton

Tell Her What She Wants to Know by Sam Phillips
Tequila by Los Lodos
Thank Heaven for Little Girls by Maurice Chevalier
Thanks for Christmas by XTC
The Best Is Yet To Come by Tony Bennett
The Boat Ashore by Michael Roe
The Candy Man by Sammy Davis, Jr
The Coffee Song By Bob Hilliard & Richard Miles
The Elements Song by Tom Lehrer
The Entertainer by Billy Joel
The Girl From Ipanema by Fantastic Strings
The Joker by Steve Miller Band
The Lathe of Heaven by Scott Abels, Aaron Owens, Matthew W. Parker, David Fuentes, Brian Dixon
The Laws Have Changed by The New Pornographers
The Little Ol' Beggar's Bush by Flogging Molly
The Man That Got Away by Judy Garland
The Music Goes Round And Round by Frank Froeba & His Swing Band
Diga Diga Doo by Mills Brothers with Duke Ellington
The Neutral by Sonic Youth
The Perfect Crime 2 by The Decemberists
The Rap Song by Daniel Palladino
The Sound of Silence by Simon and Garfunkel
The Star-Spangled Banner by Francis Scott Key

The Way You Look Tonight by Frank Sinatra
The Weakest Shade Of Blue by The Pernice Brothers
The Whiffenpoof Song by the Whiffenpoofs
Theme from Terms of Endearment by Michael Gore, Arr. Mark Northam
Then She Appeared by XTC
There She Goes by The La's
These Boots Are Made For Walkin' by Nancy Sinatra
These Foolish Things performed by the Swingin' Deacons
Thirteen by Big Star
This is Hell by Elvis Costello
This Old House by Brian Setzer Orchestra
This Town by The Go-Go's
Those Lazy Hazy Crazy Days of Summer by Nat King Cole
Through the Eyes of Love (Theme from Ice Castles) by Marvin Hamlisch and Carole Bayer Sager
Time Bomb by Rancid
Time Bomb by Rancid
Time by Tom Waits
Tiny Cities Made of Ashes by Modest Mouse
To Go Home by M. Ward
Too Much Love by LCD Soundsystem
Too Shy by Kajagoogoo
Top Of The World by The Carpenters
True by Spandau Ballet
Truly Truly by Grant Lee Phillips

Twin Cinema by the New Pornographers
Unbreakable by Daniel and Amy Sherman-Palladino, Jeanine Tesori
Under The Boardwalk by Bette Midler
Until the Real Thing Comes Along by Dean Martin
Valley Winter Song by Grant-Lee Phillips
Video by India Arie
Wake Me Up (Before You Go Go) by Grant Lee Phillips
Walk Like an Egyptian by The Bangles
Walkin' My Baby Back Home performed by the Swingin Deacons
Walking After Midnight by Patsy Cline
Walking On Sunshine by Katrina And The Waves

Waterloo by ABBA
We Are Family by Sister Sledge
We Are the Champions by Queen
We Wish You a Merry Christmas
Wedding Bell Blues by The 5th Dimension
Wedding March by Felix Mendelssohn
Wendy by Wesley Yang and Gavin McNett
Wendy composed by Wesley Yang & Gavin McNett
We're All Light by XTC
We've Got Magic To Do by Stephen Schwartz
Swan Lake, Op. 20, Suite 3 - Danse des petits cygnes by Herbert von Karajan with the Berliner Philharmoniker
Koyaanisqatsi by Philip Glass

What A Time It Was by Daniel May
What a Waste by Sonic Youth
What A Wonderful World by Joey Ramone
What Do I Do by Sam Phillips
What More Can I Say by Kurt Cobain
What's There Not To Love About Stars Hollow? Daniel and Amy Sherman-Palladino, Jeanine Tesori
Whatever Will Be, Will Be (Que Sera Sera) by Doris Day
When The Saints Go Marching In by The Dixieland All Stars
When You Tell Me That You Love Me by Diana Ross
Where It's At by Beck
Where the Colors Don't Go by Sam Phillips
Where You Lead by Carole King
White Lines by Grandmaster and Melle Mel
White Riot by The Clash
Who Will Save Your Soul by Jewel
Who's That Girl? by White and Schogger
Why by North Green
Why Does it Always Rain on Me? by Travis
Wicked Witch Theme (From The Wizard of Oz)
William Tell Overture by St. Olaf Orchestra
Wind Beneath My Wings by Bette Midler
Windy by The Association
Winter Wonderland by Bing Crosby
Winterglow by Grant-Lee Phillips
With A Little Help From My Friends by Joe Anderson and Jim Sturgess

Without a Net composed by Ken Hiatt
'Woo Hoo' by 5.6.7.8's
Work It by Missy Elliot
Working on Building Stars Hollow by Daniel and Amy Sherman-Palladino, Jeanine Tesori
Yale Bulldog Chant by Cole Porter
You and Me by Daniel May
You Can't Hurry Love by The Concretes
You Never Can Tell by Chuck Berry
You're Just in Love from Call Me Madame
You're The Top by Cole Porter
You've Lost That Loving Feeling by The Righteous Brothers
Zombie by The Cranberries
Zombie Jamboree by The Kingston Trio
Zydeco Boogaloo by Buckwheat Zydeco

Pets

Angus
Apricot
Buster
Buttercup
Cat Kirk
Chin Chin
Chowder
Cinnamon
Cletus
Coco/Co-kie/Kookie/Tookie/Paul Anka
Coligular
Cyrus
Dan
Davey's Goldfish
Desdemona
General Lee
Jimmy Jam
Legolas
Leopold
Lobe
Mudball
Murray
Papaya
Paw Paw
Petal
Petey
Princess
Rufus

Sammy
Satchimo
Sherlock
Skippy
Snuggles
Spot
Stan
Stella/Case Study #12
Terry Lewis
Unnamed dog

Businesses

Al's Pancake World
Antonioli's Restaurant and Pizzeria
Baco's: Sporting Good Store
Birch Grove Spa
Beat Records
Black, White, and Read Bookshop/Theatre
Bootsy's Newsstand
Buff Rite Inc.
Butchery
Café Coffee
CBGB
Chez Zinjustin
Chilton Academy
Churchogogue
Cider Mill
China Garden
Colonial Museum
Dante's inferno
Damen's
Dell's Bar
Doose's Market
Dragonfly Inn
Dynasty Makers
Eastside Dental
Fair Game Video and Arcade
Farmer's Market

Ferme
First National Bank
Fred's Dry Cleaning
Gabby's Flower Shop
Gallery
Gelston House
Goodwill
Groove Yard Music
Gypsy's Garage / Hewes Brothers
Hair Salon
Halfway House Café
Harry's Bar
Harry's House of Twinkle Lights
Hockey Rink
Homeless Pets on the Net
Household
Hungry Diner
Independence Inn
Jackson's Produce
Jojo's Burgers
John Skinner Medical Centre
KC's Tavern Bar and Grill
Kim's Antiques
Kirk's Diner
Kirk's Doggy Daycare
Kirk's Pedi Cab
Kirsten's
L'Aprge
Le Chat Club
Lena's Stationery
Lila's Café

Lisa's Beauty Parlor
Luger's Bait and Tackle
Luke's Diner / William's Hardware
Madison House
Malin DSL
Mailboxes, Etc.
Marry Mimi's Bridal Shop
Mediterranean Delight
Miniature Golf
Miss Patty's Dance School
Momo's Tyres
Mongolian Grill
Museum of Rocks that Look Like Famous People
Muskie's
Nancy's Cottage of Calico
No Fish Today
Old Place Gambling Hall
Once Upon a Bookstore
Ooober
Paris Fashions
Posey's
Post Office
Pretty Pastures
Quest Copying
Radio Shack
Record Breaker
Renaissance Fair
Recycling Centre
Rich Man's Show Bar and Grill
Sally's Florist
Salvation Army

Samantha Leigh's Bakery
Samuel Mudson's Apothecary
Sandeep's
Sandee Says
Sears
Seaspray Motel
Sophie's Music
Something Old, Something New Bridal Shop
Sniffy's Tavern
Stamford Eagle Gazette
Stars Hollow Bank
Stars Hollow Baby
Stars Hollow Beauty Supply
Stars Hollow Books
Stars Hollow Chamber of Commerce
Stars Hollow City Council
Stars Hollow Dairy
Stars Hollow Elementary School
Stars Hollow Fire Department
Stars Hollow Gazette
Stars Hollow High School
Stars Hollow Library
Stars Hollow Middle School
Stars Hollow Municipal Pool
Stars Hollow Museum
Stars Hollow Party Supply
Stars Hollow Pharmacy
Stars Hollow Security
Stars Hollow Shoe Repair
Stars Hollow Swimming Pool
Stars Hollow Retirement Home

Stars Hollow Video
Stars Hollow Visitor Center
Suddaby's
Taco Barn
Taylor Doose's Old-Fashioned Soda Shoppe and Candy Store
Teriyaki Joe's
Teriyaki Tokyo
Tilman Farm
The Autobody Shop
The Binser Corp
The Cheshire Cat
The Linen Closet
The Hartford Courant
The Chimney Sweep
The Good Neighbor Pharmacy
The King's Head Inn
The Learning Center
The Radio Station
The Road Crew
The Secret Bar
Tricky's Dry Cleaners
Truncheon Books
Vintage Clothing
Walmart
West Hills Market
Weston's Bakery
Winkie's Restaurant
Yale Bookstore
Yale University
Yummy Bartenders

Porcelain Unicorn Store #1
Porcelain Unicorn Store #2
Porcelain Unicorn Store #3
Porcelain Unicorn Store #4
Porcelain Unicorn Store #5
Porcelain Unicorn Store #6
Porcelain Unicorn Store #7
Porcelain Unicorn Store #8
Porcelain Unicorn Store #9
Porcelain Unicorn Store #10
Porcelain Unicorn Store #11
Porcelain Unicorn Store #12

Stars Hollow Events

Arbor Day Festival
Book Club
Buy A Book Fundraiser
Charity Rummage Sale
Christmas Caroling
Connecticut Bike Race
Corn Com Boom
Cornucopia Can Drive
Easter Egg Hunt
Edgar Allen Poe Society 'Readings of Poe'
End of Summer Madness Festival
First Annual Stars Hollow Gay Pride Parade
Harvest Festival
Hay Bale Maze
Hayride
Hodges Sports Club
Kirk in a Box
Miss Patty's Grand Recital
Monique Ashwell Bakery
Movie Night In The Square
Snowman Contest
Spring Fling Festival
Stars Hollow Autumn Festival
Stars Hollow Bid-On-A-Basket Festival

Stars Hollow High Pep Rally
Stars Hollow Spring International Food Festival
Stars Hollow Winter Carnival
Stars Hollow Winter Festival
Tennessee Williams Lookalike Competition
The 24-Hour Annual Dance Marathon
The Annual Stars Hollow Founders Firelight Festival
The Christmas Pageant
The Festival of Living Art/Pictures
The Old Muddy River Bridge Knitathon
The Revolutionary War Reenactment
The Stars Hollow Musical
Wicca Convention

Books

18 and Life on Skid Row by Sebastian Bach
1984 by George Orwell
A Bolt from The Blue and Other Essays by Mary McCarthy
A Christmas Carol by Charles Dickens
A Clockwork Orange by Anthony Burgess
A Confederacy of Dunces by John Kennedy Toole
A Connecticut Yankee in King Arthur's Court by Mark Twain
A Girl from Yamhill, Beverly Cleary; Like Water for Chocolate by Laura Esquivel
A Heartbreaking Work of Staggering Genius by Dave Eggers
A Mencken's Chrestomathy by H.L. Mencken
A Monetary History of the United States by Milton Friedman
A Moveable Feast by Ernest Hemingway
A Room of One's Own by Virginia Woolf
A Room with a View by E.M. Forster
A Streetcar Named Desire by Tennessee Williams
A Tale of Two Cities by Charles Dickens
Absolute Rage by Robert K Tanenbaum
Alice's Adventures in Wonderland by Lewis Carroll
All the Pretty Horses by Cormac McCarthy
American Steel by Richard Preston

Angels in America by Tony Kushner
Anna Karenina by Leo Tolstoy
As I Lay Dying by William Faulkner
Atonement by Ian McEwan
Babe by Dick King- Smith
Backlash: The Undeclared War Against American Women by Susan Faludi
Bad Dirt by Annie Proulx
Basic Writings of Nietzsche by Friedrich Nietzsche
Beowulf by unknown
Beyond Good and Evil by Friedrich Nietzsche
Billy Budd and Other Tales, Herman Melville
Blind Faith by Joe McGinniss
Brave New World by Aldous Huxley
Brigadoon by Alan Jay Lerner
Brothers on Life by Matt Czuchry and Mike Czuchry
Call of the Wild by Jack London
Candide by Voltaire
Carrie by Stephen King
Catch-22 by Joseph Heller
Charles Darwin, On the Origin of Species
Charlie and the Chocolate Factory by Roald Dahl
Charlotte's Web by E.B. White
Chronicles of Narnia by C.S. Lewis
Chrysanthemum by Kevin Henkes
Clifford the Big Red Dog by Norman Bridwell
Cloud Atlas by David Mitchell
Coffee at Luke's: An Unauthorized Gilmore Girls Gabfest by Leah Wilson

Complete Novels by Dawn Powell
Consider the Lobster by David Foster Wallace
Contact by Carl Sagan
Contemporary Political Fiction
Cujo by Stephen King
Cyrano de Bergerac by Edmond Rostand
David and Lisa by Dr Theodore Issac Rubin M.D.
David Copperfield by Charles Dickens
Dead Souls by Nikolai Vasilevich Gogol
Death of a Salesman by Arthur Miller
Deenie by Judy Blume
Delta of Venus by Anais Nin
Demons by Fyodor Dostoevsky; translated by Richard Pevear and Larissa Volokhonsky
Don Quixote by Miguel de Cervantes
Downpour by Nick Holmes
Dr. Dolittle by Hugh Lofting
Driving Miss Daisy by Alfred Uhry
Eat Like a Gilmore: Daily Cravings by Kristi Carlson
Eat Like a Gilmore: The Unofficial Cookbook for Fans of Gilmore Girls by Kristi Carlson
Eat, Pray, Love by Elizabeth Gilbert
Eleanor Roosevelt by Blanche Wiesen Cook
Elements by Euclid
Elmer Gantry by Sinclair Lewis
Eloise by Kay Thompson
Emily the Strange by Roger Reger
Encyclopedia Brown: Boy Detective by Donald J. Sobol

Essentials of Economics, 3rd ed., Bradley R. Schiller
Ethan Frome by Edith Wharton
Ethics by Spinoza
Europe Through the Back Door, 2003 by Rick Steves
Eva Luna by Isabel Allende
Fast Talk & Faith: A 22-Day Devotional Inspired by Gilmore Girls
Fear and Loathing in Las Vegas by Hunter S. Thompson
Firewall by Lawrence E. Walsh
First Folio by William Shakespeare
Flavor of the Month by Olivia Goldsmith
Fletch by Gregory McDonald
Frankenstein by Mary Shelley
Franny and Zooey by J.D. Salinger
Freaky Friday by Mary Rodgers
Frida by Hayden Herrera
Game of Thrones by George R.R. Martin
Gender Trouble by Judith Butler
Gidget by Frederick Kohner
Gigi by Collette
Gilmore Girls and the Politics of Identity: Essays on Family and Feminism in the Television Series by Ritch Calvin
Gilmore Girls: A Cultural History by Lara C. Stache, Rachel Davidson
Gilmore Girls: I Do, Don't I? (Book 3) by Catherine Clark

Gilmore Girls: I Love You, You Idiot (Book 2) by Cathy East Dubowski
Gilmore Girls: Like Mother, Like Daughter (Book 1) by Catherine Clark
Gilmore Girls: The Other Side of Summer (Book 4) by Helen Pai
Girl, Interrupted by Susanna Kaysen
Glengarry Glen Ross by David Mamet
Go Set a Watchman by Harper Lee
Gone with the Wind by Margaret Mitchell
Goodnight Moon by Margaret Wise Brown and Clement Hurd
Great Expectations by Charles Dickens
Gulliver's Travels by Jonathon Swift
Guys and Dolls by Jo Swerling and Abe Burrows
Haiku, Volume 2: Spring by R.H. Blyth
Haiti: State Against Nation: Origins and Legacy of Duvalierism by Michel-Rolph Trouillot
Hamlet by William Shakespeare
Harold and the Purple Crayon by Crockett Johnson
Harry Potter & the Goblet of Fire by J.K. Rowling
Harry Potter and the Sorcerer's Stone: Harry Potter - Book 1 by J. K. Rowling
He's Just Not That Into You by Greg Behrendt and Liz Tuccillo
Henry IV, Part 1 by William Shakespeare
Henry IV, Part 2 by William Shakespeare
Henry V by William Shakespeare
Hidden Romantic Gems of the Restaurant World

High Fidelity by Nick Hornsby
History of the Peloponnesian War by Thucydides
Hockey for Dummies by John Davidson
Hoover's Handbook of American Business 1996 by Gary Hoover
How the Grinch Stole Christmas by Dr. Seuss
How we are Hungry by Dave Eggers
Howl by Allen Ginsberg
Huckleberry Finn by Mark Twain
I Feel Bad About My Neck: And Other Thoughts on Being a Woman by Nora Ephron
I'm With the Band by Pamela Des Barres
In Cold Blood by Truman Capote
In Conclusion, Don't Worry About It by Lauren Graham
In Search of Lost Time by Marcel Proust
In the Shadow of Young Girls in Flower by Marcel Proust
Inferno by Dante
Inherit the Wind by Jerome Lawrence and Robert E. Lee
Into the Woods by Stephen Sondheim
Iron Weed by William J. Kennedy
It Takes a Village by Hilary Clinton
Jaglon by Asher Fleming (fictional text)
Jane Eyre by Charlotte Bronte
Jane: One Woman's Harrowing Journey to God (fictional text)
Julius Caesar by William Shakespeare
King Richard III by William Shakespeare
Lady Chatterley's Lover by D.H. Lawrence

Laroose Wine by David Cobbold
Leaves of Grass by Walt Whitman
Less than Zero, Bret Easton Ellis
Letters of Ayn Rand edited by Michael S. Berliner
Letters to a Young Poet by Rainer Maria Rilke
Lies and the Lying Liars Who Tell Them by Al Franken
Life of Samuel Johnson by James Boswell
Like Water for Chocolate by Laura Esquivel
Little Dorrit by Charles Dickens
Little House in the Big Woods by Laura Ingalls Wilder
Little House on the Prairie by Laura Ingalls Wilder
Lolita by Vladimir Nabokov
Lord Jim by Joseph Conrad
Lord of the Flies by William Golding
Lord of The Rings: The Return of the King by J.R.R. Tolkien
Love Story, Erich Segal
Macbeth by William Shakespeare
Madame Bovary by Gustave Flaubert
Madeline by Ludwig Bemelmans
Marathon Man by William Goldman
Martha Stewart Living, Holidays: The Best of Martha Stewart Living
Matisse the Master: A Life of Henri Matisse by Hilary Spurling
Memoirs of a Dutiful Daughter by Simone de Beauvoir

Memoirs of General W. T. Sherman by William Tecumseh Sherman
Mencken's Chrestomathy by H.R. Mencken
Mistress of Mellyn by Victoria Holt
Moby Dick by Herman Melville
Moliere: A Biography by Hobart Chatfield Taylor
Mommie Dearest by Christina Crawford
Monsieur Proust by Celeste Albaret
Mrs. Dalloway by Virginia Woolf
Mutiny on the Bounty by Charles Nordhoff and James Norman Hall
My First Summer in the Sierra by John Muir
My Lai 4: A Report on the Massacre and Its Aftermath by Seymour M. Hersh
My Life as Author and Editor by H.L. Mencken
My Struggle by Karl Ove Knausgaard
Myra Waldo's Travel and Motoring Guide to Europe, 1978 by Myra Waldo
Naked Lunch: The Restored Text, William S. Burroughs
Nancy Drew 33: The Witch Tree Symbol by Carolyn Keene
Nancy Drew Mysteries by Carolyn Keene
Native Son by Richard Wright
Nature's Metropolis: Chicago and the Great West by William Cronon
Nickel and Dimed by Barbara Ehrenreich
No Man is an Island by John Donne
No Mistakes: A Workbook for Imperfect Artists by Keiko Agena
Northanger Abbey by Jane Austen

Notes of a Dirty Old Man by Charles Bukowski
November of the Heart by LaVyrle Spencer
Of Human Bondage by W Somerset Maugham
Of Mice and Men by John Steinbeck
Oliver Twist by Charles Dickens
On the Contrary by Mary McCarthy
On the Road by Jack Kerouac
One Day in the Life of Ivan Denisovich by Aleksandr Solzhenitsyn
One Hundred Years of Solitude by Gabriel Garcia Marquez
Orations of American Orators
Othello by William Shakespeare
Out of Africa by Isaac Denison
Outlander by Diana Gabaldon
Oxford English Dictionary
Personal History by Katharine Graham
Peyton Place by Grace Metalious
Pinocchio by Carlo Collodi
Please Kill Me: The Uncensored Oral History of Punk by Legs McNeil and Gillian McCain
Plutarch's Lives, volume 1 or 2 by John Dryden and Arthur Hugh Clough
Poems by Alfred Lord Tennyson
Points of View by W Somerset Maugham
Pomeranian: An Owner's Guide to a Happy Healthy Pet by Happeth A. Jones
Punk: The Definitive Record of a Revolution by Stephen Colegrave and Colin Sullivan
Pushkin: A Biography by T.J. Binyon
Quiller Bambo by Adam Hall

R is for Ricochet by Sue Grafton
Rapunzel by Brothers Grimm
Rebecca of Sunnybrook Farm by Kate Douglas Wiggin
Revolution from Within by Gloria Steinem
Rita Hayworth and The Shawshank Redemption by Stephen King
Robert's Rules of Order by Henry Robert
Romeo and Juliet by William Shakespeare
Rosemary's Baby by Ira Levin
S is for Silence by Sue Grafton
Sailing Alone Around the Room: New and Selected Poems by Billy Collins
Savage Beauty: The Life of Edna St. Vincent Millay by Nancy Milford
Saving the Queen by William F. Buckley Jr.
Say Goodbye to Daisy Miller by Henry James
Screwball Television: Critical Perspectives on Gilmore Girls by David Lavery and David Scott Diffrient
Fast Talk & Faith: A 22-Day Devotional Inspired by Gilmore Girls by Mary Carver
Secrets of the Flesh: A Life of Colette by Judith Thurman
Selected Hotels of Europe
Sexus by Henry Miller
Sherlock Holmes by Arthur Conan Doyle
Slaughter-House Five by Kurt Vonnegut
Snow White and Rose Red by Grimm Brothers
Snows of Kilimanjaro by Ernest Hemingway

Social Origins of Dictatorship and Democracy by Barrington Moore Jr.
Someday, Someday, Maybe by Lauren Graham
Sophie's Choice by William Styron
Stalin: A Biography by Robert Service
Stepford Wives by Ira Levin
Story of O by Pauline Reage
Stuart Little by E. B. White
Summer of Fear by T Jefferson Parker
Swann's Way by Marcel Proust
Taken Hostage: the Iran Hostage Crisis and America's First Encounter with Radical Islam by David Farber
Talking as Fast As I Can by Lauren Graham
Tender is the Night by F Scott Fitzgerald
Terms of Endearment by Larry McMurtry
Tevya the Dairyman and the Railroad Stories by Sholem Aleichem
The Adventures of Huckleberry Finn by Mark Twain
The Age of Innocence by Edith Wharton
The Andy Warhol Diaries edited by Pat Hackett
The Apocalyptics - Cancer and the Big Lie: How Environmental Politics Controls What We Know About Cancer by Edith Efron
The Armies of the Night: History as a Novel, the Novel as History; The Executioner's Song by Norman Mailer
The Art of Eating by MFK Fisher
The Art of Fiction by Henry James
The Art of War by Sun Tzu

The Bell Jar by Sylvia Plath
The Bhagavad Gita
The Bible
The Big Love by Sarah Dunn
The Bright of Martydom (fictional text)
The Brontes by Juliet Barker
The Catcher in the Rye by J.D. Salinger
The Children's Hour by Lillian Hellman
The Collected Short Stories by Eudora Welty
The Compact Oxford English Dictionary by Henry Watson Fowler
The Complete Poems by Anne Sexton
The Complete Works of William Shakespeare by William Shakespeare
The Crimson Petal and the White by Michel Faber
The Crisis by David Harris
The Crucible by Arthur Miller
The Curious Incident of the Dog in the Night-time by Mark Haddon
The Da Vinci Code by Dan Brown
The Diary of Virginia Woolf, Volume 4: 1931-1935 edited by Anne Olivier Bell
The Diary of Virginia Woolf, Volumes 1, 3-5 edited by Anne Olivier Bell
The Dirt: Confessions of the World's Most Notorious Rock Band by Tommy Lee, Vince Neil, Mick Mars and Nikki Sixx
The Divine Comedy by Dante
The Divine Secrets of the Ya-Ya Sisterhood by Rebecca Wells

The Electric Kool-Aid Acid Test by Tom Woolf
The Executioner's Song by Norman Mailer
The Fountainhead by Ayn Rand
The Gilmore Girls Companion by A. S. Berman
The Gnostic Gospels by Elaine Pagels
The Godfather: Book 1 by Mario Puzo
The Graduate by Charles Webb
The Grapes of Wrath by John Steinbeck
The Great Gatsby by F.Scott Fitzgerald
The Group by Mary McCarthy
The History of the Decline and Fall of the Roman Empire by Edward Gibbon
The History of Tom Thumb by Anonymous
The Holy Barbarians by Lawrence Lipton
The House of the Spirits by Isabel Allende
The Human Factor by Graham Greene
The Hunchback of Notre Dame by Victor Hugo
The Iliad and The Odyssey by Homer
The Invitation by Oriah Mountain Dreamer
The Joy Luck Club by Amy Tan
The Jumping Frog by Mark Twain
The Last Empire: Essays 1992-2000 by Gore Vidal
The Last Word by Graham Greene
The Legend of Bagger Vance by Steven Pressfield
The Life-Changing Magic of Tidying Up by Marie Konde'
The Lion, The Witch, and the Wardrobe by C.S. Lewis

The Little Locksmith by Katharine Butler Hathaway
The Little Match Girl by Hans Christian Andersen
The Lord of the Rings by J.R.R. Tolkien
The Lottery by Shirley Jackson
The Lovely Bones by Alice Sebold
The Manticore by Robertson Davies
The Master and the Margarita by Mikhail Bulgakov
The Meditations by Marcus Aurelius
The Merry Wives of Windsor by William Shakespeare
The Metamorphosis by Franz Kafka
The Miracle Worker by William Gibson
The Mojo Collection: The Ultimate Music Companion by Jim Irvin
The Mourning Bride by William Congreve
The Naked and the Dead by Norman Mailer
The Nancy Drew Series by Carolyn Keene
The New Poems of Emily Dickinson by Emily Dickinson
The New Way Things Work by David McCauley
The Old Man and the Sea by Ernest Hemingway
The Oresteia: Agamemnon; The Libation Bearers; The Eumenides by W.B. Stanford
The Outbreak of the Peloponnesian War by Donald Kagan
The Outsiders by S.E. Hinton
The Persian Puzzle by Kenneth M Pollack
The Picture of Dorian Gray by Oscar Wilde

The Portable Dorothy Parker by Dorothy Parker
The Portable Nietzche by Fredrich Nietzche
The Price of Loyalty: George W. Bush, the White House, and the Education of Paul O'Neill by Ron Suskind
The Princess Bride by William Golding
The Pursuit of Love & Love in a Cold Climate by Nancy Mitford
The Raven by Edgar Allan Poe
The Rough Guide to Europe, 2003 Edition
The Scarecrow of Oz by L. Frank Baum
The Scarlett Letter by Nathaniel Hawthorne
The Second Sex by Simone de Beauvoir
The Shining by Stephen King
The Sisters: The Saga of the Mitford Family by Mary S. Lovell
The Skin of Our Teeth by Thornton Wilder
The Sonnets by William Shakespeare
The Sound and the Fury by William Faulkner
The Story of My Life by Helen Keller
The Subsect by Jess Mariano (fictional text)
The Sun Also Rises by Ernest Hemingway
The Town and the City by Jack Kerouac
The Tragedy of Richard III by William Shakespeare
The Trial by Franz Kafka
The Unabridged Journals of Sylvia Plath 1950-1962 by Sylvia Plath
The Unbearable Lightness of Being by Milan Kundera
The Vanishing Newspaper by Phillip Meyers

The Wine Bible by Karen MacNeil
The Wizard of Oz by L. Frank Baum
The Women of Amy Sherman-Palladino by Scott Ryan
The Year of Magical Thinking by Joan Didion
The Yearling by Marjorie Kinnan Rawlings
The Comedy of Errors by William Shakespeare
Theatre by W Somerset Maugham
Thunder by James Grady
Timeline by Michael Crichton
To Have and Have Not by Ernest Hemingway
To Kill a Mockingbird by Harper Lee
Trainspotting by Irvine Welsh
Trouble in Our Backyard: Central America and the United States in the Eighties by Martin Diskin
Tuesdays with Morrie by Mitch Album
Ulysses by James Joyce
Uncle Tom's Cabin by Harriet Beecher Stowe
Understanding Power by Noam Chomsky
US Foreign Policy and the Iran Hostage Crisis by David Patrick Houghton
Valley of the Dolls by Jacqueline Susann
Visions of Cody by Jack Kerouac
Waiting for Godot by Samuel Beckett
Walden by Henry David Thoreau
War and Peace by Leo Tolstoy
We Owe You Nothing- Punk Planet: The Collected Interviews edited by Daniel Sinker
Webster's Dictionary
What Color is Your Parachute? by Richard Nelson Bolles

What Happened to Baby Jane? by Henry Farrell
When Everything Changed by Gail Collins
Who Moved My Cheese? by Spencer Johnson
Who's Afraid of Virginia Woolf? by Edward Albee
Who's Who & What's What in Shakespeare by Evangeline M. O'Connor
Wild by Cheryl Strand
Written in Blood by Dianne Fanning
Written in Blood: the Story of the Haitian People 1492-1995 by Nancy Gordon Heinl, Robert Debs Heinl
Wuthering Heights by Emily Bronte
Yoga for Dummies by Georg Feuerstein and Larry Payne
You Deserve Love by D. Sherber
You've Been Gilmore'd!: The Unofficial Gilmore Girls Encyclopedia by Taryn Dryfhout
Zorba the Greek by Nikos Kazantakis

Movies

2 Fast 2 Furious (2003)
2001: A Space Odyssey (1968)
8 Mile (2002)
9½ Weeks (1986)
A Beautiful Mind (2001)
A Brief History of Time (1991)
A History of Violence (2005)
A Nightmare on Elm Street (1984)
A Room with a View (1985)
A Star Is Born (1976)
A Streetcar Named Desire (1951)
A Woman Under the Influence (1974)
Accepted (2006)
Ace Ventura: Pet Detective (1994)
Al Capone (1959)
Alice Doesn't Live Here Anymore (1974)
Alice in Wonderland (1951)
Alive (1993)
All About Eve (1950)
All the President's Men (1976)
Almost Famous (2000)
American Gigolo (1980)
American Splendor (2003)
An Affair to Remember (1957)
An American in Paris (1951)
An Inconvenient Truth (2006)
An Officer and a Gentleman (1982)
An Unmarried Woman (1978)

Animal House (1978)
Annie (1982)
Annie Hall (1977)
Anything Goes (1936)
Anywhere But Here (1999)
Apocalypse Now (1979)
Arctic Flight (1952)
Armageddon (1998)
Arthur (1981)
Attack of the 50 Foot Woman (1958)
Austin Powers: The Spy Who Shagged Me (1999)
Auto Focus (2002)
Babe (1995)
Babe: Pig in the City (1998)
Babette: "Ah! I knew it! Simba, you've been dethroned."
Baby Doll (1956)
Back to the Future (1985)
Bambi (1942)
Barbarella (1968)
Basic Instinct (1992)
Batman v Superman: Dawn of Justice (2016)
Beach Blanket Bingo (1965)
Beaches (1988)
Beethoven (1992)
Being There (1979)
Ben-Hur (1959)
Bend It Like Beckham (2002)
Benji (1974)
Better Off Dead... (1985)

Beverly Hills Cop (1984)
Blades of Glory (2007)
Blow (2001)
Blue Crush (2002)
Blue Velvet (1986)
Bob & Carol & Ted & Alice (1969)
Bonnie and Clyde (1967)
Boogie Nights (1997)
Boxing Helena (1993)
Brazil (1985)
Breakfast at Tiffany's (1961)
Breakin' 2: Electric Boogaloo (1984)
Breaking Away (1979)
Bride of Chucky (1998)
Bridget Jones's Diary (2001)
Brigadoon (1954)
Bright Eyes (1934)
Bring Me the Head of Alfredo Garcia (1974)
Bringing Up Baby (1938)
Broadcast News (1987)
Broadway Danny Rose (1984)
Brokeback Mountain (2005)
Bugsy (1991)
Bugsy Malone (1976)
Bull Durham (1988)
Bullets Over Broadway (1994)
Bullitt (1968)
Butch Cassidy and the Sundance Kid (1969)
Butterfield 8 (1960)
Bye Bye Birdie (1963)
Cabaret (1972)

Cabin Boy (1994)
Caged Heat (1974)
Camelot (1967)
Captain Corelli's Mandolin (2001)
Carrie (1976)
Casablanca (1942)
Cats & Dogs (2001)
Charlie's Angels: Full Throttle (2003)
Chinatown (1974)
Chitty Chitty Bang Bang (1968)
Christine (1983)
Christmas in July (1940)
Cinderella (1950)
Citizen Kane (1941)
Cocktail (1988)
Cocoon (1985)
Coming Home (1978)
Cool Hand Luke (1967)
Cool as Ice (1991)
Coyote Ugly (2000)
Crimes and Misdemeanors (1989)
Crouching Tiger, Hidden Dragon (2000)
Cujo (1983)
Damn Yankees! (1958)
Dances with Wolves (1990)
Dangerous Liaisons (1988)
Das Boot (1981)
David Blaine: Above the Below (2003)
David and Lisa (1962)
Dawn of the Dead (1978)
Dead Calm (1989)

Desperately Seeking Susan (1985)
Destry Rides Again (1939)
Deuce Bigalow: Male Gigolo (1999)
Dig! (2004)
Diner (1982)
Dirty Dancing (1987)
Divine Secrets of the Ya-Ya Sisterhood (2002)
Doctor Dolittle (1967)
Dog Day Afternoon (1975)
Dogtown and Z-Boys (2001)
Donnie Darko (2001)
Dorf on Golf (1987)
Double Indemnity (1944)
Driving Miss Daisy (1989)
Duck Soup (1933)
Dumbo (1941)
E.T. the Extra-Terrestrial (1982)
Easter Parade (1948)
Eastern Promises (2007)
Easy Rider (1969)
Eat Pray Love (2010)
Ed Wood (1994)
Edward Scissorhands (1990)
Elizabeth (1998)
Encino Man (1992)
Endless Love (1981)
Eraserhead (1977)
Erin Brockovich (2000)
Eternal Sunshine of the Spotless Mind (2004)
Everest (1998)
Face/Off (1997)

Fahrenheit 9/11 (2004)
Fame (1980)
Farewell My Concubine (1993)
Fast Times at Ridgemont High (1982)
Fatal Attraction (1987)
Fatso (1980)
Ferris Bueller's Day Off (1986)
Festival Express (2003)
Fiddler on the Roof (1971)
Field of Dreams (1989)
Final Destination (2000)
Final Destination 2 (2003)
Final Destination 3 (2006)
Firestarter (1984)
Flashdance (1983)
Fletch (1985)
Footloose (1984)
For Keeps? (1988)
Frankenstein (1931)
Freaky Friday (1976)
Friday the 13th (1980)
Fried Green Tomatoes (1991)
From Here to Eternity (1953)
From Justin to Kelly (2003)
Full Metal Jacket (1987)
Funny Face (1957)
Funny Girl (1968)
G.I. Jane (1997)
Galaga (1981)
Gangs of New York (2002)
Gaslight (1944)

Get Shorty (1995)
Ghost (1990)
Ghostbusters (1984)
Giant (1956)
Gidget (1959)
Gigi (1958)
Girl, Interrupted (1999)
Girls Gone Wild on Campus 2 (2003)
Give 'em Hell, Harry! (1975)
Glitter
Gone Girl (2014)
Gone with the Wind (1939)
Good Morning, Vietnam (1987)
Goodfellas (1990)
Grease (1978)
Grey Gardens (1975)
Gunga Din (1939)
Guys and Dolls (1955)
Halloween (1978)
Happy Gilmore (1996)
Hardbodies (1984)
Harold and Maude (1971)
Harry Potter and the Sorcerer's Stone (2001)
Harvey (1950)
Heathers (1988)
Hello, Dolly! (1969)
High Fidelity (2000)
High Noon (1952)
His Girl Friday (1940)
Hitch (2005)
Hoosiers (1986)

Hotel Rwanda (2004)
House of Flying Daggers (2004)
House on Haunted Hill (1959)
How the Grinch Stole Christmas! (1966)
Hudson Hawk (1991)
I Am a Camera (1955)
Ice Castles (1978)
Inside Llewyn Davis (2013)
Inside Out (2015)
Invasion of the Body Snatchers (1956)
Invasion of the Body Snatchers (1978)
Ishtar (1987)
It Happened One Night (1934)
It's a Wonderful Life (1946)
Jack Frost (1998)
Jackie Brown (1997)
Jailhouse Rock (1957)
Jarhead (2005)
Jerry Maguire (1996)
Jesus Christ Superstar (1973)
Joe Versus the Volcano (1990)
Julia (1977)
Just Shoot Me! (1997)
Kill Bill: Vol. 1 (2003)
Killer Shark (1950)
King Kong (1976)
La Dolce Vita (1960)
Lady and the Tramp (1955)
Lassie (1954)
Last Tango in Paris (1972)
Legally Blonde (2001)

Les Misérables (2012)
Less Than Zero (1987)
Life of Brian (1979)
Life with Judy Garland: Me and My Shadows (2001)
Like Father Like Son (1987)
Little Man Tate (1991)
Live and Let Die (1973)
Looney, Looney, Looney Bugs Bunny Movie (1981)
Lord Jim (1965)
Lord of the Rings: The Return of the King (2003)
Love Story (1970)
Mad Hot Ballroom (2005)
Mad Max Beyond Thunderdome (1985)
Magnolia (1999)
Mamma Mia! (2008)
Marathon Man (1976)
March of the Penguins (2005)
Mary Poppins (1964)
Mask (1985)
Master and Commander: The Far Side of the World (2003)
Mens vi venter på Godot (1965)
Midnight Express (1978)
Mildred Pierce (1945)
Million Dollar Baby (1941)
Misery (1990)
Moment by Moment (1978)
Mommie Dearest (1981)
Monster (2003)

Monty Python and the Holy Grail (1975)
Moulin Rouge! (2001)
Mr. & Mrs. Bridge (1990)
Mr. Baseball (1992)
My Fair Lady (1964)
My Left Foot (1989)
My Man Godfrey (1936)
Mystic Pizza (1988)
Nanny McPhee (2005)
Nanook of the North (1922)
Napoleon Dynamite (2004)
National Treasure (2004)
National Velvet (1944)
Nell (1994)
Network (1976)
Norma Rae (1979)
Not Without My Daughter (1991)
Ocean's Eleven (2001)
Oklahoma! (1955)
Old Yeller (1957)
Oliver Twist (1948)
On the Town (1949)
On the Waterfront (1954)
Open Water (2003)
Out of Africa (1985)
Oxford Blues (1984)
Panic Room (2002)
Paper Moon (1973)
Paris Is Burning (1990)
Patton (1970)
Peyton Place (1957)

Pippi Långstrump (1969)
Pleasantville (1998)
Pretty in Pink (1986)
Prizzi's Honor (1985)
Psycho (1960)
Pulp Fiction (1994)
Purple Rain (1984)
Queen of Outer Space (1958)
Raging Bull (1980)
Rain Man (1988)
Rebecca of Sunnybrook Farm (1938)
Rent (2005)
Reservoir Dogs (1992)
Reversal of Fortune (1990)
Riding the Bus with My Sister (2005)
Risky Business (1983)
Robert Benchley and the Knights of the Algonquin (1998)
RoboCop (1987)
Rock of Ages (2012)
Rocky (1976)
Rocky III (1982)
Roman Holiday (1953)
Romeo + Juliet (1996)
Rosemary's Baby (1968)
Rudolph the Red-Nosed Reindeer (1964)
Rush Hour (1998)
Sabrina (1954)
Saturday Night Fever (1977)
Saving Private Ryan (1998)
Saw II (2005)

Say Anything... (1989)
Scarface (1983)
Scenes from a Mall (1991)
Schindler's List (1993)
Secrets & Lies (1996)
Seven Brides for Seven Brothers (1954)
Seven Samurai (1954)
Shaft (1971)
Shakespeare in Love (1998)
Shall We Dance (1937)
Shallow Hal (2001)
Shane (1953)
Shanghai Surprise (1986)
Shields and Yarnell (1977)
Shoah (1985)
Showgirls (1995)
Sid and Nancy (1986)
Silent Movie (1976)
Silkwood (1983)
Singin' in the Rain (1952)
Sister Act (1992)
Six Candles (1984)
Sleeping Beauty (1959)
Sleepless in Seattle (1993)
Snakes on a Plane (2006)
Snow Dogs (2002)
Snow White and the Seven Dwarfs (1937)
Solaris (2002)
Some Kind of Wonderful (1987)
Song of the South (1946)
Sophie's Choice (1982)

South Pacific (1958)
Speed (1994)
St. Elmo's Fire (1985)
Stalag 17 (1953)
Star Trek: The Motion Picture (1979)
Star Wars: Episode III - Revenge of the Sith (2005)
Star Wars: Episode IV - A New Hope (1977)
Star Wars: Episode V - The Empire Strikes Back (1980)
Stop Making Sense (1984)
Stuart Little (1999)
Sudden Danger (1955)
Summertime (1955)
Sunset Boulevard (1950)
Superman (1941)
Suspense (1946)
Sweet November (2001)
Swept Away (2002)
Swing Time (1936)
Syriana (2005)
Taxi Driver (1976)
Tears and Laughter: The Joan and Melissa Rivers Story (1994)
Terms of Endearment (1983)
The 2000 Year Old Man (1975)
The 40 Year Old Virgin (2005)
The Adventures of Priscilla, Queen of the Desert (1994)
The Amityville Horror (1979)
The Arrival of a Train (1896)

The Bad Seed (1956)
The Banger Sisters (2002)
The Blue Lagoon (1980)
The Born Losers (1967)
The Bourne Supremacy (2004)
The Boy in the Plastic Bubble (1976)
The Breakfast Club (1985)
The Bridge on the River Kwai (1957)
The Bridges of Madison County (1995)
The Brown Bunny (2003)
The Champ (1979)
The Court Jester (1955)
The Crucible (1996)
The Deer Hunter (1978)
The Exorcist (1973)
The Fast and the Furious (2001)
The Fast and the Furious: Tokyo Drift (2006)
The Fly (1958)
The Ghost and Mrs. Muir (1947)
The Glass Menagerie (1950)
The Glenn Miller Story (1954)
The Godfather (1972)
The Godfather: Part II (1974)
The Godfather: Part III (1990)
The Goofy Gophers (1947)
The Goonies (1985)
The Graduate (1967)
The Grapes of Wrath (1940)
The Great Santini (1979)
The Great White Hope (1970)
The Hunchback of Notre Dame (1996)

The Hurt Locker (2008)
The In-Laws (1979)
The Incredible Shrinking Man (1957)
The Jerk (1979)
The Joy Luck Club (1993)
The Jungle Book (2016)
The Karate Kid (1984)
The Lady Is Willing (1942)
The Lake House (2006)
The Last of the Mohicans (1992)
The Legend of Bagger Vance (2000)
The Lion King (1994)
The Lord of the Rings: The Fellowship of the Ring (2001)
The Lord of the Rings: The Two Towers (2002)
The Lords of Flatbush (1974)
The Lost Weekend (1945)
The Lottery (1969)
The Machinist (2004)
The Magnificent Ambersons (1942)
The Mambo Kings (1992)
The Man Who Knew Too Much (1956)
The Man in the Gray Flannel Suit (1956)
The Manchurian Candidate (1962)
The Matrix (1999)
The Matrix Reloaded (2003)
The Meaning of Life (1983)
The Miracle Worker (1962)
The Money Pit (1986)
The Mothman Prophecies (2002)
The Muse (1999)

The Music Man (1962)
The Naughty Nineties (1945)
The Odd Couple (1968)
The Omen (1976)
The Outsiders (1983)
The Parent Trap (1961)
The Passion of the Christ (2004)
The Pee Wee Herman Show (1981)
The Perfect Storm (2000)
The Philadelphia Story (1940)
The Poseidon Adventure (1972)
The Postman (1997)
The Pursuit of Happyness (2006)
The River Wild (1994)
The Rocky Horror Picture Show (1975)
The Shawshank Redemption (1994)
The Shining (1980)
The Silence of the Lambs (1991)
The Singing Detective (1986)
The Sixth Sense (1999)
The Sound of Music (1965)
The Stepford Wives (1975)
The Sting (1973)
The Thin Man (1934)
The Thomas Crown Affair (1968)
The Treasure of the Sierra Madre (1948)
The Turning Point (1977)
The Unbearable Lightness of Being (1988)
The Way We Were (1973)
The Witches of Eastwick (1987)
The Wizard of Oz (1939)

The Yearling (1946)
Thelma & Louise (1991)
Them! (1954)
There Will Be Blood (2007)
There's Something About Mary (1998)
They Shoot Horses, Don't They? (1969)
This Is Spinal Tap (1984)
Three Days of the Condor (1975)
Titanic (1997)
To Kill a Mockingbird (1962)
Tommy (1975)
Top Gun (1986)
Touch of Evil (1958)
Trainspotting (1996)
True Grit (1969)
Tuesdays with Morrie (1999)
Up (2009)
Urban Cowboy (1980)
Valentine (2001)
Valley of the Dolls (1967)
View from the Top (2003)
Waiting for Guffman (1996)
Wall Street (1987)
Welcome to the Dollhouse (1995)
West Side Story (1961)
What Ever Happened to Baby Jane? (1962)
Where Are Your Children? (1943)
Who's Afraid of Virginia Woolf? (1966)
Wild (2014)
Willy Wonka & the Chocolate Factory (1971)
Winnie the Pooh and the Honey Tree (1966)

Wonder Woman: Who's Afraid of Diana Prince? (1967)
Working Girl (1988)
Xanadu (1980)
Yellow Submarine (1968)
Yentl (1983)
You're a Good Man, Charlie Brown (1973)
You've Got Mail (1998)
Young Frankenstein (1974)
Zoolander 2 (2016)

Television Shows

21 Jump Street (1987)
24 (2001)
60 Minutes (1968)
7th Heaven (1996)
ABC Afterschool Specials (1972)
Absolutely Fabulous (1992)
Alice (1976)
All in the Family (1971)
America's Next Top Model (2003)
Angela's Ashes (1999)
Animaniacs (1993)
Antiques Roadshow (1997)
Barefoot Contessa (2002)
Baretta (1975)
Batman (1966)
BattleBots (2000)
Battlestar Galactica (1978)
Baywatch (1989)
Behind the Music (1997)
Benson (1979)
Beverly Hills, 90210 (1990)
Bewitched (1964)
Blue Bloods (2010)
Bosom Buddies (1980)
Bozo (1960)
Brian's Song (1971)
Brideshead Revisited (1981)

Buffy the Vampire Slayer (1997)
CBS Evening News with Dan Rather (1981)
CHiPs (1977)
CSI: Miami (2002)
Captain Kangaroo (1955)
Charlie Rose (1991)
Charlie's Angels (1976)
Chico and the Man (1974)
Columbo (1971)
Cop Rock (1990)
Cops (1989)
Cribs (2000)
Danger Mouse (1981)
Daria (1997)
Dark Shadows (1966)
Dawson's Creek (1998)
Days of Our Lives (1965)
Deadwood (2004)
Def Comedy Jam (1992)
Desperate Housewives (2004)
Diff'rent Strokes (1978)
Doctor Who (1963)
Doogie Howser, M.D. (1989)
Dr. Phil (2002)
Dynasty (1981)
E! True Hollywood Story (1996)
ER (1994)
Electra Woman and Dyna Girl (1976)
Everybody Loves Raymond (1996)
Family Feud (1976)
Family Matters (1989)

Fantasy Island (1977)
Fat Albert and the Cosby Kids (1972)
Felicity (1998)
Frontline (1983)
Frosty the Snowman (1954)
Full House (1987)
Futurama (1999)
Game of Thrones (2011)
General Hospital (1963)
Get Smart (1965)
Gilligan's Island (1964)
Girlfriends (2000)
Gumby Adventures (1988)
Halt and Catch Fire (2014)
Happy Days (1974)
Hart to Hart (1979)
Hawaii Five-O (1968)
Hee Haw (1969)
Hee Haw Honeys (1978)
Hogan's Heroes (1965)
Holmes and Yo-Yo (1976)
How the Grinch Stole Christmas! (1966)
I Dream of Jeannie (1965)
I Love Lucy (1951)
Inside the Actors Studio (1994)
Iron Chef (1993)
Iron Chef America: The Series (2005)
Jazz (2001)
Jeopardy! (1984)
Joanie Loves Chachi (1982)
Johnny Bravo (1997)

Joseph Campbell and the Power of Myth (1988)
Kentucky vs. the University of Alabama, Freedom Hall - Louisville, Kentucky (January 21, 1998).
Knots Landing: Moments of Truth (1981)
Lassie (1954)
Laugh-In (1967)
Laverne & Shirley (1976)
Law & Order (1990)
Leave It to Beaver (1957)
Les Revenants (2012)
Lifestyles of the Rich and Famous (1984)
Lillehammer 1994: XVII Olympic Winter Games (1994)
Live! With Kelly and Michael (1988)
Lost in Space (1965)
M*A*S*H (1970)
Magnum, P.I. (1980)
Mahha GoGoGo (1967)
Malcolm in the Middle (2000)
Marcus Welby, M.D. (1969)
Martha Stewart Living (1991)
Matlock (1986)
Meet the Press (1947)
Mission: Impossible (1966)
Mister Ed (1958)
Monk (2002)
Monty Python's Flying Circus (1969)
Mutual of Omaha's Wild Kingdom (1963)
My Little Pony Tales (1992)
NFL Monday Night Football (1970)

NYPD Blue (1993)
Nancy Grace (2005)
Nanny and the Professor (1970)
Narcos (2015)
Nigella Bites (2000)
Outlander (2014)
Oz (1997)
Pee-wee's Playhouse (1986)
Petticoat Junction (1963)
Peyton Place (1964)
Pink Lady (1980)
Pippi Långstrump (1969)
Please Don't Eat the Daisies (1965)
Politically Incorrect (1993)
Privileged: All About Friends and Family (2008)
Project Runway (2004)
Punk'd (2003)
Puppet Playhouse (1947)
Queer Eye for the Straight Guy (2003)
Quincy M.E. (1976)
Reno 911! (2003)
Rhoda (1974)
Ricki Lake (1992)
Rock Star: INXS (2005)
Sanford and Son (1972)
Saturday Night Live (1975)
Saved by the Bell (1989)
Schindler's List (1993)
Schoolhouse Rock! (1973)
Scooby Doo, Where Are You! (1969)
Seinfeld (1989)

Sesame Street (1969)
Sex and the City (1998)
Shields and Yarnell (1977)
Smurfs (1981)
Soap (1977)
Soul Train (1971)
Soulcalibur III (2005)
South Park (1997)
SpongeBob SquarePants (1999)
Star Search (1983)
Star Trek (1966)
Star Trek: The Next Generation (1987)
Summerland (2004)
Survivor (2000)
Sábado Gigante (1962)
Taxi (1978)
Teenage Mutant Ninja Turtles (1987)
Teletubbies (1997)
That Girl (1966)
The 67th Annual Academy Awards (1995)
The 700 Club (1966)
The 75th Annual Academy Awards (2003)
The 78th Annual Academy Awards (2006)
The Addams Family (1964)
The Amazing Race (2001)
The Andy Griffith Show (1960)
The Apprentice (2004)
The Brady Bunch (1969)
The Brady Bunch Variety Hour (1976)
The Comeback (2005)
The Courtship of Eddie's Father (1969)

The Daily Show (1996)
The Dick Van Dyke Show (1961)
The Donna Reed Show (1958)
The Dukes of Hazzard (1979)
The Flintstones (1960)
The Greatest American Hero (1981)
The Gumby Show (1956)
The Honeymooners (1955)
The Jetsons (1962)
The Kids in the Hall (1988)
The L Word (2004)
The Late Show with David Letterman (1993)
The Lawrence Welk Show (1951)
The Life and Times of Grizzly Adams (1977)
The Little Rascals (1955)
The Lonely Island: Lazy Sunday (2005)
The Love Boat (1977)
The Monkees (1966)
The Munsters (1964)
The Muppet Show (1976)
The Mysteries of Laura (2014)
The O.C. (2003)
The Odd Couple (1970)
The Office (2001)
The Oprah Winfrey Show (1986)
The Patty Duke Show (1963)
The Powerpuff Girls (1998)
The Price Is Right (1972)
The Real World (1992)
The Simpsons (1989)
The Six Million Dollar Man (1973)

The Sonny and Cher Show (1976)
The Sopranos (1999)
The Tonight Show (1962)
The Twilight Zone (1959)
The View (1997)
The Voice (2011)
The Waltons (1971)
The West Wing (1999)
The Yogi Bear Show (1961)
Thirtysomething (1987)
This Is Your Life (1952)
This Old House (1979)
Toast of the Town: Episode #17.19 (1964)
Today (1952)
Top Chef (2006)
Total Request Live (1998)
Two Fat Ladies (1996)
Two and a Half Men (2003)
V.I.P. (1998)
Wheel of Fortune (1983)
Who's the Boss? (1984)
Will & Grace (1998)
Wonder Woman (1975)
Xuxa (1993)

Acknowledgements

I cannot even express how grateful I am to have had the opportunity to go on this journey. When I was in university, I dreamed of finding a way to write about *Gilmore Girls*. I even used to joke that if I could major in *Gilmore Girls*, I would gladly do it. While this book won't earn me a college degree, it certainly fulfilled a dream.

First and foremost, I am grateful to my family for their patience while I took this creative journey, watching the show with me over and over while I researched and made notes. I will be forever grateful to my husband Stephen – my partner in everything, and my rock. Thank you for helping me to do this, and for your unwavering support and encouragement in all things. You always believed this book was in me. A big thank you to my mother Debby, who is the Lorelai to my Rory. Any success I have is always a reflection of the support that I find in you, and it is mainly to your strong character, that I aspire. I am also incredibly blessed and grateful to my four beautiful children, to whom this book is dedicated.

Thank you to Sam Phillips - your music inspires me every day, and to the actors who brought the characters to life, and who continue to contribute to the fan community. Thank you to Daniel Palladino, and Amy Sherman-Palladino, for creating a series that made me want to read more, and write more, and which compelled me to start this journey. I will always be grateful for the rich characters, and compelling story arcs that you created, and for coming back years later to give us more episodes to watch over and over.

Thank you to the fans who shared their stories and photos with me for the fan section of this book, and with whom I have had many lively discussions about the show. Thank you to all those fans who came before me in the compiling of Gilmore content—creating online lists which gave me a place to start, and which set the stage for an encyclopedia of this density. Thank you also to Lori, who helped me with some of the preliminary 'sorting' early in the project.

Lastly, thank you to Erin - my best 'Gilmore' friend. You are the only person I know who can go toe-to-toe with me about anything Gilmore, and who understands that it is so much more than just a good television show.

Taryn

References

Armstrong, Jennifer. "Boys Not Alllowed" in *Coffee at Luke's: An Unauthorized Gilmore Girls Gabfest*, ed. Jennifer Crusie, Leah Wilson, 15-20. Dallas: BenBella Books, 2007.

Beail, Linda. "The City, the Suburbs, and Stars Hollow: The Return of the Evening Soap Opera." In *You've Come A Long Way, Baby: Women, Politics, and Popular Culture*, ed. Goren Lilly J., 93-114. Kentucky: University Press of Kentucky, 2009.

Diffrient, David Scott. "Introduction: "You're about to Be Gilmored"," In *Screwball Television: Critical Perspectives on Gilmore Girls*, ed. Diffrient, David Scott and Lavery, David, Xv-Xxxvi. Syracuse, NY: Syracuse University Press, 2010.

_____ "The Gift of Gilmore Girls' Gab: Fan Podcasts and the Task of "Talking Back" to TV," In *Screwball Television: Critical Perspectives on Gilmore Girls*, ed. Diffrient, David Scott and Lavery, David, 79-107. Syracuse, NY: Syracuse University Press, 2010.

Johns, Erin K. and Smith, Kristin L. "Welcome to Stars Hollow: Gilmore Girls, Utopia, and the Hyperreal" in *Gilmore Girls and the Politics of Identity: Essays on Family and Feminism in the Television Series*, ed. Calvin, Ritch. Jefferson, 23-34. North Carolina : McFarland & Company, Inc., 2008.

Jones, Caroline E. "Unpleasant Consequences: First Sex in Buffy the Vampire Slayer, Veronica Mars, and Gilmore Girls," in *Jeunesse: Young People, Texts, Cultures 5, no. 1*, 2013, 65-83.

Lizardi, Ryan. "Mourning and Melancholia: Conflicting Approaches to Reviving Gilmore Girls One Season at a Time," in *Television & New Media 19:*4, 379 –395, 2018.

Manning, Jimmie. ""But Luke and Lorelai Belong Together!": Relationships, Social Control, and Gilmore Girls." In *Screwball Television: Critical Perspectives on Gilmore Girls*, ed. Diffrient, David Scott and Lavery David, 302-20. Syracuse, NY: Syracuse University Press, 2010.

Mintz, Susannah B. and Leah E. Mintz. "Pass the Pop-Tarts: The Gilmore Girls' Perpetual Hunger." In *Screwball Television: Critical Perspectives on Gilmore Girls*, edited by Diffrient, David Scott and Lavery, David, 235-56. Syracuse, NY: Syracuse University Press, 2010.

Morrison, Sara. "Your Guide to the Real Stars Hollow Business World," in *Coffee at Luke's: An Unauthorised Gilmore Girls Gabfest*, ed. Jennifer Cruise, Leah Wilson, 85-96. Dallas: BenBella Books, 2007.

Nelson, Matthew C. "Stars Hollow, Chilton, and the Politics of Education in Gilmore Girls." In *Screwball Television: Critical Perspectives on Gilmore Girls*, ed. Diffrient, David Scott and Lavery, David, 202-13. Syracuse, NY: Syracuse University Press, 2010.

Petersen, Line Nybro. "Gilmore Girls Generations: Disrupting Generational Belonging in Long-Term Fandom", in *Celebrity Studies* 9:2, 216-230, Taylor & Francis (Routledge), 2018.

Rawlins, Justin Owen. "Your Guide to the Girls: Gilmore-isms, Cultural Capital, and a Different Kind of Quality TV." In *Screwball Television: Critical Perspectives on Gilmore Girls*, ed. Diffrient, David Scott and Lavery, David, 36-56. Syracuse, NY: Syracuse University Press, 2010.

Sborgi, Anna Viola. ""The Thing That Reads a Lot": Bibliophilia, College Life, and Literary Culture in Gilmore Girls." In *Screwball Television: Critical Perspectives on Gilmore Girls*, ed. Diffrient, David Scott and Lavery, David, 186-201. Syracuse, NY: Syracuse University Press, 2010.

Stache, Lara C. and Davidson, Rachel. *Gilmore Girls: A Cultural History*. Lanham, Maryland: Rowman and Littlefield, 2019.

Stern, Danielle M. "It Takes a Classless, Heteronormative Utopian Village: Gilmore Girls and the Problem of Postfeminism," *The Communication Review, 15:3*, 167-186, 2012.

Smith-Rowsey, Daniel. "Still More Gilmore How Online Fan Communities Remediate Gilmore Girls," in *Gilmore Girls: The Politics of Identity,* ed. Ritch Calvin. 193-204. Jefferson, NC: McFarland & Company Inc., 2008.

Sutcliffe, David. "For Madeline," *Cameo*, https://www.cameo.com/v/5e45fe5746fc9901a55dbcbd

Woods, Faye. "Generation Gap? Mothers, Daughters and Music," in *Gilmore Girls: The Politics of Identity*, ed. Ritch Calvin. 127-142. Jefferson, NC: McFarland & Company Inc., 2008.

Whiteside, Stephanie. "When Paris Met Rory", in in *Coffee at Luke's: An Unauthorized Gilmore Girls Gabfest*, ed. Jennifer Crusie, Leah Wilson, 21-28. Dallas: BenBella Books, 2007.

Wright, Katheryn. "Gilmore Girls: "Bon Voyage"." In *Television Finales: From Howdy Doody to Girls*, ed. Howard Douglas L. and Bianculli David, 142-49. Syracuse, NY: Syracuse University Press, 2018.

About the Author

Taryn is an experienced writer, English teacher, theologian, and coffee junkie who lives in New Zealand with her husband and four children.

A Rory-inspired blue-stocking, Taryn is a serial student, earning several diploma's and degrees, and now currently completing a PhD program. She works part-time as a college tutor, and has won awards for her post-graduate research and Māori leadership.

Taryn's publication record includes several non-fiction books, tertiary college courses, website content, and more than 400 feature articles, reviews, and columns published in newspapers, websites, and magazines.

When Taryn is not writing, studying, or with her kids, she can be found reading books, buying books, or watching *Gilmore Girls*.

www.TarynDryfhout.com

www.ingramcontent.com/pod-product-compliance
Lightning Source LLC
Chambersburg PA
CBHW051414290426
44109CB00016B/1294